Positive Illusions

POSITIVE ILLUSIONS

Creative Self-Deception and the Healthy Mind

Shelley E. Taylor

BasicBooks
A Division of HarperCollinsPublishers

7/93

Library of Congress Cataloging–in–Publication Data

Taylor, Shelley E.
    Positive illusions : creative self-deception and the healthy mind/
Shelley Taylor.
        p.   cm.
    Bibliography: p. 265
    Includes index.
    ISBN 0–465–06052–8 (cloth)
    ISBN 0–465–06053–6 (paper)
    1. Mental health.   2. Self-deception—Therapeutic use.
3. Medicine and psychology.   I. Title.
RA790.5.T38   1989
158'.1—dc20
                                    89–42515
                                    CIP

c.1

CONTENTS

PREFACE

As a college student, I worked in a mental hospital for several months. When I took the job, I assumed that those who are confined to such institutions had been driven by the pain of life into madness. I expected to find people suffering intolerable stress—the death of a loved one, the destruction of home and property by a natural disaster, a divorce or other wrenching separation. This, I assumed, must be what leads to mental illness. I was quickly disabused of this belief. Indeed, as I soon learned, victims of disasters—personal ones such as assault or rape, or natural catastrophes such as a fire or flood—rarely develop the signs of mental illness. When interviewed some months after what would seem to be devastating losses, these people often report that their lives are at least as happy and satisfying as they were before these disastrous events.

These facts so intrigued me that, following my graduate training, I determined to study the processes whereby recovery from a tragic or near-tragic event takes place. Such problems are not to be studied lightly. Conducting interviews with rape victims, cancer patients, and men vulnerable to sudden death—the groups that would constitute our first investigations—is a wrenching way to make a living. People who are facing death or who have recently faced it have much to say and a lot of it is hard to hear. Yet there were also remarkable stories of recovery.

Originally, I had thought of adjustment to trauma and recovery from devastation as a homeostatic process, that is, as a mental regulatory system whose function it is to maintain psychological balance and stability. I suspected that there might be mechanisms within the mind that help restore people's emotional and cognitive balance to the levels experienced before a victimizing event. A homeostatic hypothesis is a logical choice, for it applies quite well to many biological problems. The gastric system, for example, has five different methods by which hydrochloric acid can be produced, and if one or more of them is disrupted, then the others can take over, maintaining gastric functioning at approximately its previous level. Homeostasis seemed on the surface to be an apt description of the recovery processes of the mind.

In fact, what we soon uncovered was a different process altogether. Rather than being restored to their previous level of functioning, many of the people we interviewed seemed actually to have achieved a higher level of functioning than they had experienced prior to the victimizing event. Many of these victims said that their lives prior to the victimizing events had simply rolled along as a life will when one makes no particular effort to intervene actively in its course. The threatening events to which they were exposed, however, forced them to rethink their priorities and values, and many victims indicated that their lives were now self-consciously lived a moment at a time, in order to extract as much enjoyment and meaning from life as possible. They thought about the reasons behind what they did as they had never before, put value on what truly mattered to them, and in some cases, undertook new activities that left them feeling more fulfilled. As one of the cancer patients we interviewed put it, "The trick, of course, is to do this without getting cancer."

My life was changed by contact with these people. After listening to hours of interviews in which victims thoughtfully appraised their lives and their accomplishments and explained how they had restructured their activities and thinking in order to make their lives more rewarding and meaningful, one feels almost embarrassed by the lack of similar attention to one's own life. Consequently, this work has the effect of forcing a rigorous scrutiny of one's own values and a questioning of the intrinsic merit of its activities, sometimes prompting as well an unwelcome contemplation of death. At these moments, my husband comments, "You and Woody Allen . . ." and sets off to find lighter diversions. Despite these risks, I have watched with pleasure as successive waves of students who have worked with me have also found their lives enriched by contact with people who have been forced to confront the meaning and value in their lives. After four or five interviews my students come back as changed people, and years later will write letters about how important the experiences were to their development as scientists and as mature adults.

A curious picture began to emerge in our research findings. Many of the psychological recoveries recounted by these victims seemed to depend on certain distortions of their situations, especially overly optimistic perceptions concerning chances of recovery from a disease, or the belief that they could actively control the likelihood of a repeat victimization in the future. It was surprising and disturbing to listen to a cancer patient recount the meaning that the experience had brought to her life, and to hear her state with confidence that she would never get cancer again, knowing from the chart records that she would almost certainly develop a recurrence and ultimately die of the disease. But what was more surprising was the discovery that those people who maintained these overly optimistic assessments of their situations and the beliefs that they could control the victimizing events were actually better adjusted to their circumstances and not more poorly adjusted. We came to call these adaptive fictions *illusions,* and although they did not exist in every account of recovery from victimization, they were nonetheless prevalent.

Puzzled by this unanticipated role of creative imagination in recovery, we looked for a context in which to explore it further. We turned first to the mental health literature, but although it was interesting in its own right, it was not especially helpful for understanding the illusions we observed among our victims of life-threatening events. We turned next to the research on cognition and social cognition, new and fast-growing subspecialties of psychology that have attracted many of the brightest scientists in the field. And it was here that we began to find clues. First, a brief digression is required.

At different points in their histories, most of the sciences have had frameworks that, once articulated, attracted the majority of scientists and advanced the field suddenly and abruptly in an all-new direction. Cognitive psychology has represented such a development for psychology. The cognitive perspective, which focuses on how the mind is organized and how it functions, has become a dominant framework for developmental psychologists, who study the lives of children and adults across the lifespan; social psychologists, who examine how people think about social activities and interact with others; and clinicians, who attempt to understand mental health and illness. These fields have been so overwhelmed by the cognitive perspective in recent years that, in many respects, social psychologists, clinicians, and developmental psychologists are often cognitive psychologists as well.

What is the cognitive perspective? It is an understanding of how people think about themselves and the world. The cognitive perspective focuses on the person's interpretations. It examines how ordinary people think about people and how they think they think about people and why they think that way. To a cognitive psychologist, for example, it is less important to know whether someone failed a test than to know whether he or she regards failure as a setback or as a learning experience. It is less important to know if a person is Protestant, Catholic, or Jewish than to understand what purpose religion serves in the person's life. It is less important to know if a person makes a lot of money and has an exciting job than it is to know if he or she is contented with those circumstances. Interpretation is the key element in the cognitive analysis.

Ironically, this literature helped us to understand better the kinds of adaptive fictions we saw in our victims, for cognitive research documents similar perceptions in normal, everyday thought. That is, rather than being firmly in touch with reality, the normal human mind distorts incoming information in a positive direction. In particular, people think of themselves, their future, and their ability to have an impact on what goes on around them in a more positive manner than reality can sustain. Just as victims of life-threatening events seem to be motivated to recover from victimization and actively restructure victimizing events in a positive manner, so people who are confronted with the normal rebuffs of everyday life seem to construe their experience as to develop and maintain an exaggeratedly positive view of their own attributes, an unrealistic optimism about the future, and a distorted faith in their ability to control what goes on around them.

These labors and investigations have culminated in the perspective on mental health set forth in this book. I argue that the normal human mind is oriented toward mental health and that at every turn it construes events in a manner that promotes benign fictions about the self, the world, and the future. The mind is, with some significant exceptions, intrinsically adaptive, oriented toward overcoming rather than succumbing to the adverse events of life. In many ways, the healthy mind is a self-deceptive one, as I will attempt to show. At one level, it constructs beneficent interpretations of threatening events that raise self-esteem and promote motivation; yet at another level, it recognizes the threat or challenge that is posed by these events.

The viewpoint that people need to distort reality in order to adjust successfully to it would seem to be quite cynical on the surface. I hope to convey exactly the opposite sentiment. The ability of the mind to construe benefit from tragedy and to prevent a person from becoming overwhelmed by the stress and pain of life is a remarkable achievement. To a scientist, it makes the mind infinitely more interesting to study. If all our minds did was to take in information as it actually exists and represent it faithfully, the chief task of a psychologist would be to function as a historian of mundane mental activity. Exploring how the mind imposes structure and meaning on events and how it does so systematically in adaptive ways is truly an adventure. Moreover, one emerges from the exploration, not with cynical disdain for the petty ways in which people must cover up their faults and distort their tragedies, but with a huge respect for an organism that has evolved to the point that it can triumph over adversity through sheer mental effort. The mind's resources are exceptional and impressive, and their ability to help people overcome adversity is testimony to the resilience of the human spirit.

A word about the evidence on which this analysis is based. The science covered in this volume comes from three main sources: laboratory investigations from cognitive psychology, field interviews with people undergoing stressful events, and surveys of the general public. These three sources of evidence differ greatly. The laboratory is a strange, alien world in which all aspects of the environment are highly structured and the research respondent, whether child, adolescent, or adult, is required to react to those stimuli as they are presented. The work is experimental, meaning that the research investigator has manipulated aspects of the situation so as to compare the responses of one group of individuals to those of another. The atmosphere is out of Dr. Strangelove and other theatrical visions of the weird scientist at work on people. Yet the work is also compelling in ways that no other research is, precisely because it is so rigorously controlled.

In contrast, interviews with people about their life experiences are often only minimally structured, providing people with the opportunity to talk about the things that are most important to them. In interview research, the respondent often directs the work, and the investigator simply acts as a faithful recorder of the respondent's experiences. The data are time consuming to gather but rich in their detail and implications.

The survey represents another method with intrinsic advantages and disadvantages. Taking a survey involves asking a large number of people a limited set of questions about some specific aspect of their lives. The chief disadvantage of the survey method is that when large numbers of people are canvassed, typically only a few questions can be asked. The advantages, however, are manifold. When the general public is surveyed about its beliefs, people who are young and old, male and female, well educated and poorly educated, drawn from diverse geographic areas and from all occupations of life, respond to the questions. Conclusions that can be drawn about the beliefs of the general public are impressive conclusions indeed, for they cut across numerous distinctions and ways of living that otherwise divide us.

When three such different types of evidence show similar conclusions, confidence in the results rises enormously. Such is the case with the present endeavor. The experimental work in cognition, interviews from people going through stressful life events, and surveys of the general public clearly converge on a common set of life themes and mechanisms of the mind that promote mental health.

This is a propitious time to write a volume on mental health. Previous analyses have come largely from the clinical literature and have drawn extensively on case histories and observations made by clinicians in their practices with people suffering from a variety of mental disturbances and distress. Occasionally, one also finds an empirical investigation of a nonclinical well-functioning sample. For example, mental health pioneer Abraham Maslow, who described the process of self-actualization in the mid-1950s, did so through an intense examination of creative and influential leaders in the fields of politics, literature, and humanitarian enterprises, as well as through interviews with less prominent but capable, well-functioning adults.[1] For the most part, however, these investigations were isolated from each other and limited by the kinds and numbers of people investigated.

I have the good fortune to be writing at a time when psychology offers literally hundreds of well-designed, well-controlled scientific investigations that address aspects of mental health. It is hard to imagine more opportune circumstances. Yet there is also some risk entailed in offering a nonclinical account of processes that have previously been examined almost exclusively from a clinical perspective. Science often lacks the subtleties and richness of the clinical experience. The significant statistical differences that can seem so compelling to a scientist rarely carry the persuasive wallop of even a single, sensitively written case history. In this respect, the clinical case history can sometimes be dangerous, for while it is often a sensitive, faithful, and insightful description of one individual's experience, its implications for other people and situations are unknown.

Moreover, by the time science comes around to demonstrating the validity of a certain point, someone is almost certain to have voiced the idea. Consequently, a bit of the novelty of the conclusions can be undermined. Yet even using a completely different approach to the question of mental health, there is convergence with themes in the clinical literature, particularly self-psychology as formulated by Heinz Kohut and his followers, and cognitive-behavioral analyses of such problems as depression.[2] From these joint endeavors, the picture of the mentally healthy mind is slowly but clearly emerging.

Anthropologist Sol Tax of the University of Chicago was one day carrying his granddaughter on his shoulders when he encountered a colleague. The friend, who had not seen the little girl for a while, looked up at her and said, "My, my! How you've grown!" The child responded, "Not all of this is me."[3] This assessment aptly reflects my own situation in recounting the events and observations that follow. I am extremely grateful to my fellow social psychologists, on whose shoulders I sit, and who have conducted the lion's share of the careful, cautious work from which this book is assembled. I am also grateful to the cognitive psychologists and clinical psychologists whose work is also intrinsic and vital to the formulation of these ideas.

I wish to thank the National Institute of Mental Health,

which has demonstrated its confidence in me through twenty years of support from my earliest days in graduate school to the present. I am especially grateful for the ten-year Research Scientist Development Award that has enabled me to dedicate my time to the pursuit of these problems.

I wish to acknowledge the collaborative efforts of many generations of undergraduate and graduate students and postdoctoral scholars who have worked with me over the years on these problems. These students include Lisa Aspinwall, Leslie Clark, Mary Collins, Rebecca Collins, Jennifer Crocker, Gayle Dakof, Roberta Falke, Larry Feinstein, Myra Ferree, Susan Fiske, Nancy Goodban, Judith Hall, Jim Kulik, Darrin Lehman, Smadar Levin, Marci Lobel, John Lydon, Grant Marshall, Fred Miller, Buf Meyer, Geoffrey Reed, Sherry Schneider, Barry Shields, Laurie Skokan, Elliot Smith, Robyn Steer, Suzanne Thompson, Jay Wagener, Charlene Williams, Elissa Wurf, and most especially Jonathon Brown, Rosemary Lichtman, and Joanne Wood.

I am grateful to my many colleagues and friends in psychology and related fields who have influenced the development of these ideas and, in many cases, read drafts of chapters or articles and commented extensively on them. In this context, I especially thank Roy Baumeister, Edward Emery, Constance Hammen, Charles McClintock, Richard Nisbett, Lee Ross, William Swann, Charles Taylor, and Elissa Wurf. I am especially grateful to George Vaillant, who first suggested that I write this book.

I wish to thank Judy Greissman and Laura Wolff for encouraging me on this project and my editor, Jo Ann Miller, for her help in bringing this volume to fruition. Special thanks are also due Garrett Duncan Songhawke for his efforts in preparing multiple drafts of the manuscript and readying it for publication. I am grateful to my husband, Mervyn Fernandes, for his love and support. And, finally, I dedicate this volume to my children, Sara and Charlie, who have brought me more joy than they can imagine.

Positive Illusions

CHAPTER 1

Escape from Reality: Illusions in Everyday Life

> With the truth, one cannot live. To be able to live, one needs illusions.
> —OTTO RANK

WHAT is mental health? What do we mean when we say a person has a healthy mind? Philosophers and scientists have debated these questions for decades. Some have regarded the mind as an unruly pursuer of pleasure that must be tamed by social forces and the overbearing weight of its own guilt. According to this view, the healthy mind is one that is under control, its secret desires converted into socially acceptable substitutions. Others have regarded the mind as an evenhanded processor of knowledge, one that sorts out information in a relatively unbiased manner and emerges with carefully drawn conclusions and well-considered decisions. Occasionally this process might be thrown off balance by emotions such as anxiety or passion, but usually the mind is thought to perform its task quite well. In this view, then, the healthy mind is a sober little creature, seeking to find the most rational answers.

Despite the variety of views of mental health, there is one point on which most experts agree. Decades of psychological wisdom have established contact with reality as a hallmark of mental health. The well-adjusted person is thought to have a clear perception of reality, whereas someone whose vision is clouded by illusion is regarded as vulnerable to, if not already a victim of, mental illness.

In 1958, the federal government called together a group of the country's most prominent mental health experts to address the question that opened this chapter. The esteemed psychological historian Marie Jahoda was asked to distill knowledge on the topic into a volume summarizing what was known about mental health. After carefully reviewing prominent psychological theories, Jahoda concluded the following:

> The perception of reality is called mentally healthy when what the individual sees corresponds to what is actually there. . . .[1] Mentally healthy perception means the process of viewing the world so that one is able to take in matters one wishes were different without distorting them to fit those wishes.[2]

Most theories of mental health, Jahoda concluded, consider accurate perceptions of reality to be a critical component of mental health, a point echoed in the writings of Gordon Allport, Erik Erikson, Abraham Maslow, Karl Menninger, and Erich Fromm, among others.[3]

The position that one must perceive reality accurately to be mentally healthy has a certain self-evident quality. Marked distortions of reality surely must lead to poor functioning in the world. Believing incorrectly that one can swim can lead to drowning. False perceptions of one's talents can produce incorrect choices of occupations or mates. Perhaps for this reason, the assumption that accurate perceptions of reality are a critical component of mental health has continued for decades to go unchallenged. Indeed, this assumption has been so much considered the conventional wisdom that it has made its way into textbooks. One volume, for example, suggests that the ability to perceive reality as it really is is fundamental to effective functioning and is one of the main preconditions to the development of the healthy personality.[4]

One may legitimately ask whether musings on mental health have any real consequences for human thought and behavior. Indeed they do, in two important ways. First, theory largely dictates the kinds of science conducted, both in a benign fashion, by defining the questions that are considered important, and in a more insidious fashion, by suggesting the kinds of conclusions it is appropriate to draw. Those scientists who generate conclusions consistent with current theory find their articles published and cited, whereas those whose findings contradict or challenge established wisdom may find their methods, statistics, and conclusions scrutinized more closely and held to a higher standard. Scientific bias is in favor of established belief.[5]

Perhaps more important is the fact that mental health practitioners, those who work directly with patients, are trained in and guided by these established conventions of mental health. Taught that contact with reality is the sine qua non of mental health, at least some clinicians feel this to be the standard to which patients should be held. Psychologist C. R. Snyder noted that his clinical training represented accurate perception of reality as essential to mental health, a point he had not questioned until one of his patients grumbled, "What's so great about reality?"[6] Psychologist Richard Lazarus remarks of his own clinical training in the 1950s:

> To be sophisticated meant accepting *accurate reality testing* as
> the hallmark of mental health. . . . Everyone knew that
> self-deception was tantamount to mental disorder. If one

wished to manage life successfully, it was not only necessary to know the truth, however painful, but to revel in it
and even drown in it if need be.[7]

Nonetheless, despite its plausibility, this viewpoint is increasingly difficult to maintain or justify. A persistent voice
from cognitive psychology suggests a different conclusion altogether. In fact, as we shall see, a substantial amount of knowledge now testifies to the prevalence of bias and illusion in
normal human thought. Indeed, social scientists have found
that rather than perceiving themselves, the world, and the future accurately, most people regard themselves, their circumstances, and the future as considerably more positive than is
objectively likely or than reality can sustain.[8] These biased
perceptions, or *illusions,* as I call them, often involve central
aspects of the self and the environment and therefore cannot be
dismissed as inconsequential. Illusions fall into three general
categories: self-enhancement, or the perception of one's self,
one's past behavior, and one's enduring attributes as more positive than is actually the case; an exaggerated belief in one's
personal control, involving the perception that one can bring
about primarily positive but not negative outcomes; and unrealistic optimism, namely perceptions that the future holds an
unrealistically bountiful array of opportunities and a singular
absence of adverse events.

Although the view that illusion marks normal human perception is not entirely new, the scientific basis for these observations is quite recent.[9] How did this discovery come about? In
trying to understand how and why people think the way they
do, early research investigations on human thinking made the
assumption that people take in and interpret information about
the world fairly accurately. The person was said to converse
with the world much as a scientist might. He or she was thought
to gather information in an unbiased manner, put it together in
a logical and clear fashion, and reach generally good and accu-

rate inferences and decisions.[10] This view of the person as an accurate negotiator with reality quickly ran into difficulty. Indeed, scientists were startled by people's incomplete gathering of information and the shortcuts, errors, and biases they demonstrated in decision making and the formation of judgments. Some of those studying the judgment process began to wonder how it is that people survive at all, given the flaws that can be so readily documented in their reasoning.[11]

It is not simply that people make mistakes when they take in information and try to draw inferences from it. They must, of course, invariably commit errors, because of the enormity of the task before them, namely processing a wealth of information and making sense of it. Rather, the alarm these early scientists experienced derived from the fact that the mistakes consistently stray in a particular direction. Normal human thought is distinguished by a robust positive bias.

My task in this volume is to persuade the reader that normal human thought and perception is marked not by accuracy but by positive self-enhancing illusions about the self, the world, and the future. Moreover, as I will attempt to show, these illusions are not merely characteristic of human thought; they appear actually to be adaptive, promoting rather than undermining good mental health. Such a viewpoint forces us not only to reconsider the underpinnings of the concept of mental health, but to reconsider as well clinical approaches to a variety of mental health problems, such as how people learn from negative information, how they overcome adversity in their lives, and how they succumb to certain debilitating emotional disorders such as depression.

But these comments anticipate the evidence. The first step is to characterize the illusions of thought and to consider how they develop. This search begins with the science of the self, a literature that explores how people develop the sense of self in childhood and perceive their attributes in adulthood. Novelist André Gide remarked, "Each one of us has his own way of deceiving himself. The important thing is to believe in one's own importance" (Gide, 1987, p. 44). The sense of one's own importance is an appropriate place to begin.

THE SELF AS HERO

One of the first things an infant learns is that the self is a separate person. Upon seeing his reflection, the very young baby will pat his image and pat himself in return, knowing that what he is seeing is himself. Much of early knowledge involves distinguishing what is the self from other important people in the environment, especially the mother and father. As a consequence, the self helps to organize thinking around its attributes and its relationships to the social world.[12] Mental health experts suggest that the process by which this differentiation of self occurs should involve the capacity to perceive the self realistically, that is, to acknowledge faithfully both one's strengths and one's weaknesses. This is not, in fact, how the process evolves.

Before the exigencies of the world impinge upon the child's self-concept, the child is his or her own hero. With few exceptions, most children think very well of themselves. They believe they are capable at many tasks and abilities, including those they have never tried. They see themselves as popular. Most kindergartners and first-graders say they are at or near the top of the class. They have great expectations for their future success. Moreover, these grandiose assessments are quite unresponsive to negative feedback, at least until approximately age seven. Children see themselves as successful on most tasks, even ones on which they failed. They seem quite cheerfully oblivious to feedback from others that they have not performed as well as they think they have.[13] An architect friend recounts the time he took his five-year-old daughter to work with him.

As he finalized some building plans at his drafting table, the child scrupulously mimicked the behavior at a nearby desk. Amused passersby came over to see what the child had accomplished, and one kindly friend remarked, "Someday you'll be an even better architect than your daddy." The child looked up in surprise and responded, "But I already am," and went back to work.

Why do children have such unrealistically positive assessments of their abilities that, moreover, appear to be so unresponsive to feedback? Psychologist Deborah Stipek argues, in part, that children do not necessarily view failure as failure. To a child, the fact that a goal has not been attained does not mean that something bad has occurred or that the experience has any implications for the future. Eventually children learn to judge their performance as a success or failure, but in very young children these concepts have little meaning. Children have fairly short memories and may actually forget how they have done. Children also see ability and effort as very much the same thing, and so they see any activity in pursuit of a goal, whether successful or unsuccessful, as progress. As one child noted, "If you study, it helps the brain and you get smarter."[14] Young children do not differentiate very well between what they wish could be true and what they think is true, and thus they show wishful thinking in their estimations of their abilities.[15]

The view of oneself as a hero who possesses all the qualities necessary to succeed in a world filled with opportunities fades somewhat in late childhood, but it is nonetheless present in adults as well as children. Although mental health experts regard the well-adjusted person as being aware and accepting of negative as well as positive aspects of the self, in fact, most adults hold very positive views of themselves. When asked to describe themselves, most people mention many positive qualities and few, if any, negative ones.[16] Even when people acknowledge that they have faults, they tend to downplay those weaknesses as unimportant or dismiss them as inconsequential.[17] For those who are mathematically inclined, the world is awash with arithmetic problems waiting to be solved. For those with little talent in that direction, the tasks are best left undone or delegated to a spouse or an accountant. People regard activities that do not hold their interest as less important than things that interest them. To a football fan, football is an important part of life. To those uninterested in football, it is a slow-moving, bizarre contest between surreal giants who could surely think of better ways to spend their time. When people recognize their lack of talent in a particular area, they are likely to see it as a common fault shared by others. Favored abilities, in contrast, are typically regarded as rare and distinctive signs of unusual talent.[18] The child who can hop on one foot is convinced no one else can do it quite as well, while this same child would insistently argue that all her friends eat cereal with their fingers, too. Thus, far from being balanced between positive and negative conceptions, the image that most people hold of themselves is heavily weighted in a positive direction.[19]

But are these self-perceptions actually unrealistic? Is the positive self-image an illusion or a reality? An imbalance in self-perceptions does not in and of itself mean that people's self-perceptions are biased. Most people commit positive actions most of the time, and consequently people's favorable attributes and actions considerably outweigh their negative ones. There is, however, some evidence that adults' positive self-perceptions are unrealistic. Most people, for example, see themselves as better than others and as above average on most of their qualities. When asked to describe themselves and other people, most people provide more positive descriptions of themselves than they do of friends. This tendency to see the self as better than others occurs across a wide variety of tasks and abilities.[20] Because it is logically impossible for most people to be better than everyone else, the positive view that most people have of themselves appears to be, at least to some degree, illusory in nature. Most people even believe that they drive better than others. For example, in one survey, 90 percent of automobile drivers considered themselves to be better than average drivers. Indeed, these beliefs sometimes show an unresponsiveness to feedback that reminds one of the very young child. When people whose driving had involved them in accidents serious enough to involve hospitalization were interviewed about their driving skills and compared with drivers who had not had accident histories, the two groups gave almost identical descriptions of their driving abilities. Irrespective of their accident records, people judged themselves to be more skillful than average, and this was true even when the drivers involved in accidents had been responsible for them.[21]

The evaluations people offer of themselves are also typically more favorable than judgments made by others about them.[22] For example, when people's descriptions are contrasted with the descriptions of them offered by their friends or acquaintances, the self-descriptions tend to be more positive. Typically, we see ourselves in more flattering terms than we are seen by others. The perception of self that most people hold, then, is not as well balanced as traditional theories of mental health suggest. Rather than being attentive to both the favorable and unfavorable aspects of the self, most people appear to be very cognizant of their strengths and assets and considerably less aware of their weaknesses and faults. Our self-aggrandizing perceptions may result in part from biases in how we remember ourselves and our past actions.

THE SELF AS PERSONAL HISTORIAN

Our minds are constructed not only to sift through and digest the information available to us in the present, but to store and make sense of all the information that has been part of the past. In a sense each person acts as a personal historian, recording the events of which he or she has been a part. Rather than acting as a dispassionate recorder of events as they transpire, the self appears to actively fabricate and revise personal history. Moreover, this task is accomplished in a way that makes the self an important, central, and positive figure in that history.

In his landmark essay, "The Totalitarian Ego," psychologist Anthony Greenwald argues that "the past is remembered as if it were a drama in which the self is the leading player."[23] In some ways, this fact is a necessity of memory. One can remember only events in which one participated because, by definition, events from which one was absent cannot be remembered, only heard about. Moreover, memory must be limited by our own perceptions of what transpired. We cannot remember other people's interpretations of situations, only our own. We can experience only our own sensations and emotional reactions to situations and not other people's. Since memory is often enriched by the recall of particular feelings or sensations, these details will, of necessity, be egocentric, that is, centered around the self. In recalling a dinner party of the night before, I may remember that I had slightly too much to drink, told an off-color story about a colleague that might best have been censored, and was otherwise fairly outgoing and a little funnier than usual. Were I to share these perceptions with another who had been a guest at the party, they would no doubt bear little resemblance to his recollections. He might dimly remember my off-color story, have no awareness that I had slightly too much to drink, nor be particularly cognizant of the fact that I was entertaining. Rather, his own recollection of the party might involve wondering whether people noticed that he was feeling low and whether they would properly attribute this to problems in his marriage. He might remember several of the stories told, but not necessarily who told which one. He might recall wondering at ten o'clock if the party would ever end, and the relief he felt when at eleven fifteen people finally pushed their chairs away from the table to say good night. The comparison of these experiences suggests that we were at different dinner parties, which indeed is exactly what happened in certain respects. In the absence of any active reconstruction or distortion, memory is egocentric, organized entirely around the experiences of the person constructing the memory.

But memory is egocentric in more important ways as well.

Our memories of situations not only bear the traces of egocentric sensations and perspectives, but are also actively organized around our own interests and concerns. Each of us has qualities that we consider to be characteristic of ourselves. One person may think of himself as witty, musical, and hopelessly lacking in athletic ability. Another person may regard herself as kind, overweight, and intelligent. Psychologists call these enduring beliefs that people have about themselves *self-schemas*. [24] Self-schemas are important because they guide the selection and interpretation of information in social situations. The man who thinks of himself as musical will almost certainly remember that a Mozart clarinet concerto played in the background during the dinner party, whereas someone who does not consider himself to be musical might not even be aware than music was playing. The person who thinks of himself as witty is likely to interpret his barbed remark toward another dinner guest as humorous, whereas a person for whom kindness is an important dimension may interpret the same behavior as rude and unkind. The woman who thinks of herself as overweight will almost certainly remember the entire menu, what she ate and what she didn't eat, and the approximate caloric value of each food item.

Self-schemas, then, impose an additional selectivity on the information that people construe from situations and later remember about them. In recalling information that fits self-schemas, those self-schemas are inadvertently reinforced by memory. For example, each situation that a witty person interprets as an example of his own witty banter provides him with additional evidence that he is witty. If he construes three or four remarks that he made as examples of his wit, then his self-perception as a witty person is strengthened by each of these events. Other guests at the party, however, may remember only one or two of the remarks, considering neither especially funny. Self-schemas, then, enable us to take in the information that fits our prior conceptions of what we are like and what interests us and simultaneously helps cement those self-impressions.

Psychologists generally interpret the effects of self-schemas on memory to mean that memory is organized efficiently in a limited number of categories. That is, given that no one can take in all of the available information in a situation, self-schemas provide guidelines for which information should be noticed, thought about, and put away in memory. The fact that these organizing categories are related to the self is in some respects an accident of the fact that the self is taking in the information. If one takes a functional perspective for a moment, however, it is clear that the egocentric organization of information can be very useful. People make a rough cut on information as "relevant to me" or "not relevant to me." Next they interpret exactly how the information is relevant. When that information is later stored egocentrically in memory, it can be applied in extremely useful ways. For example, a woman for whom kindness is important not only uses kindness as a way of sorting people into the categories of kind and unkind, she may also use the information as a basis for her own future social interactions. Having determined that the witty man is unkind, she would be very likely to avoid him in future situations, a highly adaptive maneuver from her standpoint. Clearly, the egocentric organization of memory is useful from an economic standpoint, that is, in reducing information to a manageable load.[25] But beyond this, it may be very adaptive in helping people to construct their future activities.[26]

Most of us think well of ourselves on most attributes, so self-schemas are more likely to be positive than negative. This recognition leads to the realization that memory for past events will likely be recalled in a positive manner, one that reflects well on the self. This logical inference yields a third way in which memory is biased, namely toward positive construals of one's own attributes and roles in events gone by.[27] Indeed, the capacity of memory to recast events in a positive light almost immediately after they have transpired is almost astonishing. People who have just performed poorly on a task such as doing mathematics problems can be asked to recall their performance a scant twenty minutes later, and even in the short interval they mis-remember their performance as better than it actually was. Within a few days or weeks, the event may be forgotten alto-gether. If I rush a student in and out of my office in a few minutes, knowing that he has not had a chance to discuss his research with me fully, I may feel guilty shortly thereafter, but will likely have put the event totally out of mind within days. If I later learn that he has told other students that I am too busy to provide useful advice, I might be hurt and amazed by this betrayal, totally forgetting that I once believed it to hold a kernel of truth.

When people are asked to recall their personal qualities, they typically come up with more positive than negative informa-tion. Positive information about one's own personality is easily recalled and efficiently processed, whereas negative informa-tion about one's personality is poorly processed and difficult to recall.[28] There are, of course, qualifications to this general rule. Most of us know that in making our qualities known to another person, to brag endlessly of our talents without any assessment of our weaknesses would make us appear conceited. In order to achieve the positive picture we wish to construct for others, sometimes we may admit to certain faults. However, even the faults or weaknesses may be carefully chosen to round out a warm, human portrait, rather than one that is balanced between the positive and negative.[29] A woman may be more likely to admit to others that she is hopeless at math than to confess that she sometimes cheats on her husband. Thus, while our charac-terizations of ourselves to others may incorporate a certain so-cially desirable modesty, the portraits that we actually believe, when we are given freedom to voice them, are dramatically more positive than reality can sustain. As writer Carlos Fuentes so acutely noted, "Desire will send you back into memory . . . for memory is desire satisfied."[30]

Greenwald's characterization of these memory processes as totalitarian is apt. Unlike the academic historian, who is ex-pected to adhere closely to the facts and insert a personal evaluation only in the interpretation, the personal historian takes unbridled license with the facts themselves, rearranging and distorting them and omitting aspects of history altogether in an effort to create and maintain a positive image of the self. We control the present by using our own interests and attributes as ways of selecting and organizing available information, and then we store it in memory in ways that are both highly positive and consistent with our existing impressions of ourselves. We use the present to construct a benign portrait of the past with ourselves as central actors. In so doing, we pave the way for a similar future.

THE SELF AS CAUSAL ACTOR

Taking in and recalling information are not the only cognitive tasks that people must perform. Active interpretation of the present is also required. Perceptions of what caused events to happen are among the most important beliefs that people hold about social situations. Here, too, the self is self-serving. A consistent and ubiquitous research finding is that people take credit for good things that happen and deny responsibility for the bad things that happen.[31] This self-serving bias, as it has been called, shows up in a broad array of situations. For example, on the tennis court, after you have soundly beaten an opponent, rarely do you hear the gratifying, "Gee, you're much better than I am, aren't you?" Usually you hear that it was a bad day, your opponent's serve was off, he is still working on his backhand, or the light was in his eyes. On the other hand, when you have just been badly beaten, the smug look and condescending "bad luck" from the opponent are particularly grating because you know that he does not believe it was bad luck for a moment; he simply thinks he is better. Positive outcomes or actions tend to be attributed to one's own personal qualities, whereas negative outcomes are regarded as the result of bad luck or factors beyond one's control.

The following examples from the *San Francisco Chronicle* of drivers' explanations of their accidents to the police reveal how reluctantly people assume blame for negative events.

> As I approached an intersection, a sign suddenly appeared in a place where a stop sign had never appeared before. I was unable to stop in time to avoid an accident.

> The telephone pole was approaching. I was attempting to swerve out of its way when it struck my front end.[32]

And commenting on students' evaluations of final exams, Greenwald notes:

> I have repeatedly found a strong correlation between obtained grade and the belief that the exam was a proper measure. Students who do well are willing to accept credit for success; those who do poorly, however, are unwilling to accept responsibility for failure, instead seeing the exam (or the instructor) as being insensitive to their abilities.[33]

How do people maintain the perception that they cause good things to happen but bear less responsibility for bad outcomes? Is this simply some sleight of mind analogous to the magician's sleight of hand? Or can it be understood as an adaptive cognitive process? Perhaps when people try to understand why an event occurred, they confuse their intentions with their actions.[34] Usually we intend to cause good things and not bad things. When those good things do occur, the tendency to see ourselves as having brought them about may be quite justifiable, given that we did indeed mean to bring the outcome about. However, when our actions produce bad outcomes, we may look for circumstantial explanations precisely because no adverse outcomes were intended. The man who backs out of his driveway and hits a small child may blame the automobile manufacturers for having rear-view mirrors that fail to pick up low objects. Alternatively, he may blame the child's parents for not having trained the child to stay out of the street. He is unlikely to blame himself, because he never intended to hit the child. Whether the confusion of intention and causality underlies the tendency to attribute good outcomes to oneself to a greater degree than bad outcomes remains to be seen. The interpretational bias itself, however, is well established and constitutes yet another way in which the mind actively fosters a positive view of the self.

Self-serving biases in the perception of the causes of events are strengthened by the fact that people typically exaggerate how much of a role they have in any task, particularly one with a good outcome.[35] To take a simple example, when two people have written a book together and are asked to estimate how much of the book they are personally responsible for, the estimates added together will typically exceed 100 percent. The same feature characterizes more mundane tasks. Asked to estimate how much of a contribution they make to housework, adding together husbands' and wives' estimates of their own efforts produces a total that greatly exceeds 100 percent.[36] Even the lore surrounding Nobel Prize winners is filled with such accounts.

> In 1923, two Canadians, Banting and Macleod, were awarded the Nobel Prize for their discovery of insulin. Upon receiving the prize, Banting contended that Macleod, who was head of the laboratory, had been more of a hindrance than a help. On the other hand, Macleod managed to omit Banting's name in speeches describing the research leading up to discovery of insulin.[37]

What leads people to overestimate their role in jointly undertaken ventures? Egocentric memory appears once again to be the culprit. We notice our own contributions to a joint task because we are mentally and physically present when making our own contributions. When the other person is contributing his or her share to the joint task, we may not be physically present to observe it or we may be distracted from noticing the other person's effort. When asked to recall who contributed what to the task, it will subsequently be easier to recall one's own contributions, having attended to them better in the first place, than to recall the other person's.[38]

There will also likely be interpretational biases in what constitutes a contribution.[39] A recent tiff between two authors of a book centered on the fact that while one wrote his share of the chapters rather quickly, the other put a great deal more time into preparing his chapters. Because the first writer was more experienced, his chapters needed few revisions; but the second author's chapters required several drafts and received comments from the first author. The first author perceived that he had borne the lion's share of the effort, by both being responsible for his own chapters and critiquing those of his collaborator. The collaborator, in contrast, felt that he had done the most, because his work had taken three times as long as the first author's. Who is right? Clearly it depends on one's perspective, and one can make a case for either position.

The tendency to take more than one's share of credit for a joint outcome would appear to be a maladaptive bias, inasmuch as it creates so many opportunities for misunderstandings. However, the bias may have benefits as well as potential liabilities. By perceiving one's share of a joint product to be larger than it is, people may feel more responsible for the outcome and work harder to make it a positive one. Moreover, the process of contributing to the activity may instill a sense of commitment to the project and to one's collaborators that may undermine, at least temporarily, any feelings of having done more than one's share. The bias, too, may be more one of memory than of active construction during the time that the tasks are being performed. Often, when two people have jointly achieved greatness, the falling out over who was most responsible for the product occurs after the outcome has been achieved, not while the task is going on. Commitment and a sense of responsibility may carry the joint product through completion, but egocentric memory may distort later reconstructions of what actually took place.[40]

At this point, it is useful to take stock and reassess whether normal human self-perception is characterized by realism or not. The evidence from numerous research investigations with both children and adults clearly indicates that people's assessments of their own capabilities are ego-enhancing rather than realistic. The fact that this bias is so clearly prevalent in the normal human mind is surprising. Psychologists have typically interpreted blatant ego enhancement as the resort of weak and insecure people attempting to bolster fragile self-esteem. Weak egos are thought to need narcissism to survive.[41] Alternatively, ego defensiveness has been viewed as a handy refuge for all of us during weak or threatening moments.[42] In this view, we may need the occasional self-serving interpretation to recover from a blow to self-esteem, but not otherwise. The picture furnished by the evidence, however, is quite different and suggests that ego enhancement characterizes most perception most of the time. This fact, in itself, does not make self-enhancement adaptive, but it does make it normal. As such, this picture is in opposition to the portrait of normal functioning painted by many theories of mental health.

THE NEED FOR CONTROL

In 1971, psychologist B. F. Skinner published a book, *Beyond Freedom and Dignity*, that sparked heated debate. Among other points, Skinner argued that freedom and individual will are illusions because behavior is under the control of positive and negative reinforcements provided by the environment. The uproar created by this argument is testimony to the attachment people have to their perceptions of freedom, personal choice, and control. Indeed, Skinner may have gone too far. While there is certainly a basis for contending that freedom, control, and personal will are constructions that people impose on events rather than factors inherent in events themselves, what people construe about their behavior is of great importance. Interpretations enable people to make sense of their experience; moreover, they can have important personal consequences. As psychologist Herbert Lefcourt notes:

> To believe that one's freedom is a false myth and that one should submit to wiser or better controls contains the assumption that beliefs or illusions have no immediate consequences. . . . This assumption is specious. Illusions have consequences and . . . the loss of the illusion of freedom may have untoward consequences for the way men live.[43]

Since the days of Aristotle and Plato, philosophers have argued that a sense of personal control is vital to human functioning. Psychologists from many theoretical viewpoints, including social psychologist Fritz Heider, developmental psychologist Robert White, learning theorist Albert Bandura, and psychoanalytic theorists Alfred Adler and Sandor Fenichel, have maintained that the self-concept cannot mature without a sense of personal control.

THE CHILD'S NEED FOR CONTROL

The desire to control and manipulate the world is evident from a remarkably early age. Within weeks after birth, an infant actively explores the environment, responding to a new stimulus, such as a brightly colored rattle, with rapt attention and babbling. Soon, however, when the rattle has been fully explored, the infant shows little response when the rattle is again dangled before her, but may react with the same excitement to a new checkerboard that she has not previously seen. The infant, then, is primed to master new experiences.[44] At first, psychologists observing this behavior tried to identify what reinforcements it might bring for the child. Were the parents more likely to feed or comfort the child when he or she explored and manipulated the environment? What rewards did curiosity evoke that maintained this behavior? Soon it became evident that the child pursued these exploratory activities for their own sake. Exploration and the ability to bring about change in the environment are their own rewards.[45]

As a result of these observations, psychologists believe that even newborn infants have an intrinsic need to understand and manage the environment.[46] Even the youngest children seem to do what is good for them to bring about their own effective learning. They seek out tasks and sources of stimulation that lead to the development of new skills. Children seem to derive pleasure from engaging in this mastery-oriented behavior, and when a child has accomplished some task—that is, when mastery is attained—he or she seems to experience joy and satisfaction. Both pleasure in the activity itself and enjoyment of the sense of mastery promote similar activities in the future.

So evident is this drive toward mastery that psychologists believe the need to master the environment, or at least its basic elements, is wired in via a mastery-motivation system that instigates, maintains, and reinforces activities that lead to the development of new skills. White refers to this as competence motivation, arguing that the process of learning about the environment and gaining mastery over it is actually intrinsic to the child's development and will occur of its own accord unless disrupted by a biological malfunction or an impoverished environment.[47] Daniel Berlyne refers to a curiosity motivation by which the child constantly seeks more and varied objects to manipulate and explore.[48]

Some of the child's exploratory activities involve stretching already evident skills to try something new. For example, the infant who is able to reach and grasp a stationary toy may be stimulated more by a new toy that is moving than by another stationary toy. The moving toy forces her to extend her abilities to track the toy with her eyes and grasp it as it comes into reach.

Children seek and produce novel activity and stimulus variability. Moderately new environments that include objects the child has not seen before are far more interesting and stimulating than either radically different environments or environments full of familiar objects.

The child's mastery needs, then, have a certain orderly progression to them that is responsive both to the demands of tasks and to the limits of existing skills.[49] Any parent attempting unrealistically to throw a birthday party for a one-year-old will stumble upon this fact. As each gift is unwrapped, the child reacts not to the contents but to the wrappings, balling up the paper to make a wonderful crumpling noise and waving the brightly colored ribbons overhead. The empty box makes a perfect hat and is far more valued a toy than the train that came in it, which may not be admired and played with for another six or eight months. Children learn and perform new tasks that are just beyond their range of competence. The young child does not try to drive a car. He depresses the accelerator repeatedly. The adolescent, ready for such a challenge, rolls the car down the driveway at night and practices driving while his parents sleep. The very young child's early cooking efforts extend to baking cookies by stirring in the flour and eating too many chocolate bits. The adolescent can cook an entire meal, assuming she can be induced to do so. Mastery skills are used in a discriminating fashion, moving a step or two ahead of the child's current abilities.

By learning to master their own environments, children alter their parents' behaviors dramatically. Parents quickly learn that if they want the infant to reward them with enthusiastic sounds, the best way to achieve this goal is to gradually introduce more and varied novel experiences. Even infants are able to enlist the cooperation of the social environment to their own mastery needs.[50]

The desire to master the environment, then, appears to be a basic drive, perhaps even a fundamental need of the human organism. By learning that he or she can have an impact on the environment, the child acquires the valuable skills, crucial for adult functioning, that enable him or her to actively intervene in the world so as to bring about desired outcomes. The implicit assumption that underlies a functional interpretation of the need to master is that such early experiences provide the child with a realistic sense of self-efficacy, that is, a realization of those things that can be actively changed and controlled in order to realize personal goals. In fact, however, the sense of control that young children develop appears to be exaggerated rather than tempered by realism.

As young children are learning *how* to control the environment, so too are they learning *that* they can control it. Early in development, children gain the sense that they can make things happen.[51] This, too, may be intrinsic to the child's nature, for it can easily be observed in extreme and dramatic form in the young child. In his conversations with children, the esteemed developmental psychologist Jean Piaget discovered that children believe not only that they can master what goes on in the immediate environment but that they control the movements of the sun, moon, and stars as well.[52] The child's sense of omnipotence is so strong that when family crises arise, such as a sibling's illness or parents' divorce, young children may react very strongly, in part because they believe they brought the tragic events about.[53]

The child's sense of omnipotence extends to schoolwork and other learning tasks. When asked to guess how well they will do on tasks, young children usually substantially overestimate their performance because they believe they can master the tasks easily. Psychologist Carol Dweck and her associates argue that a mastery orientation toward tasks develops and coheres quite early in life.[54] Mastery-oriented children approach new tasks with the question, "How can this best be accomplished and what should I do to solve it correctly?" When they run into trouble on a difficult task, these mastery-oriented children talk to themselves, trying to figure out what is wrong with their performance and developing strategies to change it so they will be more effective. Often they encourage themselves, letting themselves know that they can do the task correctly.

The competence drive that one sees in the infant and young child is remarkably simple, but extraordinary in its effects. On the one hand, it requires no plan or intention. Yet it enables the child to fashion his or her environment in an increasingly complex way, enlisting the cooperation and talents of several powerful adults in the process, and to derive great pleasure and satisfaction from the results, while simultaneously building essential intellectual skills.

Over time, the child's sense of personal control diminishes somewhat, becoming responsive to realistic limits on talents and the limitations inherent in difficult tasks.[55] Despite this movement toward realism, adults not only continue to have a need and desire to control the environment, but also maintain an exaggerated faith in their ability to do so.

THE ADULT'S NEED FOR CONTROL

Most adults believe the world to be inherently controllable. They have faith that a combination of personal effort and advanced technology can solve most of the world's problems. To the extent that we have been unsuccessful in controlling natural forces or, for that matter, the economic, social, and political dilemmas we have ourselves created, we perceive it to be through lack of effort, not ability, that the problems have remained unsolved. We believe that people succeed through their own efforts, and this leads us to impute effort to those who are highly successful and laziness to those who are not.[56] Even if evidence is all around us suggesting that events are less orderly and systematic than we think they are, rarely do we develop a full appreciation of this fact. The failure to recognize the role of random, unsystematic forces in many aspects of life may come, in part, from our need to see the world as a systematic and orderly place. As Ernest Becker noted in his Pulitzer Prize– winning book, *The Denial of Death,* through the imposition of logic and order on the world we spare ourselves the constant realization of the random terror of death.

One source of faith in personal control is that the environment often cooperates in maintaining it. People are typically quite cognizant of the effects of their own actions on the environment, but are considerably less so regarding the effects of the environment on their own actions. We underestimate the degree to which our behavior is determined by social and physical forces that not only are uncontrollable but often escape awareness altogether.[57] One of my colleagues believes, only half in jest, that he can will a parking place in any lot in which he needs to find one. The reason he holds this belief is that apparently most lots into which he drives have one or two spaces left. Until recently, it had escaped his attention that building projects must create an appropriate number of parking spaces. Thus, while he no doubt overestimates the number of times he gets the last spot, it is also the case that getting one of the last spots is a highly probable event, given the small miracle of city planning.

Another source of the belief in control is that people confuse what they want to have happen with what they can actually bring about, and if the desired event occurs, they conclude that they controlled it.[58] I once observed this in a young boy who had been hospitalized for diabetes. Although not confined to bed, he remained in the hospital for observation because his blood sugar level changed erratically and required monitoring. The hospital environment was dull for this youngster, and he soon took to riding the elevators to provide himself with some semblance of stimulation. Deciding that he would become the elevator operator, he positioned himself in front of the control panel, making it impossible for others to press any but the floor numbers. At each floor, the boy would push the "Door Open" button; when the passenger had departed, the boy would push the "Door Close" button. The door obediently opened and shut. The regular passengers tolerated this unusual behavior because they could see that the boy needed to believe that something, however small, was under his personal control. No one had the heart to tell him, and he never figured out on his own, that the elevator was controlled entirely automatically, and that his button presses had no effect whatsoever on its operation. Because the door repeatedly opened and shut when he wanted it to, he mistakenly assumed that his behavior was actually bringing it about.

The process of evaluating whether or not an event is controllable is an example of a broader fallacy of reasoning, namely the search for examples that confirm prior beliefs.[59] To see how this logical fallacy operates, consider the popular belief that people can cure themselves of serious illnesses through positive thinking. Many people believe that illness results primarily from stressful events and that those who are able to maintain a positive attitude can exert control over their bodily processes and drive illness away. What kind of evidence leads people to hold such a belief? Examples of the mental control of illness are readily available. Norman Cousins's book, *Anatomy of an Illness*, describes in warm and humorous detail the methods the author used to treat himself for a disease that it usually fatal. Magazines contain stories of people who have apparently healed themselves of advanced malignancies through positive thinking. Cultural mythology abounds with examples of shamans who cured their sick neighbors through a variety of useless but dramatic ceremonies. These positive examples make compelling reading, but the logical error lies in precisely this point: they are all positive instances.

Suppose one wanted to determine scientifically whether people are able to cure their diseases through positive attitudes. What would one need to know? Most people immediately recognize the need to find examples of people who tried to cure their diseases through positive thinking and were successful. If pushed, one might come up with the observation that it would be useful to find out how many people tried to cure their diseases through positive thinking and failed. What most people miss is that an accurate sense of whether people can cure their illnesses depends on at least two more types of information: the number of people who did not try to cure their incurable illnesses and survived nonetheless, and the number of people who did not make an effort to cure their illnesses and died. In other words, to establish that people can survive a serious illness if they have effectively tried to control it, one needs all four types of information.

Unfortunately, the world of disease is full of people who have tried valiantly to cure themselves of their illnesses and have ultimately failed. Those who have worked extensively with the chronically ill also know that many people survive years longer than expected without having made any effort in their own behalf at all. These people are often just as bewildered as their physicians, family, and friends to find themselves alive some five or ten years after their initial diagnosis, when everyone expected them to die within months.

In short, it is logically incorrect to conclude that people can control their illnesses simply because one can readily find apparent examples. When one is forced to survey all of the evidence—instead of just the positive cases that are so compelling—judgments of control are considerably more muted, and enthusiasm for the initial belief is somewhat diminished.

This is not to say that people are unable to improve their health by maintaining a positive attitude. The jury is still out on this issue. Rather, the point is that people "see" their beliefs confirmed in incomplete evidence that leads them prematurely to desired conclusions. They fail to see that evidence they have ignored is also relevant. Decision theorists despair of ever getting people to avoid this error. Moreover, on this bias, the average person is in good company. The error is virtually irresistible, not only to the general public but to high-level decision makers in government and industry as well. The analysis of numerous policy decisions, such as the disastrous Bay of Pigs invasion in 1961, has implicated as the basis of the failure the tendency to incorporate primarily positive information and to ignore negative information.[60]

THE ILLUSION OF CONTROL

As the previous analysis suggests, people not only believe that the world is inherently controllable, they believe that their own ability to personally control events around them is exceptional. Psychologist Ellen Langer argues that most people succumb to an illusion of control, in which they believe they can affect events more than is actually the case. To demonstrate this point, Langer chose gambling.[61]

Gambling is a clear case in which the relative importance of personal control and chance are often confused. Sociologist Erving Goffman, who once took a job as a croupier in Las Vegas, noted that dealers who experienced runs of bad luck, leading the house to lose heavily, ran the risk of losing their jobs, even though the reason for the run of bad luck was ostensibly chance.[62] Experienced dice players engaged in a variety of behaviors suggesting a belief that they could control what numbers the dice turned up. They threw the dice softly if they wanted low numbers to come up and hard if they were trying to get high numbers. Moreover, they believed that effort and concentration were important and often would not roll the dice unless there was silence and they had a few seconds to concentrate on the number they wanted to get.[63] These kinds of behaviors make perfect sense if a game involves skill. They do not make much sense when the outcome is controlled by chance.

Most of us are not heavy gamblers. In an intriguing set of studies, however, Langer was able to demonstrate that virtually all people are subject to the same illusions of control as veteran gamblers. Beginning with the recognition that people often fail to distinguish between controllable and uncontrollable events, she argued that one reason for this fact is that the cues people use to differentiate situations of luck and skill are often confused. In skill situations, there is a causal link between one's own behavior and likely outcomes. By choosing materials appropriate for a problem, deciding what responses to make, familiarizing oneself with those materials and responses, spending time thinking about the tasks, coming up with strategies that might be used, and exerting effort, people increase their likelihood of succeeding on a skill-based task.[64] On tasks determined by chance, such behaviors have no effect at all.

Langer showed that by introducing skill-related cues into a chance situation, people came to behave as if the situations were under their personal control and not a result of luck at all. Among her observations were the following: If a person had to bet against a suave, confident opponent, he bet less money than if the opponent appeared to be meek and ineffective. When people were able to choose their own lottery card, as opposed to having it chosen for them, they were less likely to turn it in for a new lottery card that offered them a better chance of winning, simply because they felt it was now *their* card and they wanted to hold onto it. The longer a person held on to a lottery card and presumably had time to think about the likelihood of winning and what he would do with all the money, the less likely he was to turn the lottery card in for a ticket in a drawing with better odds. Langer was able to show that perfectly normal people engaged in a wide variety of superstitious and nonsensical behaviors in chance situations, when cues suggesting skill had been subtly introduced.[65]

The significance of Langer's research extends far beyond its curious but rather minor implications regarding gambling. Any situation in which a person confronts options, develops strategies, and devotes thought to a problem is vulnerable to an illusion of control. For several months, I have been plagued with a problem that until recently proved to be intractable, namely the fact that my dogs eat the pansies growing in the backyard. A variety of disciplinary actions as well as the application of foul-smelling but harmless chemicals to the flower beds have proven unsuccessful in keeping them from these meals. Now, however, I have mastered the situation, by planning to plant pansies only in the beds around the front door. In the backyard I will plant marigolds, which are not nearly as appealing to dogs. The successful solution to this problem bolsters my confidence that I am able to handle stressful events. One can legitimately ask, of course, who actually has control in this situation, me or the dogs? While in my weaker moments I acknowledge that one can probably make the stronger case for the dogs, most of the time this does not dampen my self-congratulations at having successfully mastered the problem by choosing an effective solution. The fact that this "choice" was fully constrained by the situation and was the only option remaining, other than eliminating the dogs, is conveniently forgotten.

The illusion of control has powerful effects on the human psyche. Psychologists have demonstrated that people can tolerate extreme distress if they believe they have the ability to control the source of that distress.[66] The following study conducted with college students makes this point. The students were brought into the laboratory for a study of reactions to electric shock. Half of the students were told that once the shock began, they could terminate it simply by pressing a button in front of them. The other half of the students were not given a button to press to terminate the shock. All the students were then exposed to a series of uncomfortable but harmless electric shocks. The shocks were rigged so that both groups of students received exactly the same amount of shock. Despite this fact, those able to terminate the event by pressing the button themselves experienced less psychological distress, fewer symptoms of physiological arousal, and less physical discomfort.[67] This study and ones like it have been carried out many times with different stressful events and, in every known case, those who can exert control over the stressful event experience less distress and arousal than those who cannot. In fact, those able to control the event often show no more psychological distress or physiological arousal than people receiving no aversive experience at all.[68] Clearly it is not the adverse event itself that leads people to feel physically aroused and psychologically distressed, but rather the perception that it cannot be controlled.

Why do we perceive as controllable things that either are not controllable or are much less so than we think they are? We understand control. We know what it means to seek a goal, to develop methods for obtaining it, and then to employ those methods until the goal is obtained. There is an order, logic, and process to control. There is no order or logic to randomness. Perhaps as well we need to see events as controllable and this is why our minds are predisposed to focus in selectively on instances that support our preconceptions. Perhaps it is the false belief in control that makes people persist in pursuing their goals. Would a novelist undertaking her first work want to contemplate other writers who were catapulted into success by their first works, or would she want to focus instead on the far larger group of writers whose first novels never even attracted a publisher? Clearly, the answer is the former. Our need to see things as inherently controllable may well be adaptive, and our tendency to focus on positive cases of the relationships we expect and so badly wish to see may have value, even as it distorts perceptions.

UNREALISTIC OPTIMISM ABOUT THE FUTURE

Most people are oriented toward the future. When asked to describe what occupies their thoughts, people typically mention issues of immediate or future concern.[69] Moreover, optimism pervades thinking about the future. We seem to be optimistic by nature, some of us more than others, but most more than reality can support.[70] Each year, survey researchers query the American public about their current lives and what they think their lives will be like in five years. Most surveys find people reporting that the present is better than the past and that the future will be even better. More than 95 percent of people questioned in these surveys typically believe that the economic picture will be good for everyone and that their personal economic future will be even better than that of others. People are characteristically hopeful and confident that things will improve.[71]

Although this warm and generous vision is extended to all people, it is most clearly evident in visions of one's own future. Students asked to envision what their future lives would be like said they were more likely to graduate at the top of the class, get a good job, have a high starting salary, like their first job, receive an award for work, get written up in the paper, and give birth to a gifted child than their classmates. Moreover, they considered themselves far less likely than their classmates to have a drinking problem, to be fired from a job, to get divorced after a few years of marriage, to become depressed, or to have a heart attack or contract cancer.[72]

Unrealistic optimism is not confined to the idealistic young. Older adults also underestimate the likelihood that they will encounter a large number of negative, but unhappily common, events such as having an automobile accident, being a crime victim, having job problems, contracting major diseases, or becoming depressed. Unrealistic optimism appears to be unaffected by age, education, sex, or occupational prestige. The old and young, the well- and the poorly-educated, men and women, and people in all areas of life show unrealistic optimism in their assessments of the future.[73]

When asked to predict the future, most people predict what they would like to see happen, rather than what is objectively likely. Whether it be in a volleyball game, on a driving test, or on a report prepared for one's boss, most people believe that they will do well in the future. People expect to improve their performance over time, and moreover, this optimism typically increases with the importance of the task.[74] People are more unrealistically optimistic about the prospects for their future jobs than about their gardens, for example. People are even

unrealistically optimistic about events that are completely determined by chance, such as whether they will win the lottery
and whether the weather will be good for a picnic. People seem
to be saying, in effect, "The future will be great, especially for
me."

One of the more charming optimistic biases that people share
is the belief that they can accomplish more in a given period of
time than is humanly possible. This bias persists in the face of
innumerable contradictions. Perhaps the most poignant example of this unrealistic optimism is the daily to-do list. Each day,
the well-organized person makes a list of the tasks to be accomplished and then sets out to get them done. Then the exigencies
of the day begin to intrude: phone calls, minor setbacks, a
miscalculation of how long a task will take, or a small emer-
gency. The list that began the day crisp and white is now in
tatters, with additions, cross-outs and, most significantly, half
its items left undone. Yet at the end of the day, the list maker
cheerfully makes up another overly optimistic list for the next
day, or if much was left undone, simply crosses out the day at
the top of the list and writes in the next day. This all-too-
familiar pattern is remarkable not only because a to-do list
typically includes far more than any person could reasonably
expect to accomplish in a given time period, but also because
the pattern persists day after day, completely unresponsive to
the repeated feedback that it is unrealistic.[75]

Like the overly positive view of the self and the illusion of
control, unrealistic optimism develops very early in life. When
children are asked how well they will do on a future task, their
expectations are typically very high, higher than is realistic.
Moreover, unrealistically optimistic assessments of future performance are not very responsive to feedback, such as actual
performance, grades in class, comments from teachers, or reactions of parents. By about age seven or eight, children begin to
be aware of the meaning of negative feedback. They become
more responsive to what their teachers and parents tell them.
They also know what objective tests are, and so they are able

to use both objective information and feedback from others to evaluate whether or not they have done a good job.[76] In some respects, this intruding realism is a sad aspect of growing older. Stipek notes:

> It is perhaps unfortunate that children's naive optimism declines so soon after they enter school. To some degree the development of more realistic expectations is unavoidable and even desirable. However . . . if children were only given tasks on which they could succeed with some effort, continually high expectations for success and the adaptive behaviors that are associated with high expectations might be maintained throughout the school years. Rather than lamenting children's unrealistic judgments about their competencies, perhaps we should try harder to design educational environments that maintain their optimism and eagerness.[77]

But is unrealistic optimism adaptive? Just as ego-enhancing biases have been regarded as defenses against threats to self-esteem, unrealistic optimism has been thought of as a defensive reaction, a distortion of reality designed to reduce anxiety.[78] Consider the following opinions:

> Optimism . . . is a mania for maintaining that all is going well when things are going badly. (VOLTAIRE)

> Optimism, not religion, is the opiate of the people. (LIONEL TIGER)

> The place where optimism most flourishes is in the lunatic asylum. (HAVELOCK ELLIS)

Two arguments have been made against unrealistic optimism. The first is that optimism about the future is an irrational defense against reality that enables people to ward off the anxiety of threatening events without successfully coming to terms with it. The second is related to the first in maintaining that unrealistic optimism keeps people from perceiving the objective risks of external threats and preparing for them.[79] Several points argue against the appropriateness of these concerns. If unrealistic optimism were merely a defense against anxiety, one would expect that more serious and threatening events would elicit more unrealistic optimism than minor risks. In fact, the evidence does not support this position. The degree of threat posed by a risk is unrelated to the amount of unrealistic optimism people have about their lack of susceptibility to the problem.[80]

Moreover, unrealistic optimism about the future is highly and appropriately responsive to objective qualities of events, including their frequency and whether or not a person has any past experience with that event. People are less unrealistically optimistic about their chances of experiencing common events like divorce or chronic illness than they are about less frequent events, such as being the victim of a flood or fire. Past experience with a threatening event can eliminate unrealistic optimism altogether. Children of divorced parents, for example, regard their own chances of getting divorced as higher than people whose parents were not divorced. People are also more unrealistically optimistic about future events over which they have some control than they are about those that are uncontrollable. For example, although people estimate their chances of winning a lottery to be higher than is objectively likely, they recognize that winning a large amount of money in a lottery is far less likely than having a satisfying job, an event over which they presumably have more direct control. And finally, unrealistic optimism is responsive to information. When people receive objective evidence about the likelihood of risks, they change their estimates accordingly.[81] These qualities most clearly distinguish illusion from delusion. Delusions are false beliefs that persist despite the facts. Illusions accommodate them, though perhaps reluctantly.

Unrealistic optimism, then, is not a Panglossian whitewash

that paints all positive events as equally and commonly likely and all negative events as equally and uncommonly unlikely. Rather, unrealistic optimism shows a patterning that corresponds quite well to the objective likelihood of events, to relevant personal experiences with events, and to the degree to which one can actively contribute to bringing events about. Positive events are simply regarded as somewhat more likely and negative events as somewhat less likely to occur than is actually the case.

What accounts for unrealistic optimism? Optimism seems to be intimately bound up with other illusions of life, especially the belief in personal control.[82] Most people think they can control future events more than is actually the case, and consequently they may underestimate their vulnerability to random events. A driver may perceive the chance of an automobile accident to be low because she believes she is a better than average driver who can avoid such problems. She may conveniently forget the joy-riding teenager or the drunk driver who may cause an accident. People think they can avoid health problems by getting enough sleep or eating well, forgetting that hereditary factors, chance encounters with viruses, or environmental threats of which they may be ignorant can override even the most careful program of health habits. An active homosexual man in the 1970s might have given some thought to the possibility of contracting gonorrhea, but could he possibly have anticipated the horror of AIDS? Could the people attending the American Legion convention in Philadelphia in 1976 have guessed that the air in their hotel held a deadly contaminant, producing what we now call Legionnaires' disease? When people think of the future, they think of events they would like to see happen and the ones they believe they can bring about, rather than the chance events that may disrupt goals and plans.

Reflection suggests that the failure to consider the role of chance is not as surprising as first might appear. What exactly would constitute an effective recognition of chance? Should one begin driving each day with the image of a truck out of control bearing down on one's car? Should one regard every social situation as a potential opportunity for viruses to spread? Should every walk along city streets be considered a potential encounter with a mugger or rapist? While people certainly need to incorporate a certain amount of caution and defensiveness into their daily behavior, to do so by envisioning these potentially tragic but random events is hardly appropriate. Because chance and random factors are precisely that, their importance cannot be assessed in any reasonable way for any given situation. Therefore, people quite properly do not have chance at the forefront of consciousness when they assess their risks.

The belief in personal control may also account for why people see their personal likelihood of experiencing positive events as higher and negative events as lower than those of other people. When people focus on their own behaviors that might enable them to achieve desirable outcomes or avoid bad ones, they may forget that other people have just as many resources in their own lives.[83] People misjudge their risk that negative events can befall them because they have clear-cut stereotypes of the kinds of people who typically succumb to these events.[84] People who foolishly wander down dark streets at night are people who get mugged. Passive, repressed people who do not express their feelings get cancer. With these stereotypes in mind, we are able to comfort ourselves that adverse events will not befall us. The fact that each of us is engaging in this process—that is, imagining how he or she can avoid negative events—appears to escape attention altogether.

Unrealistic optimism may result from more than simple stereotypes about the kinds of people on whom bad outcomes descend. Psychologist Ziva Kunda suggests that people actively construct theories of why positive and negative events occur; in so doing they draw on their own attributes in order to defend against the possibility that the negative events might befall them and to enhance the perceived likelihood that the positive events will happen to them. For example, upon learning that the divorce rate for first marriages is 50 percent, most people predict that they will not be in that 50 percent, but rather will remain married to their spouse throughout their lifetime. They convince themselves that this is the case, Kunda has shown, by highlighting their personal attributes that might be associated with a stable marriage and downplaying the significance of or actively refuting information that might suggest a vulnerability to divorce. Thus, for example, one might point to one's parents' fifty-year marriage, the close family life that existed in one's early childhood, and the fact that one's high school relationship lasted a full four years as evidence to predict a stable marriage. The fact that one's husband has already been divorced once—a factor that predicts a second divorce—might be reinterpreted not only as not leading to divorce in one's own case, but as a protective factor ("He knows he does not want this marriage to fail like the last one, and so he's working especially hard to keep our relationship strong"). The ability to draw seemingly rational relationships between our own assets and good events and to argue away associations between our own attributes and negative events helps to maintain unrealistic optimism.[85]

THE ILLUSION OF PROGRESS

The ability to sustain an optimistic view of the future may also come in part from the ability to misconstrue events as progress. There is a well-established bias indicating that people see themselves as having improved even when no actual progress has been made.[86] We all know that people seek out the company of others who are likely to give them positive feedback. It is only reasonable that we should want as friends people who like and value us. There is a corresponding, less obvious tendency to like others whose evaluations of us improve over time. The initially hard to get girlfriend or boyfriend may, for example, be more highly valued than an old faithful partner who was responsive all along. When people's impressions improve over time, rather than staying at a positive level, it simultaneously enhances several other positive beliefs: it encourages a feeling of personal impact, the idea that one can positively affect other people's evaluations. In so doing, it encourages feelings of interpersonal control, the belief that one can bring out in people the kinds of evaluations and judgments of the self that one would like to achieve. And it creates a future as optimistic as the one mentally constructed because just as one fantasizes that progress will occur, progress appears to be made.[87]

This tendency to construct the future so that it will be better than the past is not limited to social interaction. In an intriguing study, Michael Conway and Michael Ross invited college students who were having difficulty studying to enroll in a program designed to show them how to improve their study skills and achieve higher grades.[88] Half of the students who applied to the program were accepted immediately and the other half were put on a waiting list. The first group of students then went through a three-week study skills program. As it happens, most study skills programs are actually quite ineffective in imparting new skills and raising grades,[89] and such was the case with the study skills program initiated by Conway and Ross. The students who took the program did not differ in final grades or study skills from students who had not participated in the program.

Nonetheless, students in the program perceived that they had improved dramatically. They reported better study skills, and they expected better final exam grades. They also distorted retrospectively how bad their study skills had been before going into the program. Moreover, even after final grades had been calculated, the students overestimated their grades for the term. Thus, by revising what they had initially had, the students were able to achieve, at least mentally, what they wanted, namely improvement in their study skills and grades. Failure ("I failed the test") can be reinterpreted as progress ("but I got practice that will help on this kind of test next time"). Through such distortions, several positive biases may be enhanced. One sees oneself in a positive light and as efficacious, and one simultaneously reconstructs the past and future so as to achieve an illusion of progress.

THE EFFECTS OF OUTCOMES ON OPTIMISM

People are optimistic about the future most of the time, but when something good happens to them, they become even more so.[90] Doing well at work, for example, leads a person to believe that his children will improve their grades in school and that he will win the weekend tennis tournament. Moreover, a good event acts as a generalized opportunity signal, increasing the belief in the likelihood of all kinds of positive events. Happy events are seen as portents of yet more happy things to come. Similarly, when a bad event happens, it increases the perception that other bad events may lie ahead.[91] Getting sick, being burglarized, or failing a test all move beliefs in the direction of pessimism. Even a transitory mood can yield these same effects.[92] On a day when a person feels good for no particular reason, optimism is higher. Likewise, on a day when a person is low for no particular reason, pessimism may set in. The negative event or mood seems to act as a danger signal. Moreover, this danger signal appears to be a general one, in that it sometimes increases the perception that any bad event may follow, even ones having little or nothing to do with the negative event that has already transpired. If a person fails her driving test, she might logically fear that she may do so again, but why should her fear of developing cancer increase? Why should a burglary increase a sense of vulnerability to diabetes? Similarly, why should receiving a raise at work lead to the belief that one can improve one's marriage?

Perhaps when something good happens, it reinforces a person's belief that he or she is an effective, competent person who can make things happen. Since people exaggerate their ability to control events, even those that are determined by chance, any positive outcome may make people think that they can produce other positive outcomes. Similarly, a negative event, such as getting sick, may undermine a person's sense of control and competence by pointing out that one can get in harm's way without much effort. As the person attempts to make sense of the negative event, he or she may become aware of vulnerability in general, increasing the sense that he or she can fall victim to other negative events. Sociologist Kai Erikson describes this feeling from the standpoint of natural disasters:

> One of the bargains men make with one another in order to maintain their sanity is to share an illusion that they are safe, even when the physical evidence in the world around them does not seem to warrant that conclusion. The survivors of a disaster, of course, are prone to overestimate the perils of their situation, if only to compensate for the fact that they underestimated those perils once before; but what is worse, far worse, is that they sometimes live in a state of almost constant apprehension *because they have lost the human capacity to screen out the signs of danger out of their line of vision.* [93]

The generalized danger signal created by negative events lasts only as long as the negative event or bad mood exists. Once these unpleasant experiences pass, unrealistic optimism returns. An obvious and therefore tempting interpretation is that the generalized danger signal has a certain survival value. When the organism is in a weakened state, physically or psychologically, the generalized perception of danger may keep it appropriately timid, modest, and relatively inactive in order that it not overextend its reduced resources. Once the problem passes and physical and psychological resources are replenished, the organism is once again able to assert itself in the world. At this point, unrealistic optimism may return to diminish the sense of threat. Similarly, the generalized opportunity signal created by optimism may lead people to investigate opportunities that they might not otherwise pursue and to pay little heed to information that would suggest more caution. Optimism may, then, be a significant factor in personal progress.[94]

ILLUSIONS OF THE MIND

What we see in the normal human mind does not correspond very well to the predominant view of mental health. Instead of an awareness and acceptance of both the positive and the negative elements of their personalities, most people show a keen awareness of their positive qualities and attributes, an extreme estimation of their ability to master the environment, and a positive assessment of the future. Not only are these assessments positive, they appear to be unrealistically so. It is not just that people believe they are good, but that they think they are better than reality can sustain. Judgments of mastery greatly exceed the actual ability to control many events. Views of the future are so rosy that they would make Pollyanna blush.

Should we say simply that most people are optimists at heart? Are these so-called illusions of everyday life merely a reflection of some underlying optimistic stance, a tendency to look on the good side of things? While there is surely an optimistic core to self-aggrandizing beliefs about the self, the world, and the future, these illusions also differ in important ways from optimism. One difference is that illusions critically concern the self. While most people are optimistic, the illusions they demonstrate habitually in their thought patterns concern their own attributes, their beliefs in personal mastery, and concerns about their own futures, rather than a positive view of the world more generally. Another difference is that as a general term, *optimism* refers simply to the expectation that things will turn out well, without any consideration of how those beneficial outcomes will be achieved. The illusion of control, a vital part of people's beliefs about their own attributes, is a personal statement about how positive outcomes will be achieved, not merely by wishing and hoping that they will happen, but by making them happen through one's own capabilities. Finally, as will be seen in the next chapter, it is the specific content of illusions, namely beliefs about the self, one's mastery, and the future, that promote psychological adjustment, not simply the underlying optimism reflected in those illusions.

I have repeatedly referred to these beliefs as illusions, and a word must be said about the selection of this term. In some respects, *illusion* is an unfortunate choice, for it evokes images of a conjuror flirting with the border between reality and fantasy. Moreover, when applied to human thought, it suggests a naive blind spot or weakness. Yet *illusion* is appropriate. The terms *error* and *bias,* which one might employ instead, suggest short-term accidental mistakes and distortions, respectively, that might be caused by some careless oversight or other temporary negligence. The term *illusion,* in contrast, reflects a broader and more enduring pattern of beliefs.

> Illusion is a perception that represents what is perceived in a way different from the way it is in reality. An illusion is a false mental image or conception which may be a misinterpretation of a real appearance or may be something imagined. It may be pleasing, harmless or even useful.[95]

In this sense, then, illusion captures the essence of these phenomena. People hold mild and benignly positive illusions about themselves, the world, and the future. Moreover, they are linked in mutually reinforcing and thematically consistent ways. While illusion does not characterize everyone's thinking about all issues regarding the self, the world, and the future, these illusions are common, widespread, and easily documented.

The fact that positive illusions are so dramatic in early childhood and lessen over time is especially intriguing. It suggests that they are natural, intrinsic to the cognitive system, and become worn down and tamed through the feedback that life provides. What we see in adults is not a carefully cultivated and crafted positive glow that is provided by years of experience with the adaptiveness of viewing things in a positive light.

Rather, we see instead the residual inflated view of oneself and the future that exists in extreme and almost magical form in very young children.

The illusions that adults hold about their attributes, their capacity for control, and the beneficent future are, in fact, quite mild, nowhere near the dillusional distortions that one frequently observes in mental patients, for example. As a consequence, it is tempting to dismiss them as ultimately inconsequential, amusing peccadillos that put a pleasant twist on incoming information without many consequences for important matters. Indeed, one argument for the adaptiveness of positive illusions maintains that these biases are evident primarily when information is inconsequential and not when the stakes are higher. According to this argument, people may hold falsely positive judgments about themselves on unimportant matters that may buffer them in more serious and consequential circumstances when they are forced to become more realistic. In fact, the evidence tends to suggest the opposite conclusion: people's positive distortions often increase, not decrease, as matters become more important and consequential.[96] The more ego-enhancing a situation is, the more likely it is to evoke positive, self-serving interpretations. When outcomes are important, self-enhancing causal attributions are more likely. Positive illusions, then, are pervasive and not confined to the unimportant matters of life.

The fact that positive illusions exist in normal thought raises the larger question of why they exist and whether they serve any useful purpose. Are they simply a surprising and rather charming aspect of human thought, or are they actually adaptive? Trying to understand their prevalence leads one prematurely to suggest why they might be functional, the implicit assumption being that, like other organs, the mind does not evolve in ways that are inherently injurious to its own functioning. Yet these suggestions of adaptiveness have been speculative only, and the next task is to determine whether this is indeed the case.

CHAPTER 2

Illusions and
Mental Health

> To endure life is the primary duty
> of all living beings. Illusion is of no
> value if it makes this more difficult.
> —SIGMUND FREUD

As WE HAVE SEEN, people are positively biased in their assessments of themselves and of their ability to control what goes on around them, as well as in their views of the future. The widespread existence of these biases and the ease with which they can be documented suggests that they are normal. These findings challenge the traditional view of mental health, which maintains that people must be in touch with reality to adapt successfully to it. But mental health may be a state that few people actually achieve, and thus the beliefs of the majority may not characterize mental health generally. Alternatively, illusions about one's stature in the world and the promise of the future may not contribute to mental health, but may simply be incidental aspects of the way the mind is organized. A stronger challenge to traditional views of mental health would be posed by evidence suggesting that illusions are not only normal but actually adaptive, promoting rather than undermining mental health.

The relation of illusions to mental health is by no means self-evident. In fact, the systematic nature of illusions could be a basis for concern. If people simply make errors, some positive and some negative, these errors might cancel each other out, or at least exert some gyroscopic correction on otherwise imbalanced inferences. The fact that errors consistently stray in a particular direction, namely the positive one, raises the possibility of vulnerability to misperception and distortions of judgment.

To determine whether illusions about control, self-worth, and the future contribute to or undermine mental health, one must first establish criteria of mental health and then ask whether the consequences of positive illusions promote those criteria, undermine them, or have no effect. Fortunately, there is considerable consensus in the mental health literature regarding the attributes of the mentally healthy person. Most experts agree that the ability to be happy, or at least relatively contented, is one hallmark of mental health and well-being.[1] In her landmark work, Jahoda identified several additional criteria. The ability to hold positive attitudes toward oneself, rather than to feel distress or anguish over one's inadequacies or shortcomings, is considered a mark of mature and healthy functioning. The ability to grow, develop, and move toward one's goals is also commonly recognized as an attribute of mental health, inasmuch as mental health is not a static achievement, but rather a dynamic, evolving state of being. The capacity to develop an autonomous self-regard that does not require the reassurance of other people for meaning and sustenance is a third criterion. This is not to say that the mentally healthy person is one who can stand alone and does not need or desire the support of others, but rather that the self and its ability to function does not depend upon others for its existence and meaning. The fourth criterion Jahoda identified is environmental mastery in work and social relationships. By this, she meant the ability to engage in productive and meaningful work and the capacity for warm and satisfying relationships with others. Finally, Jahoda argued that the integration and harmony of the forces of personality are essential to the development of mental health.

A recent reconsideration of the mentally healthy person by Sidney Jourard and Ted Landsman came up with a similar viewpoint:

> [The healthy personality] is guided by intelligence and respect for life, so that personal needs are satisfied and so that the person will grow in awareness, competence, and the capacity to love the self, the natural environment, and other people.[2]

Taking these viewpoints together yields a common set of attributes of the mentally healthy person: a positive view of the self, the ability to be happy or contented, the ability to care for and about others, the capacity for productive and creative work, and the ability to grow and achieve within the context of a challenging and sometimes threatening environment. One can now inquire whether the positive illusions that are held by most people promote or undermine these other qualities traditionally associated with mental health.

ILLUSIONS, HAPPINESS, AND CONTENTMENT?

Since the birth of philosophy and its scientific offspring, psychology, happiness has been held to be one of the highest states the human being can achieve. What happiness is has been a subject of some debate, however. Philosopher Jean-Jacques Rousseau considered happiness to be the result of "a good bank account, a good cook, and good digestion." Both Aristotle and Thoreau believed that activity is essential to human happiness.

On one point, there is agreement. As Marcus Aurelius said, "No man is happy who does not think himself so." Happiness consists at least in part of the awareness that one is happy. Moreover, unlike other qualities of mental health, happiness is a subjective experience. People know when they are happy and when they are not.[3]

Most people say they are happy most of the time. When surveys are undertaken to assess the public's mood, 70 to 80 percent of the people queried respond that they are moderately to very happy. Moreover, positive illusions about one's personal qualities, degree of control, and likely future appear to promote happiness. People who have high self-esteem and confidence in their abilities say that they are happy, happier than other people are. People who believe that they have a lot of control in their lives and who believe that the future will bring them even more happiness are happier by their own reports than people who lack these perceptions.[4]

Psychologists have compared happy people with mildly depressed people concerning their perceptions of themselves and the world around them. Happy people have higher opinions of themselves; they are more likely to make self-serving causal attributions; they are more likely to demonstrate an illusion of control; and they show more unrealistic optimism. Perhaps the point is not even worth discussion. It scarcely seems necessary to prove that people who think well of themselves, who believe they can control what goes on around them, and who are optimistic about the future will be happier than people who lack these perceptions. Nonetheless, a wealth of evidence exists to indicate that these relationships are true.[5]

Happiness and the good mood that accompanies it are important not only in their own right but because of the pervasive effects they exert on other aspects of a person's life.[6] A good mood, such as that produced by a lovely piece of music, a view of the mountains, or a pleasant social gathering, can quickly be dissociated from the specific event that gave rise to it and be attached to many other aspects of life, often subtly and without awareness. When one's view of the mountains is uplifting, the conversation of one's companions can seem more brilliant and the wine, more flavorful. Writer Katherine Mansfield captured this feeling in her account of Bertha, the heroine of "Bliss," who reflects on her life.

> Really—really—she had everything. She was young. Harry and she were as much in love as ever, and they got on together splendidly and were really good pals. She had an adorable baby. They didn't have to worry about money. They had this absolutely satisfactory house and garden. And friends—modern, thrilling friends, writers and painters and poets or people keen on social questions—just the kind of friends they wanted. And then there were books, and there was music, and she had found a wonderful little dressmaker and they were going abroad in the summer, and their new cook made the most superb omelets. . . .[7]

Although people are typically unaware of the specific instances in which good mood has an impact on their other thoughts and behavior, they are aware of the phenomenon. Rodgers and Hammerstein described some of the common strategies people use to lift their spirits, such as to "whistle a happy tune" or to think about one's "favorite things." A negative mood, unfortunately, can have opposite and pervasive effects as well.[8] A day of rain may remind a person that his checkbook balance is low, he must attend a boring meeting in the afternoon, and his children's rooms continue to be in shambles despite efforts to get them to pick them up. He feels cross and pessimistic, and behaves in ways likely to arouse antagonism or at least chilliness in others.

Psychologists have developed some ingenious methods for studying the effects of good mood on people's beliefs and behavior. Like Peter Pan teaching the Darling children how to fly, they lead people to think happy thoughts by surprising them with an unexpected gift, inducing them to concentrate on experiences to make them happy ("Think of Christmas, think of snow"), or asking them to recall a time in the past when they were very happy. Before long, people exposed to these techniques, though unable to fly, report that they feel more cheerful, even euphoric.[9]

The psychologist's bag of tricks includes ways of putting people into bad moods as well as good moods, by exposing them to an unexpected and gratuitous insult, leading them to focus on an unhappy or frustrating time in the past, or just concentrating on all the things that are going badly in their lives. One of the most successful techniques involves having a person read a series of statements that suggest a progressively happier or unhappier state of mind.[10] For example, if one were trying to induce a bad mood, one might have the person read the following set of statements:

> I don't seem to be quite myself today.
> In fact, I'm feeling a little low.
> My work isn't really going as well as it could.
> I'm feeling a little discouraged about it.
> In fact, you could say that I'm sort of blue today.
> It's hard to see how things are going to get better.
> In fact, if anything, they'll probably get worse.
> I'm really down today.
> I'm feeling so discouraged.
> There doesn't seem to be much hope.

After reading twenty or thirty of these progressively more depressing statements, even the most cheerful person will find herself considerably less so. By comparison, people induced to adopt a happy mood read sentences reflecting an ever more positive mood, like the following:

> I'm feeling pretty good today.
> Things have been going quite well for me.
> I think today will be a good day for me.

I've been able to accomplish a lot lately.
I'm feeling quite happy about myself.
My work is really going well.
I think if I put my mind to it, that I can do just about
anything.
In fact, I'm feeling really great right now.

After one reads twenty or thirty of these statements, one's
mood is typically somewhat more positive. The impact of these
mood-induction techniques, as they are called, is quite dramatic. In one study, shoppers in a mall were given a free gift
and then later interviewed for a consumer survey that asked
them how their cars functioned, their televisions performed,
and their washers and dryers behaved. Those who had received
the free gift reported that they were happier with their autos
and other appliances than people who had not received the
gifts.[11]

When people have been put in a good mood, they become
even more unrealistically optimistic about the future than
usual. When asked to predict their performance on a future
task, they show higher expectations for success. When they feel
they have performed well on a task, they will reward themselves more generously and report that they like themselves
more.[12] Moreover, most of these effects of mood seem to occur
without any awareness.[13]

The question arises as to whether positive illusions about the
self, personal control, and the future lead to happiness and
positive mood, or whether the reverse direction of causality is
more plausible. It is easy to imagine that feeling happy or contented might lead people to feel better about themselves, their
ability to control what goes on around them, and the future. In
fact, the scientific evidence suggests that both causal directions
are likely. Studies that have manipulated positive mood have
found a corresponding positive impact on other perceptions,
such as on one's view of one's self. And studies in which people
have been induced to think better of themselves reveal corre-

sponding positive effects on mood. Thus, although positive mood may contribute to positive illusions, there is also evidence for the reverse, namely that illusions promote happiness and good mood.[14]

Positive illusions about oneself, one's personal control, and the future, then, are significant because they promote an important attribute of mental health, namely the ability to be happy or contented. At least as important, however, may be the fact that illusions foster positive mood in general, which in turn can promote other aspects of mental health, such as the ability to care for and about others and the ability to engage in creative and productive work.

ILLUSIONS AND CARING FOR OTHER PEOPLE

Whether positive illusions foster the ability to care for and about other people is not so obvious. One can argue persuasively at least two lines of thought. First, one might imagine that people who think especially well of themselves, their abilities, and their personal futures are so self-centered as to be unable to show affection and regard for others. Perhaps the presence of positive illusions actually interferes with developing and fostering social bonds. Too much attention to the self may prevent people from recognizing the needs of others. Too much concentration on their own goals and plans may prompt people to see others as vehicles for their own personal achievements, rather than as companions to be thought about, cared for, and loved. One reason why this argument is so easy to construct is that the portrait of the ruthlessly aggressive individual, striving to get to the top and manipulating everyone in the way, is a cultural stereotype. Whether it characterizes the relationship between positive illusions and the ability to care for and about others remains to be seen.

There is another, more benign viewpoint that suggests exactly the opposite relationship. This view argues that without positive self-regard, it is difficult if not impossible to care for and about others. A person who is psychologically distressed and doubts his or her self-worth is unable to show feeling for and caring about other people, because contact with other people simply inspires more distress and feelings of inadequacy. The person who feels badly about himself and who doubts his talents and questions his ultimate worth may be too preoccupied with his own problems to meet the needs of others and thereby be unable to show affection and love. This viewpoint also reflects a cultural stereotype, one widely touted in the popular literature of the "me generation" of the 1970s. Books that argued for the need to watch out for number one and to take care of me first, maintained, sometimes quite convincingly, that by taking care of one's own needs first, one would be better able to meet the needs of others.[15] Perhaps the most familiar advocate of this position is Carl Rogers, who argued that people with feelings of self-worth regard others in a positive manner as well, whereas people who have negative attitudes toward themselves must disparage others in an attempt to ameliorate their own chronic feelings of inadequacy.[16] In this view, then, positivity simply begets more positivity without the invidious comparisons to others that high self-regard might otherwise imply.

Fortunately, we do not have to rely upon the relative strength of stereotypes to resolve this issue, inasmuch as scientific investigation has provided evidence. Generally, the evidence points toward the latter explanation. People with positive self-regard seem to achieve better social relationships. They have higher regard for others generally. For example, people with high self-esteem are generally better liked by others than people with low self-esteem. Even among children, those who think well of themselves are more likely to be popular with their peers.[17] Of course, one could argue that high self-esteem does not lead to popularity as much as being popular leads people to develop high self-esteem. Indeed, one can make a plausible case for both directions of causality. Research that has adopted a more fine grained analysis of the impact of self-esteem on social interactions, however, suggests that people who are depressed or low in self-esteem may engage in behaviors that drive others away; therefore it would seem that even if popularity does enhance self-esteem, self-esteem can also exert a direct effect on popularity.[18]

When people find themselves in situations in which they lack close social ties, those with positive beliefs about themselves and the future seem to take more effective action to solve these problems. Psychologist Carolyn Cutrona studied lonely freshmen shortly after their entrance to a large university.[19] Loneliness is a common problem plaguing these students because many have been uprooted from their communities and are thrust into a large and somewhat impersonal environment in which the necessity to make friends is clearly present and the ability to do so entirely dependent upon one's own actions. Cutrona found that the students who had high self-esteem and a more optimistic view of the future were better able to cope with their loneliness at college than were the students who did not hold these beliefs. Those with high self-esteem and an optimistic view of the future were able to see, quite appropriately, that their current loneliness was a short-term state that would pass once they had the opportunity to meet more people and find some friends. Accordingly, they were not immobilized and debilitated by their temporarily lonely state.

Some of the evidence suggesting that people with positive illusions are better able to care for and about others comes from research on the effects of mood on social behavior. People in whom a positive mood has been induced typically show more positive social behaviors than people in whom a negative mood has been induced. Happy people are more likely to help others, to initiate conversations with other people, to express liking for them, and to voice positive evaluations of people in general.

People in a good mood are more likely to approach a stranger, to help someone in need, and to believe in the ultimate goodness of mankind. When people who are in a good mood are placed in potentially competitive situations, they are less likely to use contentious strategies, and instead cooperate to increase their joint benefits. Psychologist Alice Isen, who has conducted much of this research, notes: "Positive affect is associated with increased sociability and benevolence."[20]

Just as a positive mood promotes sociability, a negative mood tends to undermine it. People put in a negative mood via a mood-induction method have more negative views of other people, indicate that they like other people less, and interpret ambiguous feedback about themselves more negatively.[21] But negative mood does not always have adverse effects on thought and behavior. What distinguishes negative and positive moods is that people in a positive mood usually try to think thoughts and perform actions that will maintain that mood, whereas people in a negative mood often try to escape it.[22] For example, a person in a bad mood will sometimes help someone in need, apparently for the purpose of making himself or herself feel better for the act of charity. Whereas positive mood leads people to do nice things for themselves and others, negative mood does not have the opposite effect. People who are feeling low are not more likely to trip other people or rob banks. A bad mood simply seems to reduce activity level overall. It may be that people in a bad mood can think of all the negative consequences that might result from any action, whether good or bad, and consequently generally inhibit their behavior. Negative mood, then, has irregular effects on thought and behavior: negative moods have the potential to be self-correcting, assuming that the person has available some strategy for improving mood; however, a bad mood, particularly a chronic bad mood, may make it hard to remember these strategies and thus may leave the person mired in inactivity.

Optimism also seems to enhance social relationships. Most people would rather spend time with someone who is optimistic, not pessimistic. Studies of spouses and friends of people suffering from mild or severe depression find that the unrelenting pessimism of the depressed person often drives social support away.[23] In contrast, optimistic people seem to be able to draw upon and make effective use of social support when they need it.

What, then, do we know about the impact of self-enhancing illusions on social relationships? Clearly, people who think well of themselves and who are optimistic are better liked than people who lack these positive perceptions. This is not, in and of itself, evidence of personal caring, however. The work on mood comes somewhat closer by showing that when people feel good about themselves, they have more benign views of other people, and they are more likely to help people in need. Yet these behaviors, too, have a certain transitory quality, rather than the enduring commitment to others that we would want to see in the mentally healthy person. Do illusions contribute to this more enduring form of caring as well?

In *Optimism: The Biology of Hope,* anthropologist Lionel Tiger poses the paradox of parenting, asking how an intelligent and otherwise self-interested being can be a parent.

> When all is said and done, the act of being a parent involves a set of radically unselfish and often incomprehensibly inconvenient activities. Two adults who could otherwise employ their time and resources in pleasurable activities of various kinds elect to seek housing and provide food and other facilities for completely dependent organisms whose personal schedules, furthermore, could not be at greater variance with adult ones, and who will involve their parents literally for decades in a compromise between a program of work or pleasure and the requirements of their offspring. It is not altogether remarkable that parents may have one child, if only in error or because of confused expectations of bliss. What is truly remarkable is that most parents have more than one child.[24]

To resolve this paradox, Tiger argues that positive illusions, optimism in particular, may make it possible for people to make certain sacrifices on behalf of others that they might be less willing to make if they were less positive about their own attributes and less optimistic about the future. If one believes that the future holds a wealth of good things, then present privations and sacrifices may seem to be bearable, even essential, steps on the way to a more promising future. In fact, a host of illusions may contribute to sacrifice. Presumably, the beliefs that one's own children are talented, attractive, and generally appealing helps make people willing to sustain sacrifices so that these remarkable offspring can realize their potential. The belief that one is a good and effective parent may contribute to these sacrifices, and the capacity to imagine a better future, however dimly, once these youngsters have been released to the world, may help people survive psychologically through the more trying times.

ILLUSIONS AND CREATIVE, PRODUCTIVE WORK

The ability to be creative and productive has been included in most formulations of mental health. In essence, this position maintains that the mentally healthy person is able to find a set of life tasks—through employment, family roles, or other activities—that enable him or her to use the imagination effectively and to be persistent and productive. The skills involved are many; hence, the ability to perform creative and productive work is a broad criterion that must be analyzed in terms of its component parts. Most successful work consists of at least three sets of skills or attributes: ability or creativity in the chosen task, the motivation to pursue it, and the organizational skills that facilitate performance. The positive illusions that normal people hold about themselves, their personal control, and the future seem to facilitate all three aspects of the ability to accomplish creative and productive work, at least in some respects.

ILLUSION AND MOTIVATION

Some of the most dramatic effects of self-enhancing perceptions, a belief in personal control, and optimism concern motivation and persistence. The confidence that one can successfully accomplish a task, the belief that one has the means to do it, and the optimism that success will eventually ensue leads people to attempt tasks that they otherwise might avoid. Moreover, because these often unrealistic assessments of the likelihood of success may lead people to stick to tasks until they do succeed, illusions can create a self-fulfilling prophecy. Some years ago, I was a visiting scholar in the laboratory of a prominent psychologist for a brief period. I was struck by how he and his students seemed to feel that the center of psychology was right there in their research investigations. Assistants reported empirical developments almost hourly. The students and postdoctoral scholars were keenly aware of who was working on which problems and which papers were being written. The level of excitement, energy, and enthusiasm was infectious and clearly contributed to the long hours everyone put in. I almost began to believe that psychology really *was* centered in their lab.

Evidence for the impact of self-enhancing beliefs on motivation, persistence, and performance comes from several sources. A positive view of the self typically leads a person to work harder and longer on tasks. Perseverance, in turn, makes performance more effective and increases the likelihood that one's goals will be attained. Moreover, people with high self-esteem evaluate their performance more positively than people with low self-esteem, even when their performance is actually the same. This fact suggests not only that people who think well of themselves are more likely to succeed, but that they are also more likely to judge their performance as successful, whether or not it actually is. The positive evaluations of performance that people with high self-esteem typically make can, in turn, feed back into enhanced motivation. People with high self-esteem rate the likelihood of success on future tasks as high and rate their ability to perform those tasks as high, even when their previous performance records would suggest that such optimism is unrealistic.[25] The sales representative with high self-esteem works longer and harder than someone of comparable talents who has lower self-esteem. In so doing, she may judge her performance to be more successful than others might, but she will also probably perform better in the future than her low-self-esteem counterpart.

The significance of sheer persistence for attaining goals is evident in numerous dramatic case histories. Lee Iaccoca took over a company that many thought would—perhaps should— fail and, through a combination of determination and savvy business moves, brought it from bankruptcy back to being one of the major auto companies in the United States. Asked to explain his stunning success at Chrysler, he was quoted as saying, "Decide what you want to achieve and then work tirelessly to achieve it."[26] Irving Wallace wrote daily for twenty years, amassing hundreds of rejection slips (including twelve in one day) before he achieved major success as a writer.[27] With one hundred dollars in the bank and a pregnant wife, Sylvester Stallone turned down an offer of $250,000 for his script, *Rocky*, and waited to find a producer willing to cast him as the lead.[28] Greenwald reminds us:

Thomas A. Edison's recipe for success was "One percent inspiration and ninety-nine percent perspiration," and Edison was a perfect example of how effective the trait of perseverance could be. He invented the light bulb by spending two years applying electric current to every substance that he could manage to shape into a filament between two electrodes. At last he found that carbonized thread would illuminate without immediately burning itself up. This sort of effective perseverance can come only from a person who is convinced, perhaps unreasonably, of the likelihood of eventual success.[29]

The explanations that people offer for their successes and failures also contribute to motivation, performance, and persistence. Psychologist Martin Seligman and his associates have developed the concept of explanatory style, arguing that people who explain the good things that happen to them with reference to stable and pervasive qualities of themselves will have higher motivation and persistence than those who do not. In one study, Kamen and Seligman found that college freshmen who explained their good grades as due to such factors as their own abilities had higher grade-point averages than those who explained good grades with reference to external, unstable, or specific factors, such as luck, easy tests, or low grading standards. Moreover, this was true even when the effects of previous grades and test scores were ruled out. That is, given two people exactly the same in their academic abilities, the one who explains success as due to his or her personal, enduring characteristics will probably be more successful than the one who explains success as an unexpected bountiful outcome of random environmental forces.[30]

Differences in explanatory style also predicted productivity and the likelihood of quitting among life insurance sales agents. Selling life insurance is a particularly good situation in which to investigate these factors since agents continually encounter rejection, indifference, and confusion in potential clients. The turnover rate among life insurance agents is very high: one study found that 78 percent of them quit within three years.[31] In a study of agents' explanations for the often discouraging conditions, those who explained temporary setbacks as due to their own poor qualities were more likely to quit and have poorer sales records than those who attributed work setbacks to external and temporary factors.[32]

Perhaps the most impressive evidence for the adaptive value

of a self-serving explanatory style comes from a study that analyzed the nomination acceptance speeches of Democratic and Republican candidates for president from 1948 to 1984. Candidates who focused on negative factors concerning the future of the country were more likely to lose the election than those who focused on positive factors. Moreover, this was true even when the candidates' standing in the polls was taken into account.[33] Consider, for example, these comments made by Adlai Stevenson in his unsuccessful bid for the presidency in 1952: "The ordeal of the 20th century—the bloodiest, most turbulent era of the Christian age—is far from over. Sacrifice, patience, and implacable purpose may be our lot for years to come." Contrast this with Dwight Eisenhower's 1952 acceptance speech, in which he promised that if elected, "I will go to Korea"—a statement that reflects the intention to solve problems through direct action. Overall, those presidential candidates who were pessimistic in their nomination acceptance speeches lost nine of the ten elections examined. Stevenson, George McGovern, Jimmy Carter, and Walter Mondale, all pessimistic ruminators, lost in landslides; of the four most optimistic candidates—Harry Truman, John F. Kennedy, Barry Goldwater, and Ronald Reagan—all but Goldwater won in upset victories. How a person explains positive versus negative events, then, can have powerful effects.[34]

Belief in personal control has also been related to motivation and persistence. A belief in one's own efficacy and ability to accomplish tasks leads to higher motivation to pursue tasks and more efforts to succeed. People who have a strong desire to control respond more vigorously to challenging tasks, and they persist at them longer. They also have higher expectations for their performance than individuals who have little desire for control.[35] For example, the entrepreneur faces a difficult task, one that often seems like an impossible dream. The task is to build from scratch some new technology, product, or service. In the early stages, when objective accomplishments are lacking, often the entrepreneur and his or her staff must ride solely on the energy, optimism, and blind faith that the project will be successful. Alan Carsrud and his associates have studied successful entrepreneurs and found that certain of the illusions that characterize normal thought are exaggerated as well as adaptive in this group. In particular, the need to master situations was more characteristic of successful than unsuccessful entrepreneurs.[36]

Optimism, including unrealistic optimism, also leads to a high level of motivation. When people expect to succeed on a task, they work longer and harder than if they doubt their ability to succeed. People who orient themselves toward the future, rather than the present or the past, report more motivation to work, more efforts to fulfill their goals, more direct action toward their goals, more daily planning, and a more optimistic vision of the future.[37] Optimism may also be highly functional when a person encounters setbacks during the course of attempting to achieve a goal. Inevitably, particularly for difficult goals, there will be times when vital elements of the goal seem unattainable or at best difficult. When an optimist confronts a setback or barrier, he or she is more likely to believe that the impediment is surmountable and that he or she must simply try harder to overcome the setback.[38]

Just as positive judgments about the future lead to higher motivation and performance, so unfavorable judgments about the future inhibit motivation, persistence, and performance. Pessimism is one of the central attributes of depression, and one of the chief symptoms of depression is inactivity. Negative mood, such as that experienced during depression, seems to depress effective action, perhaps because pessimism highlights the potential negative consequences of any action.[39] This pessimism, then, may reduce motivation and consequent activity toward a goal. One of the tips Donald Trump passed on about his success is this: "I never think of the negative. All obstacles can be overcome."[40]

The positive mood and euphoric feeling that are often a part of exaggeratedly positive illusions about the self and the future also help to foster motivation and persistence. A good mood helps a person to focus attention on a task. People who are in a good mood are more likely to evaluate their performance as successful and to reward themselves accordingly. When offered an incentive for improving performance, people who are in a positive mood actually exert more effort than people in a negative mood. In laboratory studies that have manipulated negative mood, those whose mood is lower have lower expectations for future success and are more likely to attribute their successes to unstable factors such as chance or the simplicity of the task. They also reward themselves less when they have succeeded, perhaps because they do not see the success as evolving from their own talents and efforts.[41] Motivation and mood appear to influence each other reciprocally. Being active elevates mood, and a good mood increases involvement in activity.[42]

Overall, the research evidence indicates that self-enhancement, exaggerated beliefs in control, and unrealistic optimism typically lead to higher motivation, greater persistence at tasks, more effective performance, and, ultimately, greater success. A chief value of these illusions may be that they help to create self-fulfilling prophecies. They may lead people to try harder in situations that are objectively difficult. Although some failure is certainly inevitable, ultimately the illusions will lead to success more often than will lack of persistence.

The capacity of illusion to enhance motivation and persistence may be one of its most adaptive features. For human beings to have evolved to their current state of technological and scientific advancement required enormous motivation and persistence, particularly when the objective likelihood of advancement was fairly low. Moreover, from the standpoint of the individual, unrealistic optimism, exaggerated faith in one's abilities, and a belief in personal control often do not pay off. History is filled with anonymous scientists, inventors, and other visionaries who had faith in dreams that ultimately went unrecognized or proved to be wrong. And yet, some of those unrealistically optimistic people with high positive self-regard were right, or at least right enough to be accepted and to define the technologies, sciences, and advances of the future. The links between positive illusions and cultural advancement, then, may be critical.

ILLUSIONS, INTELLIGENCE, AND CREATIVITY

The capacity of illusions to foster motivation and persistence has a certain intuitive appeal. What may be harder to understand is how exaggerated perceptions of the self, personal control, and the future could contribute directly to intellectual functioning, that is, the ability to be more creative or simply smarter in one's work. Yet there is amassing evidence to suggest that this may be the case.

Much of this thinking focuses on the egocentricity of memory and other cognitive processes. Greenwald offers an intriguing, if somewhat speculative, evolutionary argument for the intellectual adaptiveness of egocentric cognitive processes.[43] In effect, his argument maintains that the ideal cognitive system for the organization of memory should be one that is complex and highly articulated, so as to provide a maximum number of categories and associations among the elements within and across categories. The self, he argues, provides just such a system.

In making this argument, Greenwald likens the egocentrically organized mind to a totalitarian governmental system, in which "the true goal . . . is not persuasion, but organization. . . . The organization of the entire texture of life according to an ideology can be fully carried out only under a totalitarian regime."[44] The fact that the totalitarian ego assimilates information as it relates to the self essentially accomplishes this goal. Information is organized primarily around the self-system and that organization extends to every aspect of life. Egocentric biases in the recall and interpretation of information essentially function to preserve organization and protect the integrity of knowledge.

Because we know more about ourselves than any other element, the self is complex, ensuring that the interconnections among material organized egocentrically will be rich and dense.[45]

Greenwald likens the functioning of the egocentric mind to a library. In essence, the egocentric mind preserves organization in the same way that a library develops categories for books and makes additions to those categories. Each new acquisition the library makes does not lead to a new set of categories, but is assimilated to the old set of categories, and the same is true of the human mind. Just as a library develops more topics and greater numbers of volumes that deal with a particular topic, so the human mind grows in breadth and depth within categories as well. Egocentrism provides a " 'protective belt' that preserves the 'hardcore' belief that all of one's memory is the interrelated experience of a single identity—the one called myself."[46]

Despite the speculativeness of his theoretical position, Greenwald is in good company. Many prominent psychologists have emphasized the importance of the integrated and unified self in intellectual functioning. Gilbert Brim, for example, states:

What humans learn during life are axioms, concepts and hypotheses about themselves in relation to the world around them. We can think of the sense of self as a personal epistemology, similar to theories in science in its components and its operations, but dealing with a specific person.[47]

Similarly, Seymour Epstein argues:

The self-concept is a self-theory. It is a theory that the individual has unwittingly constructed about himself as an experiencing, functioning individual and is part of a broader theory which he holds with respect to his entire range of significant experience.[48]

Greenwald suggests that the existence of egocentrically organized cognition derives, in part, from its success as an intrapsychic organization system. In essence, it wins out over its competitors. In early childhood, the individual's nervous system evolves into a highly structured organizational system which is used to gather, interpret, and store information. Egocentricity is one of several competitors for this organizational system. Greenwald argues that egocentricity wins out because, compared with other cognitive systems, it is a more efficient and effective cognitive structure that preserves the organization of knowledge in relation to a highly valued and already complex system, namely the self. Intrapsychic evolution, Greenwald argues, may itself depend upon genetic evolution. A cognitive system that is relatively ineffective in recognizing, interpreting, and storing important information may literally die out over generations, whereas a cognitive system that is more effective in performing the same tasks will meet with reproductive success, remaining characteristic of the species for generations to come. The biologic evolutionary advantages of a cognitive system organized around the self may be evident if we take a simple but pointed example. Consider an early primitive person who sees a lion on the savannah while searching for food. If his first thought is, "The lions are back. It must be spring," he is less likely to survive than if he interprets the information egocentrically: "The lions are back. I must run or I will be killed." Organizing information around its adaptive implications for the self maximizes the likelihood that an organism will make most effective use of that information, at least from the standpoint of individual survival.[49]

Greenwald's position, then, is that there are cognitive benefits to an egocentrically organized cognitive system. The self as a well-known, highly complex, densely organized system allows for the rapid retrieval of information and extensive links among the stored information. It contains a set of categories that may be maximally useful and flexible for extracting information from the environment.

Egocentric cognitive processes may not be the only ways in which intellectual creative functioning is fostered by positive illusions. Positive illusions help create and maintain happiness, and this positive mood may also facilitate intellectual and creative functioning. The mind organizes information in many ways. Some information exists in the form of specific events, such as the time my mother and I went out in the rowboat and caught a fish. The same event may also be coded in several other ways simultaneously. The fish story, for example, may be endowed with particular meaning: my mother always had time to do things with me that I wanted to do. It may also be encoded emotionally, so that a strong feeling of happiness comes over the person when he or she recalls the event. Indeed, memory experts now believe that emotions are an important way in which information is organized in the mind. Emotions do not replace other organizational systems, but rather constitute another network of associations by which events are understood and, more important, linked to each other. Remembering one's childhood, for example, can evoke a series of happy memories, including the rowboat event, all of which may come flooding into mind in rapid succession.[50]

There are several important implications of the theory that emotions help organize information in the mind. One is that when people are in a particular mood, such as a happy one, they will remember and think about information that is primarily congruent with that mood, that is, other happy thoughts and events. New information consistent with the mood should also be learned more quickly and thoroughly. For example, a happy person would be more likely to learn happy than sad information and should be better able to recall that happy information when he or she is again in a happy mood. In other words, people learn happy material better when they are happy, and they are more likely to be able to recall it when they are happy.[51]

The idea that people learn mood-congruent information more easily than mood-incongruent information, and that they are able to remember information better when they are in the same mood as when they learned it initially, has some curious implications. As an example, it suggests that if one succeeds in curing a person of chronic depression, she might well develop amnesia. Nonetheless, there is consistent evidence that people recall information more easily and quickly when they are in a good mood than when they are in a bad mood. This is especially likely if the information itself has positive connotations or was learned originally when the person was in a positive state of mind.[52]

Does this mean that someone in a bad mood will think and remember primarily negative thoughts and events? Although this would seem to be an obvious implication of the affective theory of memory, in fact negative and positive moods do not parallel each other very well. When a person is in a bad mood, he or she is motivated to get out of it, and one way that a person can dispel a bad mood is by self-consciously trying to think about happy things. Consequently, people in bad moods often do not show the kinds of negative thinking that one might expect, precisely because they are working actively to dispel the bad mood. For that reason, the effect of a sad mood on learning is quite negative. A sad mood inhibits the learning and recall of positive material without promoting the learning or retrieval of negative content.[53]

In addition to its beneficial effects on memory, a good mood seems to speed up mental processing. Ideas come faster and more smoothly when one is happy. A good mood increases the likelihood that a person will use efficient and rapid problem-solving strategies.[54] Some might argue that being able to solve a problem efficiently is less important than being able to do so accurately or effectively. Certainly this is true, but there is little evidence that positive mood promotes the use of inappropriate strategies. Rather, a matching process seems to occur whereby people in a good mood are somehow better able to pick the most effective strategy for solving a problem more quickly than people who are in a negative mood.[55]

A happy state of mind also produces more creative problem

solving. Because ideas come somewhat more quickly when people are in good moods, they are more able to associate bits of information to each other, creating a cognitively more complex mental environment for making judgments and decisions. Moreover, positive mood leads to more unusual and diverse perceptions of relations among ideas. The ability to derive unusual associations is often regarded as an important condition for creative thought.[56]

ILLUSIONS AND THE SKILLS OF ACHIEVEMENT

Typically, success at any task depends upon more than simple motivation and ability. It also requires a set of skills that can advance one from a current state to the desired goal. Scientists have long noted that what we generally refer to as intelligence—what is measured by intelligence tests and, somewhat more indirectly, by grades in school—does not tell us who will be successful and why. Objective measures of intelligence are, in fact, only weakly related to ultimate success in a field, whether assessed by stature or income. What this means is that some set of skills intervenes between intelligence and success, making some people highly successful and others less so.

Psychologist Seymour Epstein has studied these processes, which he calls constructive thinking.[57] One might think of them as effective intelligence. Epstein measures constructive thinking by means of an inventory of items to which people respond true or false, depending upon whether the item is self-descriptive. The items measure skills, including the ability to control emotions such as anxiety or worry; the ability to set challenges and to make plans for accomplishing them; the absence of categorical thinking (which would include dividing people into those who are for me and those who are against me); the absence of superstitious thinking; and the absence of negative thinking (such as the tendency to believe that anything undertaken will ultimately fail). The goal of Epstein's research has been to identify the attributes of people who are most likely to show the constructive thinking that helps in the attainment of goals.

He found first, and somewhat to his surprise, that people who regarded themselves and others in a positively biased way were more constructive thinkers. In other words, self-aggrandizing illusions foster constructive thought. The relationship of optimism to constructive thinking, however, is more complex. Epstein found evidence for two quite different types of optimism. One, which might be thought of as effective optimism, is closely tied to a belief in personal control and involves expectations that one can master goal-related tasks. The other optimism, which he called naive optimism, reflects a belief that things will somehow turn out all right without active coping by the self. The effective optimism, Epstein found, was highly related to constructive thinking. Apparently, the belief that one has the skills to accomplish goals, coupled with the optimism that the use of those skills will be successful, helps to lead people to develop effective thinking skills. Naive optimism, on the other hand, was not related to constructive thinking. Simply having faith that things would turn out well does not appear to be adaptive.

However, the picture may actually be somewhat more complex. Consider, for example, the beginning stages of a long-term ambitious project that may not come to fruition for months or even years. At the outset of the project, it may be very valuable to have a certain naive optimism that the goal will be accomplished. The ability to keep that final state in mind may provide motivation and persistence when otherwise one might be tempted to turn away from the task because the goal is so far off. However, as work toward the goal progresses and the goal comes into sight, effective optimism may be more functional. In the last stages of a project, as a goal is coming to fruition, what becomes important is the ability to see exactly what tasks remain to be accomplished and to put one's mind to doing them, rather than to keep an overly optimistic assessment of the future in mind.

Over time, too, the goal that is envisioned may itself change somewhat as realism sets in. The initial aspirations of a novelist may be to make the bestseller list, and this view can inspire persistence at the outset. However, when the novel is two-thirds written, the novelist may adopt a more realistic assessment of its likely impact and recognize that it will probably sell fewer copies than the earlier vision suggested. By this time, the somewhat more modest assessment of the book's likely success may not affect motivation because the project is so close to fruition. In fact, it may keep the writer from being disappointed when the book is actually finished. In the end stages, then, naive optimism about a major success might actually be dysfunctional, as the discrepancy between what the person would like to achieve and what is actually achieved becomes evident.

Perceptions of mastery or self-efficacy may also be related to the skills necessary to bring motivation and creativity to fruition. People who believe that they have the means to accomplish their goals are better able to choose tasks that are appropriate, to estimate how much effort they need to expend, and to determine how long they should persevere at the task.[58] As the maxim "nothing ventured, nothing gained" suggests, risk taking is another skill that influences whether motivation and creativity will lead to success. A good mood increases the willingness to take risks, perhaps by reducing the awareness of what can go wrong.[59]

Another of the skills that must be learned in life in order to achieve goals is the willingness to postpone gratification. Most long-term goals worth having involve sacrifices of time, effort, and money. There are always attractive activities lurking on the sidelines, attempting to lure a person away from a goal. The desire to save for a new car may be undermined by an attractive compact disc player, a lavish vacation or other treats.

One might question whether the self-aggrandizing beliefs that people hold promote or undermine the ability to delay gratification. In fact, they appear to foster it. As any parent knows, one of the hardest things to teach a child is to postpone some positive event, be it eating candy, going to a party, or visiting a friend. It now appears that positive mood may actually help children delay these gratifications. Happy children are less likely to insist upon immediate rewards and seem better able to wait for reward than children in bad moods. Indeed, the child in a bad mood may use tempting gratifications to improve his or her mood rather than being willing to set those temptations aside in favor of a long-term goal. Positive mood seems to help adults, too, tolerate frustration better. It may be the vision of a better long-term outcome or the good mood itself that enables people to postpone gratification.[60] When in a bad mood, most people adopt a short-term focus toward tasks and will sometimes do things that actually undermine their long-term goals. For example, the person attempting to save money for a down payment on a home may, on a bad day, spend a portion of that money on a fancy dinner and some new clothes to boost morale. Yet this understandable but perhaps unwise self-indulgence both depletes the resources that are designated for the long-term goal and undermines the commitment to the savings program that the person may previously have been able to keep in mind.

The ability to evaluate one's performance and to reward oneself is another pair of skills that bring motivation and creativity together in goal attainment. These are especially important skills for children to acquire. They must learn to look at their performance, determine whether it is successful, and then verbally evaluate that performance through self-condemnation or self-congratulation which, in turn, produces an emotional reaction. As noted earlier, mastery-oriented children seem to learn appropriate verbal self-evaluation earlier than do children who are failure-oriented. They learn not only how to tell themselves that they have done a good job, but also what to tell themselves when they have not. They tell themselves that they need to try harder or attempt a different strategy; they talk to themselves about the meaning of both successful and unsuccessful outcomes, and in the case of unsuccessful ones, what to do about correcting them.[61]

In short, people who hold positive illusions about themselves, the world, and the future may be better able to develop the skills and organization necessary to make their creative ideas and high level of motivation work effectively for them. They seem more able to engage in constructive thinking. They can tie their illusions concretely to the project at hand, developing a task-oriented optimism and sense of control that enable them to accomplish more ambitious goals. They are more likely to take certain risks that may enable them to bring their ventures to fruition. And they seem better able to choose appropriate tasks, gauge the effort involved, and make realistic estimates of their need to persevere. Moreover, by developing the ability to postpone gratification, they are able to commit themselves to a longer term task that may involve sacrifices and delayed rewards along the way.

ILLUSIONS AND PERSONAL GROWTH

ILLUSIONS AND FUNCTIONING UNDER STRESS

A good theory of mental health must explain not only how people function under normal and optimal conditions, but how they function under stress as well. This point has several implications. First, it suggests that mental health is dynamic. Mental health is not a static set of attributes that an individual carries from situation to situation, but may better be thought of as resources, skills, and personal attributes that become effective tools as needed, depending upon the situation. The effectiveness of personal resources cannot be fully assessed without some sense of whether the individual is able to use those capabilities to deal with stressful events. Consequently, any theory of mental health must speak not only to the qualities that characterize the mentally healthy person generally, but also to their dynamic role in meeting the challenges of the environment.

Not all theories of mental health have fully recognized the importance of this criterion, although it is embodied in Jahoda's assertion that one component of mental health is the ability to tolerate and master the environment. This criterion implicitly acknowledges that the environment often brings stresses and challenges with which any individual must deal creatively and adaptively. A person who is mentally healthy should be able to do so to a greater degree than one who is not.[62] In fact, there is substantial evidence that positive illusions about the self, personal control, and the future are adaptive, not only in normal or optimal circumstances, but during stressful times as well.

For decades, psychologists have explored the psychological experience of stress. Early research used animals to identify objective determinants of stressful events, such as pain and discomfort, and their impact on physiology.[63] When research was subsequently conducted on people, it became evident that the experience of stress depends heavily upon how people interpret events.[64] An event that may seem stressful to one person may not be perceived as so stressful by another. One person who loses a job, for example, may regard the experience as an unmitigated tragedy, whereas another may regard it as an opportunity for personal growth. Understanding stress requires understanding why people perceive events as stressful.

Typically, events experienced as the most stressful are unexpected, negative, and difficult or impossible to control.[65] Of these, control is centrally important in the experience of stress. When an event—even a painful or upsetting event—is perceived to be under personal control, the event does not produce as much stress as one perceived to be uncontrollable. When people experience uncontrollable stressful events, they react more negatively. Their physiological systems respond dramatically, leading to an increase in adrenalin secretion, which in turn has accompanying side effects such as the pounding of the heart, nervousness, and sweatiness. Psychological distress is greater when a stressful event cannot be controlled. People who are under stress that they cannot control also perform more poorly on other tasks. Concentration is limited, so it may be difficult to attend properly to what they need to do.[66]

Not only do uncontrollable stressful events cause people to feel more stress while the event is going on, they also interfere with people's behavior after the stressful event is over. For example, if you are attempting to complete your income tax return and a radio is blasting from a neighbor's window, it may be difficult to complete the tax forms not only while the noise is going on, but also after it has stopped. The residue of the stressful experience, both emotionally and biochemically, makes it hard to focus attention on the task at hand. However, if the radio playing is yours, or you know you can control its volume simply by stepping into the next room and asking someone to turn it down, it will not only have less effect on your performance while it is on, but it will produce few, if any, aftereffects.[67]

Environmentalists have been concerned with the impact of increased crowding, noise, pollution, and other adverse environmental phenomena on people's behavior patterns and ways of living. In 1972, David Glass and Jerome Singer systematically explored the impact of noise. They noted that the noise level in major cities around the country had increased dramatically in the previous decade, and that many people were exposed to large amounts of noise in the workplace, in school, and at home. Yet until then no one had explored whether noise had a negative impact on performance and learning. To address these important research questions, Glass and Singer brought people into the laboratory and asked them to complete certain simple tasks, such as doing arithmetic problems and reading simple articles. One-third of the people were exposed to sudden bursts of loud noise over which they could exert no control. Another group of subjects was exposed to the same amount of noise, but they were able to terminate it by pressing a button. The third group completed the same tasks without being exposed to noise. The investigators then looked at performance, including whether or not people were able to complete the arithmetic tasks and understand what they were reading. The results showed first what one would expect, namely that performance on even very simple tasks is superior when unaccompanied by noise. But when the two groups of subjects exposed to noise were compared, there were dramatic differences. Those who were able to control the noise showed performance far superior to that of those who were unable to control the noise, despite the fact that the absolute amount of noise to which the two groups were exposed was the same. Thus, the experience of psychological control is intrinsic to the effects that potentially stressful events have on emotions, physiological responses, and psychological distress.[68]

If control is introduced into stressful circumstances, is the stress of those experiences reduced? The answer appears to be yes.[69] Psychologists have trained people facing stressful events in a variety of methods designed to help them control stress. Some stressful events lend themselves to direct efforts at control. For example, physicians have identified particularly unpleasant medical procedures and developed interventions to help people cope better with those stressors. One such procedure is the endoscopic examination, in which a patient swallows a tube that allows for viewing the esophagus and stomach. This procedure is very uncomfortable for most people, and produces gagging and sometimes vomiting. Researchers discovered, however, that if patients are systematically informed about the sensations associated with the procedure and then instructed in methods they can use for swallowing the tube more effectively, the procedure is less unpleasant and gagging is reduced.[70]

People need not engage in specific behaviors in order to feel a sense of control. Most of us know that when we are facing some kind of stressful event, calming ourselves down by taking deep breaths and relaxing our body will reduce at least some of the physiological arousal that usually accompanies stress. Pregnant women are often trained in techniques of breathing that will help them adjust to the different phases of labor. Thinking about a stressful event differently will also reduce the experience of stress. Most of us have learned to practice some forms of cognitive control in our own lives. A student may decide to put herself through four grueling years of medical school because she is able to maintain a vision of herself as a future physician during discouraging moments. During an awkward moment or argument with a spouse, one may become intensely aware of the details of the wallpaper pattern or a particular crack in the ceiling.

There are two quite different mental strategies for controlling the stressful of an aversive event.[71] One is to distract oneself by focusing on some other activity. Some examples of control techniques that rely on distraction are provided by children describing how they deal with stressful or painful events.[72] An eleven-year-old boy describes how he reduced pain by distracting himself while in the dentist's chair: "When the dentist says, 'Open,' I have to say the Pledge of Allegiance to the flag backwards three times before I am even allowed to think about the drill. Once he got all finished before I did." An eight-year-old boy also describes the value of distraction:

I can get through most anything as long as there's something to count—like those little holes in the squares on the ceiling at the dentist's. When I got sent to the school office for getting into trouble, I saw all the Principal's freckles. The whole time he was giving it to me, I started at the top of his face and counted his freckles all the way down.

The other kind of mental strategy for controlling stressful events is to focus directly on the events but to reinterpret the experience. The following is a description from an eight-year-old boy who confronted a painful event directly:

> As soon as I get in the dentist's chair, I pretend he's the enemy and I'm a secret agent, and he's torturing me to get secrets, and if I make one sound, I'm telling him secret information, so I never do. I'm going to be a secret agent when I grow up, so this is good practice.

According to Albert Bandura, who reports these stories, occasionally the boy "got carried away with his fantasy role-playing. One time the dentist asked him to rinse his mouth. Much to the child's own surprise, he snarled, 'I won't tell you a damned thing,' which momentarily stunned the dentist."

What research there is on these mental methods of control suggests that intuitive reactions of how to reduce stress are correct. Both distraction and reinterpretation of stressful events reduce the experience of stress before the event occurs, ameliorate distress during the event itself, and reduce the often debilitating aftereffects of stress. Distraction seems to be particularly good for improving coping before and during an event. For example, the expectant mother who focuses her attention on preparing the crib, clothing, and other essentials for the baby's arrival, instead of rehearsing what may be required during labor itself, may actually go into labor a calmer person than the woman who rehearses how to behave during labor. And for a time, the strategy of distraction may be successful as labor progresses. However, distraction seems not to be very successful in reducing distress toward the end of a stressful event or afterward. The woman who failed to prepare herself for labor could find herself in extreme pain and distress as hard labor comes on. In contrast, those who cope with a stressful event by focusing directly on it may show distress beforehand but deal more successfully with the event and its aftermath.

Which, then, is better: distraction or confrontation? There is no clear answer. Overall, the best strategy may be to focus on what one can actually do to alleviate a stressful event, and when one has done all one can to prepare, to put it out of mind.[73] The point is that both mental strategies are efforts to control the aversive stimulus. What one does by directly tackling and re-structuring the event, the other does by controlling emotional responses to it. Working in tandem, they can maximally reduce a person's experience of loss of control that is often the result of a stressful event.

Clearly, then, the experience of control is central to the experience of stress. When aversive events are seen as uncontrollable, they are more stressful, dramatically more so, than when they are regarded as subject to personal control. Moreover, the impact of a stressful event is muted, sometimes altogether, when the person undergoing the event is given some semblance of control over it. Sometimes this "control" is merely information about the event, and at other times the control may be minimal or even illusory.[74] The effectiveness of any sort of control suggests that it is the psychological sense of control and not the direct impact on stressful events that achieves the beneficial outcomes.

What of the other illusions of normal thought, namely high self-regard and optimism? Do these psychological resources— for that is what they seem to be—also blunt the effects of stress? People who have high self-esteem do, in fact, seem to manage stressful events more successfully than those low in self-esteem. It may be that high self-esteem facilitates seeing the actions that one must take to confront a stressful event directly. Or people with high self-esteem may be more positive in their outlook regarding these stressful events, and thus manage their emotional responses to stress more successfully. Exactly how self-esteem acts as a buffer against stress is not yet known, but its ability to act in this capacity is established.[75]

Evidence concerning the role of optimism in buffering people against stressful events is also accumulating. Studying optimists' and pessimists' strategies for dealing with a wide variety of stressful events, psychologists Michael Scheier and Charles

Carver found several advantages to optimism. Optimists engage in more active coping than pessimists. While pessimists spend time mulling over a stressful event and attempting to manage their emotional responses to it, optimists begin to tackle the stressful event directly in an attempt to make it more tractable or to overcome it altogether. For example, a pessimistic college student receiving an unexpectedly poor final grade might well be debilitated by the anxiety the surprise has produced, whereas the optimist would be more likely to go to the professor to arrange for another exam or an optional paper to improve her grade. Optimists also use more complex coping strategies than pessimists. Whereas the pessimist's response to setbacks is often to withdraw from the goal and focus on his or her unpleasant emotional state, the optimist is more likely to try several methods of overcoming the setback, including enlisting the aid of others.[76] Although research on the role of optimism as a stress buffer is relatively recent and there are few studies from which to draw, the evidence to date suggests that optimists cope more effectively with stressful events than pessimists.

ILLUSIONS AND THE CAPACITY FOR PERSONAL GROWTH

Many theories of mental health have represented the capacity for change and personal growth as one of the central qualities of the mentally healthy person. The research relating illusions to the capacity to deal effectively with stress speaks in part to the question of personal growth. The need to grow, change, and adapt to life is often thrust upon a person by unexpected and stressful events. The mentally healthy person may be one who can cope with stressful events, not only by minimizing their direct and immediate physiological and psychological effects, but also by integrating them into his or her life more generally to cull from them what is valuable, integrating the accommodations necessitated by stress into the evolving self-concept. Certain research on stressful events has adopted this framework and reveals that beliefs in personal control and mastery not only improve the ability to adapt to stressful events but also seem to promote personal growth.

Psychologist Suzanne Kobasa has identified a personality style she calls hardiness. Hardiness has three components. The first is a sense of commitment, that is, the ability to involve oneself both physically and psychologically in activities. The second factor is a belief in control, the sense that one causes the events of one's life and that one can influence those events. The third component is challenge, or a willingness to undertake and confront new activities that represent opportunities for personal growth. Kobasa argues that the people who adapt best in life, both psychologically and physically, are those who are hardy. Hardy people are curious about their environment and find their experiences interesting and meaningful. They believe that they have an impact on their environment and they expect change in their lives, welcoming it as an impetus for personal development. Hardy people perceive the future optimistically, and they make changes because they expect to succeed and because they see change as a natural, meaningful outgrowth of their current stage of development and planning. Hardy people take action decisively, incorporating change into their ongoing life plan and learning from their experiences in ways that will be valuable for the future. In essence, hardy people are able to transform potentially stressful events into personal challenges and opportunities for growth.[77]

In contrast, people who are low in hardiness tend to think of both themselves and their environment as boring, meaningless, and threatening. They may feel overwhelmed by the forces in their lives, believing that routine and lack of change is best. They have few expectations regarding their future personal development, and they are unlikely to take dramatic action to change their circumstances. Rather than seeing the future with optimism and taking an active role in creating it, they tend to be pessimistic, passive recipients of the environment. Moreover, because their personalities provide them with little or no

way of transforming potentially stressful events into opportunities for growth, these events may often have a debilitating
effect on them. Indeed, in studies of lawyers, business executives, and other people in high-stress occupations, Kobasa and
her associates have found evidence that those with high levels
of hardiness appear to tackle stressful events more successfully
than those who are not hardy.[78]

That hardiness is a buffer against stress is intuitively compelling. Hardiness suggests a cheerful, optimistic enthusiasm
about life. It conjures up images of Teddy Roosevelt and other
robust, charismatic figures who have successfully involved others in their causes. Researchers who have scrutinized hardiness
most closely have suggested that the most important aspect of
hardiness may be the feeling of control. A sense of control,
more than a sense of commitment or challenge, may enable
people experiencing stressful events to overcome their potentially adverse effects by transforming what others may see as
uncontrollable stressors into ones that are amenable to control.
In so doing, they may reduce the physiological arousal and
psychological distress that are often associated with stressful
events.

Of significance, too, is the fact that hardy people are more
likely to welcome a challenge and thereby admit certain stressors into their lives. In this sense, the effects of hardiness on
stress are paradoxical, because hardy people may actually increase their level of stress, at least for a time. But, as Salvador
Maddi notes:

> Though adjustment may be strenuous and difficult, change
> lends both excitement and possibility to life. Resilient peo-
> ple tend to find some meaning and interest in whatever
> they are involved in; they are actively engaged and infre-
> quently bored, apathetic or alienated. Strong in a sense of
> control, hardy individuals believe that they can exert a
> positive effect on what happens to them through their own
> initiative and resources. They rarely feel like passive vic-

tims but are capable of the inner peace that comes from doing all they can in the face of life's unchangeable givens.[79]

Avoiding or minimizing stress altogether is impractical because many of life's most rewarding and challenging experiences involve admitting stress into one's life. In many respects, this aspect of stress is the key to psychological growth. As psychiatrist Frederic Flach states:

> Thinking and acting creatively involve the ability to respond to change with a period of emotional distress during which time you may need to leave behind certain self-defeating attitudes and outmoded behaviors, all the while working to replace them with more valuable and productive ones. This continual process of emotional disruption and reintegration is the very basis of psychological growth and proves enriching in itself.[80]

Just as stress, change, and challenge sometimes foist growth experiences on a person, so can a person also actively create opportunities for growth by envisioning a new future. Inspired by a compelling vision of a different life, the homemaker can open a home business, the teacher can move into real estate, or the sedentary fifty-year-old train for a marathon. Thus, much personal growth is a positively inspired process, undertaken for the sheer joy in the challenge that it produces. Psychologist Hazel Markus and her colleagues have written about this process in their analysis of "possible selves," people's ideas of what they might become, what they fear they may become, and what they would like to become.[81] Most possible selves are positive ones: the smarter, thinner, more successful, and desirable me. Indeed, in some respects, the future provides the greatest opportunity for illusions to operate, because maintaining them requires no distortions of real events. In contrast, to maintain positive past and present selves, facts and events must sometimes be rearranged or forgotten. Images of the future self, then, can be taken on with abandon because one is not tied to concrete reality.

Markus and her colleagues argue that possible selves can serve an inspirational function. As people form a clear vision of what they would like to become, the vision guides their movements toward it, helping them to define goals along the way and to take steps to meet them. At times when motivation seems to flag and a goal seems far off, the ability to envision that future self may rekindle the desire to achieve it. Although many possible selves, such as the image of oneself as a featured concert cellist or the winner of Wimbledon, may ultimately not be achieved, those who envision such far-off dreams may become better cellists or tennis players. Thus, just as self-aggrandizing distortions of current attributes enable people to feel good about themselves and others and encourage them to persist in the effective pursuit of goals, so illusions about the future self help provide a mechanism whereby people grow and change, moving from a present situation to a far-off desirable future one, by keeping in mind the self they wish to become.[82]

CHAPTER 3

A Healthy Body

> I believe that if you're a positive
> person, your attitude has a lot to do
> with it. I definitely feel I will never
> get it again.
>
> —Cancer patient

THE QUALITY OF LIFE people enjoy is heavily influenced by their mental health. Clearly, people who are happier, who have rewarding social relationships, and who engage in productive, meaningful work have more pleasurable and rewarding lives than those who do not. The positive illusions that characterize normal thought contribute directly to mental health and to psychological well-being. Quality of life, however, is also heavily influenced by the state of one's physical health, for without freedom from illness and disability, the enjoyment of other aspects of life is undermined.

Do the positive beliefs that people hold about themselves, the world, and the future contribute to physical health, as they contribute to mental health? Are people with high self-esteem, a sense of personal efficacy, and an optimistic belief in the future more likely to be physically as well as mentally healthy? Curiously enough, the answer appears to be yes. Such findings pose challenges for scientists trying to show exactly how these mental factors affect the body. To the nonscientist, however, such findings come as no surprise. Surveys show that most people believe that stress and ways of coping with it heavily determine physical health. The boundary between science and wishful thinking is sometimes thin and never more so than in the realm of the mind's effect on the body. Witch doctors, charlatans, incurably ill self-healers, and serious scientists work side by side seeking the same outcome, but often rejecting each other's efforts to obtain it.

PSYCHOLOGICAL FACTORS IN ILLNESS: A CAUTION

The scientist has several roles in our society. Chief among these is the obligation to discover and describe truth. A secondary task is to monitor what the general public believes about the sciences, and what the media would have us believe, to see that these portrayals are reasonably accurate, neither in opposition to the truth nor an exaggeration of it. The task of a psychologist is particularly significant in this regard. Unlike the fields of chemistry, physics, and biology, about which the general public has relatively few intuitive and firmly held theories, most people consider themselves to be amateur psychologists, untrained certainly, but insightful nonetheless. In many cases, people's intuitions about psychology are quite accurate and appropriate. Moreover, nonscientists sometimes come up with useful observations that have eluded scientists mired in theoretical models. In other cases, however, the public holds beliefs about psychology that are not true or that represent a risky overstatement of the truth. To the extent that the media reinforce these beliefs by publishing stories that support them, the beliefs often come to be widely shared and take on the status of truth, even when the scientific basis for them is meager.

So it is with the impact of mental factors on physical health. Both the public and the media maintain that stress is a major cause of illness and that people's ways of dealing with it, including their attitudes, their personality styles, and their ability to maintain a fighting spririt, will enable them to avoid or overcome threatening diseases. As I write this chapter, the current issues of *Glamour, Business Week,* and the *New York Times Magazine* all have articles on how the mind controls the body and how people can improve their health by controlling their reactions to stress. The remarkable presence of books such as Bernard Siegel's *Love, Medicine and Miracles* and Norman Cousins's *Anatomy of an Illness* on bestseller lists around the country testifies to people's readiness to be persuaded that they can control their physical health and heal themselves from life-threatening diseases.

It is a wonderful idea. It will be very exciting if it is ultimately shown to be true. But the fact is that the evidence relating personality styles, coping techniques such as relaxation or imaging, and mental attitudes such as a fighting spirit to disease and the ability to cure oneself is faintly suggestive, but by no means definitive. It is astonishing that not one study has unambiguously addressed the question, "Can people heal themselves through their mental attitudes and ways of coping?" The reason is that this question is not yet amenable to scientific investigation. Scientists can answer questions more limited in scope, which together can help address the larger question, but the larger question itself remains unanswered.

What, then, is the appropriate position to take for the scientist who observes the public embracing this idea so completely but prematurely? The answer, I believe, is that one must exert a cautious and corrective influence. Anthropologist-physician Melvin Konner expressed the point well in the *New York Times.* He argued that although there may be evidence for relationships between certain psychological states and health outcomes, almost certainly the public believes that people can exert far more mental control over their health states than is actually the case. Many factors influence a person's state of health. A particular attitude or way of coping will be only one of these, and is unlikely therefore to be a conclusive one. It may, as Siegel suggests, give a patient an edge in a battle that is difficult and that may ultimately be lost. But it can never be the entire armament. As Konner notes, it may be not only unwise but actually cruel to lure people into believing that they can cure themselves of their advanced and debilitating diseases. Some patients blame themselves, wondering what they did wrong, why some people are able to cure their diseases and they are not. Dying can become the ultimate failure instead of an honorable ending to life.[1]

At the risk of belaboring the point, the following account illustrates the potential risks of these beliefs. A colleague was called in as a psychological consultant on a very difficult medical case involving a twenty-eight-year-old graduate student with an inoperable brain tumor. The physicians knew that the patient was virtually certain to die within the next few weeks. Understandably, the young man resisted this prognosis and turned to an alternative treatment center for hope, inspiration, and help in curing himself. The counselor asked him to describe his life, in an apparent effort to determine what had brought on the tumor at such a young age. Most of the events of the man's life had progressed rather normally, except that his mother had died when he was sixteen. The counselor latched on to this as an explanation for the tumor, informing him that he had never successfully come to terms with the loss and adjusted to it. Only by doing so now would he be able to free himself of the cancer. The young man was given some mental exercises to perform that involved imagining the tumor gradually shrinking. He was also urged to come to terms with the loss, but not told exactly how to do so.

Within days, the young man was seriously distressed, agitated over his apparent inability to manage the loss. He had always believed that he had done so successfully, but the counselor had persuaded him otherwise. He worked himself into a near-frenzy, so much so that his friends were alarmed and came to seek help for him. The psychologist met with him, and the young man recounted what he had been told at the alternative treatment center. The psychologist explained that no one can identify the cause of any particular tumor. Although there may be factors that predispose people to cancer in general, it is impossible to know what factors are involved in any particular case. The psychologist suggested that the counselor at the alternative treatment center may have read articles suggesting that early loss, like the death of a parent, can predispose people to cancer. The fact that this young man had had an early loss, however, did not mean that the loss had brought on the tumor. Moreover, she pointed out, there was no reason to believe that a failure to come to terms with the loss had anything whatsoever to do with the cancer growth, nor would becoming obsessed with his mother's death improve his health now. As for the imaging exercises that had been prescribed by the counselor, the psychologist pointed out that, while many people find such exercises to be soothing emotionally, there was no reason to think that by doing the exercises incorrectly he would fail to shrink the tumor.

These words, which might seem discouraging to some, had a remarkably helpful effect on the young man. Once freed of the guilt that he had brought it on himself, he was able to function normally. He did not succeed in shrinking his tumor, and he died several weeks later. But he was calm and peaceful, ready to face death with the support of those close to him, a state he could not have achieved without the psychologist's help.

Other patients give harsher voice to some of the same feelings, particularly the pressure to survive. A thirty-six-year-old man with malignant melanoma described his unsuccessful effort to join a social support group for patients like himself. "They were so depressing—not because they were going to die, but because no one would let them die. I wish just once someone had told me, 'It's okay to die.' Instead, you're made to feel like you're doing something wrong if you die; you're letting down your friends and your family, even your doctors."[2]

What is the nature of the evidence? Within limits, certain aspects of psychological control and optimism appear to influence health, health behaviors, immunologic functioning, and biochemical functioning in ways that make the body more resistant to illness and better able to recover from existing disease. These are not the nearly magical outcomes that sensational articles and books envision. One cannot wish a tumor away. However, there is increasing evidence to suggest that the same illusions of normal thought that seem to facilitate mental health may also facilitate physical health, at least to some degree.

PSYCHOLOGICAL CONTROL AND PHYSICAL HEALTH

A voluminous amount of research from diverse fields within psychology and medicine testifies to the importance of belief in personal control in health outcomes. It includes work that examines personal control and the practice of good health habits, and personal control as a buffer against stress; other research addresses vulnerable populations including the elderly, or the role of abrupt loss of control in sudden death; and some studies tie uncontrollable stressful events to cancer and to compromises in immunologic functioning. Taken together, the evidence suggests two important ways in which beliefs about control may have direct or indirect effects on health. First, a belief that one can control adverse events in one's life may lead one to practice good health habits and to cope effectively with the stresses of life, thereby minimizing or ameliorating adverse effects on health. Second, the belief that one lacks or has lost control in a stressful environment may undermine health, leading to a high likelihood of illness or even death.

In recent years, media attention has focused heavily on lifestyle and its relationship to illness, and for good reason. Until the twentieth century, the health problems of the United States involved the treatment and elimination of infectious diseases. At the turn of the century, the major causes of death were tuberculosis, pneumonia, and influenza. Largely because of public health advances in sewage control, water purification, and the containment of infection—and, to a lesser extent, developments in immunization and medical treatment—these problems were made tractable, virtually eliminating them as major causes of death by the 1940s. The conditions that currently account for most death and disability in this country are coronary artery disease, cancer, diabetes, stroke, and automobile accidents.[3] What distinguishes these disorders from the infectious diseases that previously dominated medical concern is the fact that they are controllable, at least to some degree. They are substantially influenced by the health behaviors that people practice, beginning early in life and extending into adulthood.

Chronic disease and accidents, then, are the preventable disorders. Twenty-five percent of all cancer deaths and a substantial number of deaths from heart attacks could be avoided by eliminating just one unhealthy behavior: smoking.[4] A mere 10 percent weight loss among men aged thirty-five to fifty-five would produce a decrease of 20 percent in coronary heart disease. Not incidentally, it would also lower the rate of arthritis, gastrointestinal cancer, diabetes, strokes, and heart attacks.[5] An overall estimate is that half the deaths from the ten leading causes of death in this country are due to modifiable lifestyle factors over which people have personal control.[6]

A logical question, then, focuses on what role a sense of personal control may have in promoting (or undermining) healthy behaviors. One can envision at least two possibilities.

Perhaps people who have an exaggerated perception of their ability to control the environment believe they can control the likelihood of illness as well. They may think that because they are potent people generally, they can stave off disease through sheer dint of will. If this is an accurate portrayal, it would suggest that unrealistic faith in personal control may actually interfere with the practice of good health behaviors. Such people may believe that they can go on smoking because if early symptoms of lung cancer or emphysema were to develop, they could control them. They may permit themselves to become overweight in the belief that should weight control become essential to their health, they could lose the extra pounds.

An alternative viewpoint paints a more attractive picture of the effects of control on health habits. People who have faith in their ability to control the environment may be better able to see what aspects of a situation can be controlled, and thereby exert their control over health habits as well. From this viewpoint, then, such people might actually be more likely to practice a healthy lifestyle because they regard that lifestyle as instrumental in continuing their good health.

Current evidence favors this more adaptive viewpoint. To begin with, a general belief in personal control appears to foster good health habits. Psychological research that assesses individual differences in control reports that people who believe they can control events in the environment are more likely to practice good health habits than those who do not.[7] Moreover, the specific belief that one can effectively engage in a particular healthy habit greatly enhances the likelihood that one will actually practice it.[8] People who think they can stop smoking, change their diet, or exercise regularly are much more likely to do so. Moreover, the reverse is also the case. If a person doubts his ability to achieve a particular health goal, such as stopping smoking, he will be very unlikely to succeed at quitting, even if he knows he should quit, fears the consequences of not quitting, and believes that quitting would greatly reduce his risk. The belief in self-efficacy, that is, the capacity to perform a particular behavior, is critical in the practice of healthy behaviors.[9]

Beliefs in personal efficacy are important not only for health habits practiced prior to the development of any disorder, but also for those initiated after a disorder is detected. A study conducted by Bandura and his associates clearly indicated how valuable the perceptions of self-efficacy could be in recovery from myocardial infarction (heart attack). One of the problems that physicians, nurses, and others who work with heart attack victims experience during the rehabilitation process is that patients often believe that their hearts are damaged and become invalids as a consequence. They believe they cannot handle the stress in their work life and social life; they abandon physical activity; they fear they will collapse in the middle of sexual relations; and so they remain sedentary. In fact, most heart attack patients are capable of much more activity than they think is possible, activity that may actually contribute to their recovery.

Bandura and his colleagues reasoned that perceived inefficacy, namely the perceived inability to engage in vigorous physical activity, was leading these people into premature and needless invalidism. They developed an intervention to convince male heart patients and their spouses that the patients actually had more stamina than they themselves believed or than their spouses believed. Several weeks after the patients suffered their heart attacks, they were given treadmill tests. Wives were asked to observe so they could see their husbands' stamina and performance. Patients are usually surprised when they see how well they are able to cope with the stress of the treadmill test, and such was the case in this study. Subsequent to the treadmill activity, both patients and their wives came to realize that the husbands' cardiac capability was greater than they assumed. In the coming weeks, the patients resumed a more active life than they had had previously, thanks to the perceptions of self-efficacy that had been induced by the feedback of the treadmill test.[10]

THE POWER OF BELIEF

Can a belief in control actually keep people from developing illness? Research on personality suggests that, within limits, it can. Chapter 2 introduced the idea of the hardy personality, which is characterized by a belief in personal control, a willingness to confront challenge, and a sense of commitment to projects and activities. To determine whether this constellation of attributes protects people against ill health, Suzanne Kobasa studied middle- and upper-level male business executives to find out how they appraised the challenges in their lives and how they dealt with them. She divided the executives into those who had experienced a lot of stress in the previous three years and those who had experienced less stress. Looking only at these executives under the most stress, she probed further to see who had experienced a lot of illnesses and who had experienced relatively few illnesses. She found that the highly stressed but healthy executives were distinguished by their hardiness. Because of the amassing evidence to suggest that, of the three components of hardiness, control may be the most potent, Kobasa's studies provide indirect evidence that a sense of psychological control can actually buffer people against the adverse health effects of stress.[11]

CONTROL AND THE ELDERLY

Much of the evidence suggesting an important role for control in physical health comes from findings that the absence of control has major and often dramatic adverse effects on health. Some studies implicate the absence of belief in control as the pathogen in poor health, whereas others suggest that experiencing a sudden loss of control adversely affects health. Some of the most dramatic evidence for these points comes from studies with the elderly.

Elderly people, especially those who are frail, often experience little control. Most of us have, at one time or another, visited a nursing home. We may have gone caroling at Christmas as children, taught crafts to older people, or visited an elderly relative. The first reaction to such a visit is often shock. Here are once-vigorous adults sitting in rockers with little but television to occupy their time. Nursing homes often have limited financial resources that do not allow for many activity programs or much personal liberty. Of necessity, the nursing home staff may behave in ways that deprive the inhabitants of freedom. In so doing, they may inadvertently contribute to the development of health problems or exacerbate existing ones.

In 1976, two psychologists, Ellen Langer and Judith Rodin, attempted to see whether they could introduce elements of control in a nursing home and thereby improve the morale and health of the institutionalized elderly people.[12] The intervention was, in many ways, a very simple one. Patients on one floor of the nursing home were given small plants to care for and were asked to select when they wished to participate in some of the nursing home's activities, such as movies and bingo. Patients on another floor of the nursing home were also given plants, but they were told that the staff would care for them. They participated in the same activities as the first group of patients, but were assigned the activity times. These interventions—caring for a plant and choosing activity times—were the sole controlling actions made available to the patients.

Several weeks later, nurses rated the mood and activity level of the people who had participated in the study. The residents were also asked how they were feeling, and they were surreptitiously observed to see how active they were. Those who had been given some control were more active and had a greater sense of well-being than the residents in the comparison group. Moreover, a year later, the former were still psychologically and physically healthier than the people who had not participated in the intervention. There were also somewhat fewer deaths among the participants in the intervention than among the comparison group.[13] This rather simple study has profound implications. It shows how very little control is needed to achieve beneficial effects. The steps introduced in the intervention were small, inexpensive, and easy to implement, but their impact was substantial. Moreover, they had discernible and long-term positive effects on health.

Just as control interventions can have beneficial effects on patients, the withdrawal of control or its loss can have unhappily negative consequences. Some nursing homes attempt to improve the morale of their residents by having visitor programs, in which students from nearby high schools or colleges spend time with the residents and act as regular companions. In one such program, some of the elderly people were permitted to schedule their own visiting times with the students. A second group was told in advance when the volunteers would be coming and for how long, but they did not make the arrangements themselves. A third group was not told when the volunteers would be coming or for how long, but knew that visitors would come from time to time. A fourth group of patients did not receive visitors. The short-term effects of this intervention were very positive. Those who were able to control or anticipate when their visitors would arrive improved in physical health, needed fewer medications, were more active, and were psychologically healthier than the patients who received no visitors or who were not warned when the visitors would be coming. Unfortunately, however, the program had to be terminated at the end of the school year. When this occurred, the patients who had been able to control or predict the students' visits lost ground both physically and emotionally, as compared with patients who had not received visitors or who had not been able to predict or control the visits. Moreover, more of the patients who had been able to control and anticipate their visitors' arrivals died following the termination of the program.[14]

One might look at these two interventions and wonder why they achieved such different results. In Langer and Rodin's study, the elderly were given control over areas of their lives which then became self-sustaining. They could continue the behaviors on their own without the help of the research investigators. Moreover, there was some evidence that the interventions generalized to other aspects of the residents' lives, so that they became more assertive and sought to control activities beyond those involved in the interventions. In contrast, the college visitor program could not be maintained when the students left for the summer and hence, the residents' control could not be maintained. The environment returned to its previous level of inactivity and lack of control with devastating health effects.

Despite the apparent vulnerability of the elderly to experiences involving loss of control, they are often subjected to such experiences. More than any other group in the population, they are involuntarily relocated, moved out of their own homes into nursing homes, and moved from one nursing home to another, as their health status and psychological needs change. A particular elderly person may no longer be able to take care of herself in her own home, and her family may feel that it is essential to move her. An indigent patient may need to be moved to another hospital as his health deteriorates. Older buildings may be judged to be no longer safe, requiring that the occupants be shifted to a new location. A fire that devastates a portion of a hospital may lead to the relocation of many residents. There are a number of reasons why the elderly might find themselves unwillingly moved from their personal homes to an institution or from one institution to another.

As the population in our country is aging, psychologists and policy makers have become increasingly concerned about what the impact of this involuntary relocation might be. There have now been several investigations, and the picture is not a good one. Involuntary relocation is a stressful event. People who are relocated to a new environment, particularly when it is not one of their choosing, appear to suffer adverse health consequences, psychological distress, and even death.[15] This sad situation indirectly provides evidence that loss of control can harm health and that restoration of a semblance of control can help reverse these effects.

Since July 1977, the CDC (Centers for Disease Control) in Atlanta has been investigating a strange phenomenon of sudden, unexpected night deaths among Southeast Asian refugees to the United States. To date, more than one hundred men and one woman, most of them young and apparently healthy, have died suddenly, often within the first few hours of sleep. All of the victims were from Vietnam, Laos, or Cambodia. Typically, the victim begins to gurgle and move about in bed, but cannot be awakened, and dies shortly thereafter. To date, autopsies have revealed no specific cause of death.

Family members and friends have sometimes reported that the victim experienced a dream foretelling the death. Among these refugees, dreams are taken seriously, and although ritualistic measures were sometimes offered to avert the death, anxiety from the dreams may have played a role in the deaths. Hence the term "nightmare death" was coined to describe this phenomenon.

As yet, the nightmare deaths remain a mystery. A possible contributing factor is a rare genetic malfunction of the heart's rhythm. This theory has some credibility, because the sudden deaths occur primarily in men of particular ethnic groups and also seem to cluster in particular families. The existence of the nightmares and the significance attached to them by these often superstitious people may also be contributing factors. Night terrors can produce abrupt and dramatic physiological changes that, in conjunction with a genetic malfunction, can trigger death.

Stress may also be implicated in these deaths. Many of the victims were early arrivals to the United States who had run themselves into exhaustion, combining full-time jobs with demanding night school classes or other efforts to make a living and adjust to the new culture. Some of the victims may have been overwhelmed by cultural differences, language barriers, problems finding jobs, and dependency on welfare, humiliating for these once proud and hard-working people. Although it is still uncertain why these sudden deaths occurred, cultural and psychological factors leading to the experience of extreme and uncontrollable stress may well be an important contributing factor.[16]

Sudden death is not a new phenomenon to researchers. Scientists have documented intriguing but puzzling instances of it for decades, as in the case history of this psychiatric patient reported in a monograph on sudden death.

A female patient who had remained in a mute state for nearly 10 years was shifted to a different floor of her building along with her floor mates, while her unit was being redecorated. The third floor of this psychiatric unit where the patient in question had been living was known among the patients as the chronic, hopeless floor. In contrast, the first floor was most commonly occupied by patients who held privileges, including the freedom to come and go on the hospital grounds and to the surrounding streets. In short, the first floor was an exit ward from which patients could anticipate discharge fairly rapidly.

All patients who were temporarily moved from the third floor were given medical examinations prior to the move, and the patient in question was judged to be in excellent medical health though still mute and withdrawn. Shortly after moving to the first floor, this chronic psychiatric patient surprised the ward staff by becoming socially responsive such that within a two-week period she ceased being mute and was actually becoming gregarious. As fate would have it, the redecoration of the third-floor unit was soon completed and all previous residents were returned to it. Within a week after she had been returned to the "hopeless" unit, this patient, who like the legendary Snow White had been aroused from a living torpor, collapsed and died. The subsequent autopsy revealed no pathology of note, and it was whimsically suggested at the time that the patient had died of despair.[17]

Other cases provide similar arresting accounts.

A dramatic example is the death of the 27-year-old Army Captain who had commanded the ceremonial troops at the funeral of President Kennedy. He died 10 days after the President of a "cardiac irregularity and acute congestion," according to the newspaper report of the medical findings.

A 64-year-old woman who was said never to have recovered from the death of her son in an auto accident 14 years earlier died four days after her husband was murdered in a holdup.[18]

Sudden death seems to result from two main factors. The first is some preexisting bodily weakness, such as incipient heart disease or an infection. The second is a precipitating event, usually an unexpected, uncontrollable, and severe shock, such as the death of someone close, the loss of a job, or the ending of a marriage.[19] George Engel, the psychiatrist who first documented the sudden death syndrome, suggested that shock produces a sense of total loss of control, producing intense feelings of helplessness and hopelessness. He labels this pattern the "giving up-given up" syndrome, referring to the fact that the person gives up all desire to carry on and feels given up on by everyone else. The somatic weakness and the uncontrollable event operating in concert can produce a dramatic, rapid change in a person's health.[20]

Sudden death is rare. It is easy to exaggerate how common these events are because the incidents are so colorful. But, although uncommon, they are not particularly mysterious, and in many ways they are similar to other disease processes that occur in response to stress. In sudden death, the process of disease development occurs rapidly and fatally. These cases are dramatic examples of the powerful effects that loss of control can have on health.

CONTROL AND CANCER

Psychological control, or at least certain aspects of it, may also be implicated in the development of cancer. Most people think of cancer as a single disease, but actually cancer refers to more than a hundred different diseases. All of them, however, result from a malfunction of the DNA, that part of cellular programming that controls growth and reproduction. Instead of ensuring the regular slow production of new cells, this malfunction in DNA causes excessively rapid cell growth and proliferation. Thus, cancer cells multiply at a far faster rate than do normal cells. Moreover, they provide no benefit to the body. They merely sap it of resources.

Although the causes of some cancers are known, many of the factors that lead to cancer remain speculative or uncertain. Some, like breast cancer, run in families, and thereby seem to have a genetic component. Others, such as cancer of the colon or pancreas, seem to be at least partly dependent upon diet. Cancers are more common among people who are malnourished, among those whose diets include a lot of fats and additives, and among those who consume a lot of alcohol. The likelihood of cancer is also related to certain social factors. Married people, for example, are less likely to develop cancers of all kinds than single people, with the exception of cancers of the reproductive system, to which married people are somewhat more vulnerable.[21]

More recently, scientists have posed the question, "Is cancer related to stress?" For decades, there has existed a stereotype of a cancer-prone personality as easygoing and acquiescent, repressing emotions that might interfere with smooth social and emotional functioning. The cancer-prone person has been described as inhibited, conforming, oversocialized, compulsive, and depressive. He or she is said to have trouble expressing tension, anxiety, or anger, instead presenting the self as pleasant, calm, compliant, and passive. Some have argued that cancer patients use particular defense mechanisms and express their emotions abnormally, coping with stress by using denial and repression. These individuals, then, may be more likely to confront stressful events by giving in to them than by confronting them directly or attempting to master them.[22]

A major problem with exploring whether personality factors are related to cancer concerns how to study the issue.[23] If one assesses the personalities of cancer patients and patients who do not have cancer and finds cancer patients to be more repressed, acquiescent, and inhibited, have the emotions produced the cancer or has the cancer produced the emotions? Until recently, no evidence was available to answer this question. Now, however, scientists are in a position to look at the results of personality tests administered earlier in life and relate them to cancers that occur decades later. Many colleges give personality tests as part of their admissions program and keep these scores on file, providing scientists with the opportunity to go back to these files, retrieve the personality scores, and then ask whether these individuals, now in their forties and fifties, have developed cancer. At least one study has found that a tendency toward depression at age eighteen predicts the likelihood of cancer later on in life.[24]

Researchers have been even more successful in relating personality factors to the *course* of cancer, that is to whether an existing cancer progresses rapidly or slowly. A rapid course of cancer, terminating in an early death, is more common among polite, unaggressive individuals, whereas a longer illness appears to be more common among patients who adopt a combative, angry stance toward illness and toward medical practitioners. Those who actively attempt to assert some control over the cancer and its management may actually live a little longer.[25]

Stress and cancer also seem to be related. Animals that have been exposed to crowding or noise show higher rates of malignant tumors than animals not exposed to these stressors.[26] Studies that examine the frequency of stressful life events have found that cancer patients experienced a greater number of such events than people who did not develop cancer.[27] Of course, it is possible that people who discover that they have cancer are more likely to remember all the stressful events that happened to them prior to its development than people not so motivated to reconstruct their past in a stressful manner. Some studies, however, reveal that people undergoing stressful events are more likely to develop cancer in the future, making this alternative explanation unlikely.[28]

Uncontrollable events produce more stress than controllable ones, and the development of cancer has been more clearly tied to uncontrollable than controllable stressful events. A study conducted with rats made this point clearly. Three groups of rats were operated on and a cancerous tumor preparation was inserted, rendering them vulnerable to cancer. One-third of the rats were then exposed to electric shock that could not be avoided. Another third of the rats were exposed to the same amount of electric shock, but by pressing a bar, they were able to terminate it. A third group received no shock. The rats exposed to uncontrollable stress were more likely to develop full-blown cancers, whereas rats not exposed to uncontrollable stress were sometimes able to reject the tumors altogether.[29]

Psychiatrist Arthur Schmale uncovered similar patterns among people. He described a helplessness-hopelessness syndrome (similar to the giving up-given up syndrome discovered by Engel in sudden death victims) that may characterize cancer patients. Experiences with feeling helpless, Schmale argued, lead people to feel hopeless, which in turn can contribute to the development of cancer. People who feel hopeless, have few activities in their lives, have little devotion to causes, little sense of responsibility for their achievements, and a high susceptibility to failure appear to be more likely to develop cancer, according to Schmale's work. Hopelessness is often expressed by feeling doomed or finished, which may occur in response to a highly stressful event, such as the death of a spouse or loss of a job.[30] Socially stressful events that cannot be controlled may also be important in the development of cancer. Children who lacked close family ties in childhood may be vulnerable to cancers in adulthood. Adults who have little social support seem to have a higher incidence of cancer to begin with, and a more rapid course of illness once the cancer develops.[31]

Despite the mounting evidence relating lack of control to cancer, caution is merited in drawing conclusions. People exposed to uncontrollable stressful events may fear unnecessarily that they will develop cancer. Likewise, cancer patients may uselessly search their past for *the* uncontrollable stressful event that may have given rise to the tumor. For example, a woman with breast cancer may blame her ex-husband for the tumor, arguing that his bullying, insensitive behavior left her vulnerable.[32] It is doubtful that such simple relationships exist. Scientists continue to regard cancer as an outcome of a multifaceted process. Although uncontrollable stress may be one of those factors, it is doubtful that it is either a necessary condition for a cancer to develop or sufficient to produce cancer in the absence of other contributing factors.

Nonetheless, uncontrollable stressful events and cancer do appear to be linked, and it is useful to ask how this relationship may come about. At present, the immune system is the most likely culprit.[33] Immunity serves a general surveillance function in the body, customarily guarding against the development of cancerous or precancerous cells. Prolonged or severe stress may reduce immunologic competence at a critical point in time, permitting mutant cells to grow.

CONTROL AND THE IMMUNE SYSTEM

The human body is under continuous assault by bacteria, viruses, funguses, and parasites of all kinds. What protects us from constant illness and infection is the immune system, comprised of roughly a trillion specialized cells regulated by dozens of chemicals that monitor the bloodstream and tissue for early signs of foreign invaders and incipient disease. Evolution has produced a remarkably effective, efficient, and refined system. The protective cells of the immune system must recognize quickly whether an unfamiliar body is a dangerous enemy or a friend, and if an enemy, they must ingest and destroy it. What is remarkable about the system is that it can recognize invaders that have never been in the body before and know whether or not they belong there.

Drawing any generalizations about the immune system and its functioning is risky, for invariably such observations will be out of date, given how rapidly the field is progressing.[34] Nonetheless, certain findings are emerging regarding the impact of loss of control on immunologic functioning. Stress generally has paradoxical effects on the immune system. Sometimes stressful events can actually augment immunologic functioning, whereas in other cases, they can so tax and debilitate the immune system that its functioning is compromised. As yet, scientists are uncertain about what factors of stress lead to these opposite effects. One fact does seem clear, however. Exposure to uncontrollable stress seems to have consistently adverse effects on the immune system. In animals, for example, uncontrollable events such as exposure to loud noise or electric shock, separation from the mother, and separation from peers reduces immunologic functioning, especially the production of a particular type of cells called lymphocytes.[35]

Stress seems to increase the likelihood of infectious disorders in people as well. Children, for example, show an increase in all kinds of infectious disease when their families are under stress.

Adults under stress are more likely to develop the common cold, trenchmouth, herpes recurrences, and mononucleosis. Students may take grim satisfaction from studies showing that college exams can lead to supression of the immune system and increased susceptibility to infectious disorders.[36]

Readers of Tom Wolfe's *The Right Stuff* may remember the Apollo astronauts' frustration over their limited role in the manned space flights. Singled out to be heroes, they felt foolish for being unable to perform any of the actions that "real" pilots perform as a matter of course. Although they were all superior pilots, the flight program considered them to be the human counterparts to the monkeys that had flown before them, and at least in the early stages, gave them no control of their capsules. Instead, they had to sit passively as the space vehicle took off, orbited, and splashed down, bobbing in the water until one of the rescue ships picked it up. A more perfect situation for immunocompromise could hardly be imagined—a stressful, even life-threatening, event over which the victim has no control. In fact, analyses of blood drawn after splashdown showed precisely this situation: the astronauts experienced suppression of their immune functioning apparently due to the uncontrollable stress.[37]

The stressful event that has been most consistently related to a reduction in immunologic functioning has been the death of a spouse, which is generally considered to be the most stressful life event. Not only is one deprived of a longtime companion, but because of the coordination that is usually required between spouses to manage a home and family, the departure of one-half of the team thrusts the burdens of these joint tasks on the other partner at precisely the time when the survivor may be least able to assume the additional obligations. Loss of a spouse may also be one of the least controllable stressful events. Both the event itself, which is often sudden and unexpected, and its aftermath can tax a person's abilities and produce a sense of loss of control that far exceeds that produced by other stressful events. After a spouse has died, the surviving spouse is more likely to become ill and to die in the period following the bereavement. Bereaved people are simply less able to fight off invaders than those who have not been subjected to this shock.[38]

CONTROL AND HEALTH: AN ASSESSMENT

Belief in a sense of personal control, then, appears to have a direct and positive impact on health, just as the experience of lack or loss of control has an adverse effect on health. What is clearly implicated in these studies is the importance of *beliefs* concerning control, not simply whether control is in fact present or absent in these stressful situations. Studies in which people have been led to believe that they have control over stressful events (even when they, in fact, have no control) demonstrate that the belief in control produces dramatic effects on neuroendocrine functioning. Compared with those who believe they are undergoing the same events with no control, people undergoing stressful events that they perceive as controllable look little different in neuroendocrine functioning from people who report that they are under no stress at all. However, among people undergoing stressful events that they perceive as uncontrollable, neuroendocrine functioning is dramatically altered in ways that can have a direct impact on immune functioning.[39] It is no wonder, then, that controllable and uncontrollable stressful events have such different effects on health. Moreover, it is the belief or illusion of control, and not simply the existence of control, that is implicated in these relationships.

OPTIMISM AND HEALTH

Does optimism promote health? It is possible to envision two ways in which optimism could be related to a healthy lifestyle. First, it may be that optimism leads people to see themselves as invulnerable to health risks—or at least less vulnerable than objective evidence would warrant. If so, they may see little need to practice good health habits, because they may regard the outcomes of bad health habits as so unlikely. Perceiving lung cancer to be something that other smokers get, an unrealistically optimistic person may continue to smoke in the naive faith that he or she will be spared this disease. The alternative viewpoint adopts a more instrumental view of optimism. Optimists from this vantage point would look into the future, identify potential risks, and then take steps to minimize them. If optimism operates in this functional manner, then we might expect optimistic people to practice more healthy lifestyles than pessimistic people. Pessimistic people, by implication, might see the future as more dark, thereby rendering useless any actions they might take to offset the future.

In fact, the evidence on optimism suggests that both views may have some validity. People are unrealistically optimistic about health risks.[40] They see themselves as less likely to develop heart disease, cancer, diabetes, or stroke than the average person. Moreover, when people with poor health habits are directly confronted with their bad habits and asked if they are aware of their risks, they will typically respond with an unrealistically optimistic assessment of the likelihood that the habit will give rise to injury, disease, or death.[41] Smokers know that smoking causes lung cancer and heart disease, but when asked their own chances of developing these disorders because of their smoking, they minimize their personal risks. In this case, optimism is operating defensively to justify the behavior that is so difficult to abandon. But was it unrealistic optimism that initially gave rise to the poor health behavior? Was it the failure to appreciate personal health risks that led the person to begin or continue smoking, or was it the inability to give up smoking that led to a personal distortion of the health risk? Merely observing that two factors, such as optimism and smoking, occur at the same time does not tell us which factor is causing which. Optimism can be defensive as well as adaptive and may arise in response to situations that are perceived as threatening or difficult to change. Optimism, in effect, becomes the justification for the failure to engage in healthy lifestyle change, but not necessarily the cause of the failure.

Important as this finding is, it does not address the larger question, namely, What is the effect of optimism on the likelihood that a person will develop a healthy lifestyle? Does optimism typically exert positive effects on health by directing people toward activities they can undertake to assure themselves of a beneficial future? Or does it exert a poor effect on health by blinding people to objective risks for which they should actively prepare themselves? As just noted, people do have unrealistically optimistic assessments of their vulnerability to both common and rare health risks, but this optimism is not naively unresponsive to objective estimates of risk. Assessments of vulnerability show a patterning that corresponds very closely to objective health risks.[42] For example, people quite properly realize that they are more vulnerable to common diseases such as cancer or heart disease than they are to rarer diseases such as multiple sclerosis or Parkinson's disease. People also incorporate systematic personal vulnerabilities into their assessment of their own health risks. Thus, for example, a man whose father and grandfather died of heart disease typically will assess his own chances of dying from heart disease as much higher than someone with no family history of heart disease.

Unrealistic optimism about health risks, then, is not a response to the anxiety generated about a disorder. If it were, one would expect to see that threatening and common health risks would generate the most unrealistic optimism, whereas the reverse is true. Similarly, estimates of personal vulnerability are more responsive to actual vulnerability than to the degree of threat posed by a disorder. Thus, for example, although the chances of developing cancer are both considerably higher and more threatening than the chances of developing an operable aneurism, people nonetheless quite properly see that they are more vulnerable to cancer than an aneurism. People are also more optimistic about risks that fall under their personal control than they are about random threats. If they perceive that they can reduce the risk of a particular health problem through health habits, such as stopping smoking to avoid heart disease or cancer, then they are more optimistic about this risk than about one over which they can exert less control, such as developing Parkinson's disease. In short, unrealistic optimism shows a significant realistic overlay.

Research concerning the relationship of optimism to physical health is in its infancy, and relatively few investigations have been undertaken to this point. However, what evidence exists suggests that optimistic people may be somewhat healthier. People higher in optimism report fewer physical symptoms, for example, than people who are low in optimism.[43] Optimistic people also recover faster from surgery than people who are not optimistic.[44] In an alcohol treatment program, optimism predicted success. Those alcoholics who were optimistic, not just about the likelihood of their treatment being effective but about life in general, were more likely to be successful abstainers from alcohol following the treatment than those alcoholics with a generally pessimistic outlook on life.[45] One may again raise the question of whether optimism causes recovery from these events or whether faster recovery leads to more optimism. In the case of the studies just examined, the direction of causality is quite clear, inasmuch as optimism measured at an earlier point in time predicted subsequent recovery among the surgical patients and the alcoholics.

Chapter 2 described how a pessimistic explanatory style predicts college students' grades, life insurance agents' sales records, and the outcome of presidential elections. The pessimistic explanatory style has now also been related to poor health. Interviews completed at age twenty-five by graduates of the Harvard University classes of 1942 to 1944 were analyzed to see how they habitually explained the negative events in their lives. Specifically, the men were asked about difficult experiences they had encountered during the Second World War, such as combat situations, relations with superiors, and battles in which they were actively involved, and they were asked whether they felt they had dealt successfully or unsuccessfully with those wartime situations. Some of the men also talked about difficulties they were having getting established in careers and relationships. Their answers were coded as reflecting an optimistic or pessimistic style. An example of explaining a negative event in terms of a pessimistic explanatory style is provided by one man who was to die before age fifty-five: "I cannot seem to decide firmly on a career . . . this may be an unwillingness to face reality." Another man, also to die prior to age fifty-five, stated that he disliked work because he had a "fear of getting in a rut, doing the same thing day after day, year after year." In contrast, one of the healthy men referred to his army career as follows: "My career in the army has been checkered, but on the whole, characteristic of the army." Another referred to his effort to deal with a difficult situation. "I tried to bluff my way through a situation. . . . I didn't know the facts, a situation common to all green junior officers when they are first put in charge of men." The difference between the two sets of responses is that the first two men referred to negative events in terms of their own stable qualities, with no apparent hope of escape. In contrast, the two healthy men also described negative experiences, but with reference to external factors ("That's the army") or by maintaining that a less-than-capable response was one that any "green junior officer" would have made.[46] Those men who explained bad events by referring to their own internal, stable, pervasive negative qualities had significantly poorer health at ages forty-five through sixty, some twenty to thirty-five years after the survey. This was true even when physical and mental health at age twenty-five were taken into account. Thus, pessimism in early adulthood seems to be a risk factor for poor health in middle and late adulthood.

Unrealistic optimism is not a blind spot in people's recognition of risk, but rather a modestly overoptimistic assessment that is otherwise responsive to the factors that objectively increase risk. Optimism may also have certain positive effects on health such as the ability to recover faster from disorders, and a pessimistic bent may be related to poor health. Moreover, there is now evidence that chronic pessimism, as embodied in the psychological state of depression, can have adverse health consequences.

DEPRESSION AND HEALTH

For centuries, people have believed that personality states are linked to disease. In ancient Greece, Hippocrates, the founder of medicine, maintained that there were four humors of the body—blood, black bile, yellow bile, and phlegm—and that the balance among these determined both personality and a predisposition to particular diseases. The personality type that resulted from an excess of black bile was depression. Melancholic types, it was believed, would eventually waste away from the rotting disorder within them, succumbing both emotionally and physically to their imbalance. Perhaps Hippocrates' observations had a kernel of truth. If positive illusions actually promote physical health and these illusions are virtually absent in depressed individuals, one might expect to see a higher rate of physical illness among the depressed. Until recently, there was relatively little evidence for this position.

Psychologists Howard Friedman and Stephanie Booth-Kewley have reviewed more than a hundred research investigations relating emotional states to diseases. They focused particularly upon coronary heart disease, asthma, ulcers, arthritis, and headaches. Somewhat to their surprise, they found strong relationships between depression and all five diseases. The results particularly startled scientists, because all five are diseases in which depression had not previously been suspected of playing any significant role. Depression was not the only emotional state implicated in the development of disease. Anxiety, anger, and hostility were also found to play significant roles, although with the exception of anxiety, the relationships of these last states to the five diseases were weaker.[47]

Sometimes research investigations are more exciting for what they do not find than for what they do find. Although the significance of depression in the development of illness was a major finding of the Friedman and Booth-Kewley work, of greater surprise was the fact that roughly the same factors were involved in the development of all five diseases. The results are particularly unexpected with respect to heart disease. Research investigating the impact of personality and behavior on the development of heart disease has focused almost exclusively on the Type A behavior pattern, embodied in the hard-driving, competitive, impatient workaholic. Perhaps we must rethink this profile. The true coronary-prone individual seems to be a person engulfed by negative emotions: depressed, aggressively competitive, easily frustrated, anxious, and angry. Friedman and Booth-Kewley argued cautiously that this cluster of negative attributes may represent a disease-prone personality in that anxiety, depression, anger, and hostility often go together.

Depression appears to exert an adverse effect on health in part by compromising immune functioning. Depressed people appear to be more vulnerable to a host of infectious diseases.[48] In particular, depressed people have significantly lower levels of suppressor T-cells that help combat latent infection.[49] It would appear, then, that just as positive emotional states and perceptions may help maintain good health or buffer a person against disease, the absence of these positive states may give rise to it.

Knowing that emotional states contribute to disease does not say exactly how this process occurs. Being depressed, anxious, and otherwise upset could lead people to practice poor health behaviors, leaving them vulnerable to disease. Depressed people may eat poorly, drink too much, and get little sleep. Alternatively, adverse emotional states such as depression or anxiety may produce biochemical changes in the body that are conducive to the development of illness. Depression and anxiety are both related to imbalances in the catecholamines, which include epinephrine and norepinephrine. Both depression and a propensity for illness may be caused by some other factor, such as a genetic predisposition to both melancholy and illness. Or, depressed and anxious people may simply recognize that they are ill more quickly and seek out treatment more readily. Without further research, it is difficult to know which of these explanations, if any, accounts for the relationship between depression and disease.

The relationship between emotions and illness is also not a perfect one. Merely because someone becomes depressed does not mean that he or she will develop an illness. Emotional states are only a contributing factor in the development of disease. Others include susceptibility, exposure, and health practices. But the presence of a small but consistent relationship between depression and illness adds another intriguing piece to the picture that is emerging of the relationships among beliefs, emotions, and disease.

THE POWER OF THE PLACEBO

Perhaps the clearest evidence for the beneficial impact of unrealistic optimism on health is the powerful and widely documented placebo effect. In the early days of medicine, few drugs or treatments produced any real physical benefits. As a result, patients were treated with a variety of bizarre and largely ineffective therapies. Ancient Egyptian patients, for example, were medicated with "lizard's blood, crocodile dung, the teeth of a swine, the hoof of an ass, putrid meat, and flyspecks," concoctions that were not only ineffective, but actually dangerous. Patients who did not succumb to the disease had a good chance of dying from the treatment. Medical treatments of the Middle Ages were somewhat less lethal but not much more effective. These European patients were treated with ground-up "unicorn's horn" (actually ground ivory), bezoor stones (supposedly a "crystallized tear from the eye of a deer bitten by a snake," but actually an animal gallstone or other intestinal part), theriac (made up from ground-up snake and between thirty-seven and sixty-five equally exotic ingredients), and, for healing wounds, powdered Egyptian mummy. As late as the seventeenth and eighteenth centuries, patients were subject to bloodletting, freezing, and repeatedly induced vomiting to bring about cures.[50]

These accounts of early medical practice make it seem miraculous that anyone survived, but people did, and moreover, they often seemed to get relief from these peculiar and largely ineffective remedies. Physicians have been objects of great veneration and respect for centuries, and this was no less true when few of their treatments were actually effective. The fair level of success that these ineffective treatments provided and widespread faith in the abilities of physicians are most likely examples of the tremendous power of the placebo.

Most people think of placebos as ineffective measures that were given to patients prior to the discovery of effective medical treatments. As such, they are sometimes considered part of medicine's past. In fact, placebo effects continue to be powerful today, even though medicine now boasts a large number of effective treatments. A placebo is "any medical procedure that produces an effect in a patient because of its therapeutic intent, and not its nature."[51] When asked to envision a placebo, we may imagine a harmless pill that a patient takes faithfully, if uselessly, to achieve relief from a largely fantasized problem. In fact, any medical procedure, ranging from drugs or surgery to psychotherapy, can have a placebo effect, and the effects of these placebos are substantial for reducing pain and discomfort. Many who ingest useless substances or who undergo useless procedures find that as a result their symptoms disappear and their health improves.

Placebo effects extend well beyond the beneficial results of totally ineffective substances. Many active treatments that produce real improvement on their own also have a placebo component. That is, their effectiveness is real, but it is enhanced by the faith the patient and the physician have in its ability to

achieve improvement. A study of the use of morphine to alleviate pain makes this point clearly.[52] Patients complaining of pain
were injected with either morphine or a placebo, a substance
that should exert no effect on the pain. Morphine was substantially more effective in alleviating the pain than was the placebo. However, 35 percent of the patients who received only
the placebo reported that their pain lessened. Physicians conclude from such information not only that placebos can be
effective in reducing pain, but that some portion of the positive
impact of morphine would have occurred even if morphine
were not an effective reducer of pain. Medical historian Arthur
Shapiro summarizes the placebo effect:

> Placebos can be more powerful than and reverse the action
> of potent active drugs. . . . The incidence of placebo reac-
> tions approaches 100% in some studies. Placebos can have
> profound effects on organic illnesses, including incurable
> malignancies. . . . Placebos can mimic the effect usually
> thought to be the exclusive property of active drugs.[53]

Siegel provides a dramatic example of the efficacy of the
placebo effect in his description of a cancer patient, Mr. Wright.
The patient thought he was being given injections of a contro-
versial drug, Krebiozen, about which his physician was highly
enthusiastic. In fact, knowing that Krebiozen was not an effective treatment, the physician gave Mr. Wright daily injections
of nothing but fresh water. The effects were astonishing.

> Tumor masses melted. Chest fluid vanished. He became
> ambulatory and even went back to flying again. At this
> time he was certainly the picture of health. The water
> injections were continued since they worked such won-
> ders. He then remained symptom-free for over two
> months. At this time the final AMA announcement ap-
> peared in the press—"Nationwide Tests Show Krebiozen
> to Be a Worthless Drug in Treatment of Cancer."

Within a few days of this report, Mr. Wright was read-mitted to the hospital in extremis; his faith was now gone, his last hope vanished, and he succumbed in less than two days.[54]

How does the placebo effect occur? Our stereotype involves some nearly magical process whereby a person thinks she is going to get better after ingesting a placebo, and either does or thinks she has. In fact, the placebo effect is not purely psycho-logical. People do not get better simply because they think they are going to get better. Rather, believing that one will get better releases a number of chemicals in the body that may actually promote healing. Placebos typically reduce the anxiety as-sociated with many illnesses and consequently, they may also dampen the release of chemicals associated with anxiety, such as epinephrine. Reduced anxiety gives chemical resources a chance to build up again in the body; in this way, placebos may exert direct restorative efforts on the body's neurochemistry.[55] Some placebos may stimulate the release by the brain of endor-phins, naturally produced bodily chemicals that typically re-duce pain and improve mood, at least temporarily. If placebos also promote the release of these chemicals, and research evi-dence suggests that at least some placebos do, then they like-wise may produce a feeling of greater physical comfort and emotional well-being.[56]

Placebo effects are so powerful that no new treatment or drug can be approved for general use in the practice of medicine unless its effectiveness has been evaluated against that of a placebo. Every drug's effectiveness must be compared with the outcomes produced by a placebo, much as in the study of mor-phine's effectiveness just described. In this sense, then, unreal-istic optimism has made its way into the legislative process. The laws governing the release of new drugs recognize the fact that people are unrealistically optimistic about their chances for re-covery following medication, and must consequently be pro-tected from their own lack of realism.[57]

The placebo effect is most likely to take place when it is introduced into a carefully crafted theatrical production designed to enhance unrealistic optimism. To begin with, the person administering the placebo should exude warmth and confidence in the treatment. When the practitioner radiates reassurance that the condition will improve, the placebo effect is stronger. Signs of doubt or skepticism can be communicated subtly, even nonverbally, and when they are, they reduce the strength of the placebo effect. For the placebo effect to work, the trappings of medical treatment must all be in place. For example, the shape, size, color, taste, and quantity of a placebo influence its effectiveness. Foul-tasting peculiar little pills that are taken in precise dosages ("take two" as opposed to "take two or three") and that are taken at prescribed intervals show stronger placebo effects than do candylike pills, the dosage levels and intervals for which are only roughly indicated ("take one whenever you feel uncomfortable"). Medical treatments that seem "medical" and that include precise instructions show stronger placebo effects than regimens that do not seem very medical. A placebo effect is maximized in a theatrical conspiracy in which those who administer and receive it are ready to witness a cure.[58]

How common are placebo effects? Placebos clearly achieve their greatest success in the absence of real physical disorders. Physicians estimate that about 65 percent of the patients who seek treatment actually have problems that are primarily emotional in origin.[59] Distressed people experience a wide variety of symptoms. Depression may lead to loss of energy, fatigue, and a heightened sensitivity to pain. Anxiety produces diarrhea, jitters, sleeplessness, and upset stomach. Action and caring by a physician can have a direct impact on the emotional state of a patient, and any placebo administered to such a patient, therefore, can have the immediate effect of clearing up all these emotion-related symptoms.

But placebo effects are by no means reserved for inert drugs or pills. Many surgery patients show improvement after having had unnecessary surgery that actually has no direct effect on the symptoms reported. Psychiatry and clinical psychology also show placebo effects. Some patients simply feel better knowing that a psychiatrist or psychologist has found a cause for their problems, even if the cause is not the real one. The knowledge that someone is analyzing the problem and coming up with interpretations may be at least as helpful as the therapeutic procedure itself.[60]

The effectiveness of placebos should not be thought of either as a medical trick or as a purely psychological response on the part of the patient. Placebo effects merit respect. The placebo achieves success in the absence of truly effective therapy. It increases the effectiveness of therapies that have only modest effects of their own. It reduces substantial pain and discomfort. It was the foundation of most of early medicine's effectiveness, and it continues to account for many of medicine's cures today. As such, it is powerful testimony to the adaptive impact of unrealistic optimism on health.

CHAPTER 4

Creative

Self-Deception

> The final belief is to believe in a
> fiction which you know to be a
> fiction.
>
> —WALLACE STEVENS

To THE EXTENT that people seek to preserve their positive images of themselves, their personal control, and the future, they would seem to need to guard against information that challenges these perceptions. How, then, is it possible for people to maintain self-aggrandizing views of themselves while simultaneously making adaptive use of negative information from the environment?

Some critics charge that the illusions so readily documented in normal thought may actually be nothing more than mild forms of repression and denial, temporarily useful but ultimately maladaptive ways of dealing with discrepancies between what one would like to be true and what is actually true. This viewpoint maintains that illusions give the appearance of being successful distortions of reality, but that when a person must come to terms with negative information, illusions will stand in the way of making effective use of that information and will prevent a person from learning appropriately and growing as a result. As a central adherent to this point of view, Freud stated:

> One can try to recreate the world, to build in its stead another world in which its most unbearable features are eliminated and replaced by others that are in conformity with one's own wishes. But whoever, in desperate defiance, sets out upon this path to happiness will, as a rule, obtain nothing. Reality is too strong for him. He becomes a madman who, for the most part, finds no one to help him in carrying through his delusion.[1]

This viewpoint was also central to the conceptions of ego psychology developed by the neo-Freudians in the wake of Freudian psychology.[2] If a person is unable to come to terms with his or her limitations as a person and ultimately with mortality, the ego psychologists maintained, neurosis would result. Accurate self-awareness, consequently, was thought to be a central requirement of the mentally healthy person. As Abraham Maslow wrote:

> Our healthy individuals find it possible to accept themselves and their own nature without chagrin or complaint or, for that matter, even without thinking about the matter very much. . . . They can accept their own human nature with all of its discrepancies from the ideal image without feeling real concern. It would convey the wrong impression to say that they are self-satisfied. What we must rather say is that they can take the frailties and sins, weaknesses and evils of human nature in the same unquestioning spirit that one takes or accepts the characteristics of nature.[3]

The maladaptiveness of illusions, from this standpoint, derives from two consequences. The first is the self-evident point that people need to be able to make adaptive use of negative information. Failing to do so renders one vulnerable to a host of irrational decisions and beliefs. The second derives from the fact that in maintaining benign fictions about the self, one must delegate cognitive energies to the task of keeping these discrepancies out of awareness. That is, according to the argument, maintaining benign fictions about one's self, the world, and the future is an active process requiring commitments of cognitive and emotional resources so that reality can be continually kept at bay. Consequently, to maintain that the positive illusions of normal thought are adaptive, one needs to make two arguments. First, one must show that illusions are not simply recreations of repression and denial and that, unlike repression and denial, they are positive in their consequences. Second, and more important, one must demonstrate how people can maintain self-aggrandizing views of themselves, the world, and the future while simultaneously making appropriate use of negative information.

ILLUSIONS VERSUS REPRESSION AND DENIAL

The idea that normal human thought is marked by occasional gaps and distortions as well as by outright denial of reality is not a new one. Freud argued that the primitive portion of the mind, the id, gives rise to unacceptable impulses that must be repressed. At the same time, the environment provides negative information, including mild rebuffs regarding one's limitations as a person, as well as potentially tragic victimizing events, the implications of which must be denied.

DENIAL

Denial is one of the most primitive of human defenses. It can involve a distortion of negative experience so complete that it blocks out memory of the unpleasant experience altogether. Most of us have had experiences that reflect or border on denial. When something we counted on fails to occur—as when we are rejected by a school or abandoned by a lover when we thought all was well—denial can result. The inability to admit this negative information may occur in part because people make plans for the future and envision how things will be. When these visions are dramatically disconfirmed by a negative event, these cognitive and emotional commitments to the future must be withdrawn and a new future must be constructed. Doing so takes some time, and during that process it may be difficult, even impossible, to acknowledge that the event has occurred.

Denial is most common early on, when an upsetting event has just occurred, and it is widely regarded as the first stage in reactions to severely bad news, such as the diagnosis of a chronic illness or the loss of a loved one.[4] The immediate response is that some mistake has been made. The person receiving a diagnosis of a terminal illness may believe that the test results or X rays were mixed up with somebody else's and that the diagnosis will shortly be changed. If a child is hit by a car and killed, the mental response may be that the bodies were mixed up, that the child's friend, not one's own child, has died. Precisely because the dramatic and sudden bad news alters life so profoundly in so many ways, denial can serve a protective function while these changes are sorting themselves out. Thus, early on in adjustment to a life-threatening or shocking event, denial can be both normal and useful. For most people, denial of the event lasts a short time, perhaps no longer than a few days.

Sometimes denial lasts longer, and when it does, it may require therapeutic intervention. The perception that "this is not happening to me, it is happening to someone else" may be manifested by terrified people who are unable to confront the shock of the stressful event. Denial may give the appearance of being a successful psychological shelter from reality, but it may mask anxiety without making it go away. The person who denies the existence of a threatening event can appear to others as rigidly overcontrolled, as if a crack in the defense would cause the entire facade to crumble. Moreover, reality often breaks through for a few minutes or hours at a time, leaving the person vulnerable, frightened, and hysterical. Long-term denial, then, is a defensive pattern from which people must be gently coaxed through therapeutic intervention.[5]

Most psychologists have studied denial as part of a maladaptive system of defenses employed by people who are psychologically distressed. However, psychologist Daniel Goleman in a recent provocative book, *Vital Lies, Simple Truths,* notes that denial may be more common in mental life than has previously been assumed.[6] He argues that there are many life experiences, ranging from physical pain to psychological distress, that we characteristically mute with denial. He makes a compelling case that there are biochemical underpinnings to this process. When people experience psychological or physical pain, their brains direct the release of endorphins, natural opiates that enable people to tolerate the distressing circumstances in which they are involved. In so doing, Goleman maintains, we sometimes rob ourselves of important life experiences by failing to adequately notice and realize the implications that these events have for ourselves and our lives.

REPRESSION

Just as denial involves the inability to recognize the existence and meaning of threatening events in the external world, repression is the inability to deal fully with threatening events from the internal world, that is, unacceptable impulses from within oneself. Individuals often experience conflict between what society demands of them and their own internal impulses. In the process of adjusting behavior to correspond to the expectations of society, one must often repress internal impulses that conflict with these standards. Repression inhibits the full experience of emotional responses by pushing contradictory impulses into the unconscious. Essentially, repression eliminates the discrepancy between what one should feel and what one actually feels.[7]

Freud argued that as people grow older, they develop strong conceptions of how they would like to be: the ideal parent, the successful worker, the gracious and amiable social companion. Any experience that produces a discrepancy between the ideal self and actual behavior produces negative emotions. Repression is one strategy for dealing with such discomfort. As a defensive maneuver that pushes unacceptable impulses into the unconscious, it deals with negative affect by failing to recognize it. Repression does not actually obliterate the memory of negative events altogether; rather, the affect associated with them is repressed because it might bring to full awareness the threatening implications of the information.[8]

ARE ILLUSIONS DEFENSE MECHANISMS?

Illusions are not simply particular forms of repression and denial. There are conceptual, theoretical, and empirical bases for making the distinction. Repression and denial alter reality, whereas illusions simply interpret it in the best possible light.[9] Defenses distort the facts, leading people to hold misperceptions of internal or external reality. Through illusions, on the other hand, people make the most of bad situations by adopting a maximally positive perspective. Ambiguous elements of situations enable people to impose their own interpretations on events and to give themselves the benefit of the doubt, framing events in ways that promote hope and positive self-appraisal. Psychologist Daniel Weinberger, for example, argues that illusions represent a distortion of statistical reality, in that people hold beliefs that are more positive than reality can sustain; however, he argues that hoping for the best, believing you can beat the odds, and thinking very well of yourself do not represent misconstruals of the facts.[10] Defenses, in contrast, are maladaptive because of the internal dissociation process whereby part of the brain will not deal with what another part "knows."

In a theoretical attack on the psychoanalytic view of defense mechanisms, psychologist Harold Sackeim argues that representing self-aggrandizing distortions of reality as necessarily defensive in nature is both fallacious and a logical contradiction of psychoanalytic theory.[11] He maintains that the mild self-deceptions that can be so readily observed in normal thought should be construed as "offense mechanisms," distortions that enable people to express their drives and court pleasure. But psychoanalytic theory has no way to accommodate the idea of pleasure-directed distortions. Rather, the analysis of defense mechanisms maintains that such distortions are necessarily displaced attempts to avoid pain.

> The argument is nefarious in that it stipulates that an unconscious and perhaps undiscoverable fear is behind every wish fulfilling distortion. If one demonstrates empirically and/or produces clinical evidence that some distortions result in gain, the charge can be made that analysis or understanding of the distortions is incomplete until there is identification of the hidden motive, the avoidance of mental contents behind the "screen" motive of gain.[12]

The logical contradiction comes, Sackeim argues, in the viewpoint that self-deception is necessarily a defense to avoid threat, and not a method of self-advancement. He argues that since psychoanalytic theory posits that human motivation is dictated by the pursuit of pleasure and that people have well-developed self-deceptive strategies in the form of defense mechanisms, it is logically inconsistent to maintain that people will use such strategies only when they face danger and not to advance themselves.

After reviewing the evidence for benign self-deception and considering the logically untenable position in which such observations are placed by psychoanalytic theory, Sackeim concludes:

> Through distortion, I may enhance my self-image, not because at heart I am insecure about my worth but because no matter how much I am convinced of my value, believing that I am better is pleasurable. Such self-deceptions may prove to be efficient in constructing or consolidating a solid and perhaps even "healthy" identity. I may misconstrue situations as presenting opportunities for sexual, intellectual or other advancement, not because these possibilities are dangerous or because I am otherwise warding off drives but because such distortions permit pleasurable drive expression.[13]

Sackeim's argument is a valuable one in pointing out the logical inconsistency of considering self-aggrandizing interpretations of reality necessarily as defensive maneuvers. Even more convincing, however, is evidence to suggest that the illusions of normal thought can be distinguished readily from repression on empirical grounds. Weinberger makes this case particularly well in contrasting the repressive defensive style with normal thought. In the main, he points out that those who make characteristic use of the repressive defensive style look worse, not better, on attributes characteristically associated with mental health, the exact opposite of the pattern observed with respect to illusions.[14]

Initially, distinguishing those who cope with the problems of life through repression from those who deal with life through positive illusions is not as easy as one might suppose. In many ways, the two groups look very similar. Repressors typically report low levels of negative emotion; they report not being as angry, hurt, upset, or confused as other people. On personality tests that do not distinguish the repressive coping style, repressors come out looking quite healthy—indeed, like normal people. Weinberger suggests that as many as one-third of the people who report low levels of distress in their lives, such as freedom from anxiety, depression, and questioning of self-worth, are actually repressing the negative affect that they experience, rather than being free from it. When asked about their personal happiness, people who cope through repression describe themselves as not upset by unpleasant events, but not as people who enjoy themselves and meet the challenges of life head-on. Repressors regard themselves as rational, controlled, and stable, whereas people who are truly free of anxiety describe themselves in terms suggesting a jubilant, flexible enjoyment of life. The fact that repressors actively avoid negative emotions of all kinds may retard their experiences of positive affect as well. For example, repressors report fewer positive as well as negative memories of their childhood. The illusions associated with normal thought, in contrast, appear to facilitate a fluent recall of positive memories, although specific memories for childhood experiences have not been assessed. Thus, with regard to the mental health criteria of happiness and positive self-worth, those with positive illusions seem genuinely to be happy and to think well of themselves. In contrast, those who cope with life via repression report an absence of negative experience, but no corresponding feelings of happiness and self-worth; moreover; maintaining the absence of negative emotion seems to require active management.

There is also evidence that repression interferes with certain aspects of social competence. For example, in a study in which students were asked to disclose personal information to others, those high in the repressive style appeared to have little insight into their behavior and consequently made a poor impression on those to whom they disclosed.[15] The gaps that repressors demonstrate in their self-knowledge and ability to express themselves socially are also reflected in a limited understanding of the experiences of others. When asked to play the role of a counselor by listening and responding to another person's problems, for example, repressors did significantly more poorly than people who do not characteristically use repression.[16] They appear to view the social environment in less complex terms and generally seem to notice less in the social environment.[17] In contrast, as has been noted, positive illusions appear to foster many aspects of social competence, although self-disclosure and role playing have not been directly investigated.

Certain aspects of the ability to engage in creative and productive work, another feature of mental health, appear to be undermined by the repressive style. Repressors need to use so much of their cognitive capacity to monitor negative affect that they may inhibit their cognitive flexibility, particularly the "spontaneous playful aspects of concept formation."[18] In binding up their energies in repression, there is less available capacity for motivation, persistence, and activity in the pursuit of goals. In contrast, the illusions of normal thought actually appear to facilitate motivation, persistence, and activity level. When repressors are confronted with cognitive and perceptual tasks that are sensitive to the effects of anxiety, their performance is impaired. In contrast, the illusions associated with normal thought seem to facilitate intellectual performance, including performance on challenging tasks. The defensiveness that repressors evince, then, may be associated with certain deficits in intellectual functioning, a pattern opposite to that observed in those who hold positive illusions.[19]

Some of the most startling and clear evidence for the distinction between the repressive style and normal illusions comes from their respective relations to physical health. Whereas positive illusions appear to promote better health overall, there is increasing evidence that repressors are at risk for many illnesses, including hypertension, asthma, and cancer, as well as a general propensity for somatic symptoms, including vague and diffuse aches and pains.[20] In one study, the repressive personality style actually predicted cancer progression, along with feelings of helplessness and hopelessness.[21] The repressive personality style may also interfere with or undermine effective health behavior. Repressors are less likely to seek medical care when they need it, and they delay longer for serious symptoms. They are also less likely to report symptoms that have serious implications. As a consequence, they may permit medical conditions to go unchecked longer, thus interfering with effective care.[22] Again, this pattern is the opposite of that observed in people who hold normal illusions.

Perhaps the most important characteristic that distinguishes repression and denial from positive illusions is how they respond to the threat inherent in information and the anxiety generated by it. Defensive reactions increase in response to threat, whereas normal illusion appears to respond realistically to threat.[23] Although normal people may not perceive their vulnerability to an event accurately, an increase in threat leads realistically to an increase in perceived risk. For example, a study of Southern California students' reactions to the prospect of an earthquake found that all of the students considerably underestimated the probability that one would occur. However, the students accurately perceived their risk relative to one another: those who lived in seismically unsafe buildings were aware that their risk was greater than that faced by students in buildings that were structurally more sound.[24] In contrast, repression and denial increase in magnitude as the threatening content of information increases. The greater the threat, the more rigidly one adheres to defended beliefs. This maladaptive quality of repression has been characterized as "a car that maintains a low speed because the driver is leaning heavily on both the brakes and the accelerator."[25]

There are several reasons why the phenomena of repression and denial are not synonymous with the self-aggrandizing illusions observed in normal thought. First, the exposition of repression and denial maintains that people normally have fairly good contact with reality and that these defenses arise when reality becomes too painful to bear, that is, under conditions that evoke anxiety or threat. In contrast, normal illusions appear to be present most of the time and do not appear to be invoked in response to anxiety or threat. Second, repression and denial are judged to be mixed in their psychological consequences: on the one hand, they serve a temporary, benign function by blunting the harsher side of reality; on the other hand, they hinder the ability to make full use of and profit from whatever useful information may be inherent in negative experiences. In contrast, positive illusions do not have these liabilities. For example, the illusion of control often leads people to directly tackle or confront adverse events that they anticipate, and thus promotes a confrontative rather than a repressive response to stress. Thus, in important ways, the person whose illusions are intact responds to challenging or threatening circumstances in a manner exactly opposite to that of the person who characteristically employs repression or denial as a defense mechanism. Third, the mechanisms of repression and denial have been described in a way that suggests differential responsiveness to threat but not to the utility of information. In contrast, the illusions of normal thought are very responsive to the usefulness of negative information and to its implications for the future. Thus, the subtlety and patterning of responses to negative information that seem to be characteristic of illusion are not observed in the defense mechanisms of repression and denial. Finally, on the criteria associated with mental health—happiness, productivity, social competence, intellectual functioning, and the ability to deal with stress effectively—the person whose characteristic defenses are repression and denial does not look as healthy as the person whose thought is marked by normal illusion.

Illusions, then, are not synonymous with repression and denial, which deal with threatening information by pushing it out of awareness. The adaptiveness of illusions still creates a paradox, however. To the extent that people seek to preserve their positive images of themselves, their personal control, and the future, they would seem to need to guard against negative information that challenges these perceptions. How is it possible for people to maintain self-aggrandizing views of themselves while simultaneously making adaptive use of negative information from the environment? A beginning answer is that, rather than thrusting harsh reality onto a person, the social environment more commonly mutes and blunts the impact of negative information.

ILLUSIONS AND THE SOCIAL WORLD

The most potentially destructive adversary to grandiose self-conceptions is the social environment. The people we encounter daily—family, friends, and co-workers—are very powerful because, if they chose to, they could deflate our carefully constructed positive conceptions of the self. Certainly there are times when family and friends do deflate self-evaluations and aspirations, but more commonly they reinforce them.

The social environment conspires to provide positive feedback. Normal social interaction is governed by informal rules and norms which dictate how people will behave toward one another.[26] Typically, people tell each other what a nice time they've had, how well they look, how attractive their home is, and how well behaved their children are. People who come to your home for dinner do not tell you your beans were overcooked, your dessert did not gel, and you have a stain on the back of your dress. They tell you your hors d'oeuvres were fantastic, they want the recipe for your chicken, and your new haircut looks great. Indeed, after giving a party, it is sometimes difficult to tell how it went, and one must draw upon such indirect measures as how quickly people left after dinner, whether there were lulls in the conversation, and whether one enjoyed the occasion. Normal social behavior provides remarkably few opportunities for candor.

Were our assessments of each other to be voiced frankly, the threat to the social fabric would be substantial. In the sciences there is a procedure for evaluating research articles called peer review. One submits a scientific manuscript to a journal, which is then sent out to between two and five reviewers in the field who will pass judgment anonymously on the research. Typically, the reviewers are in one's field, and so one knows them personally. Reviews that are furnished anonymously provide rare opportunities for frank feedback. One of the tasks of a scientific mentor is to prepare graduate students for their first set of reviews. The conditions of anonymity, coupled perhaps with some rivalry, often produce feedback that under other circumstances would be considered vicious and cruel. Graduate students are frequently devastated by these uncensored assessments and sometimes leave the field in response to this harrowing rite of passage. Even seasoned research investigators find that they must read the reviews in bits and pieces over a few days in order to absorb them without pain.

The point is not that under conditions of anonymity, people can be cruel and malicious. Anonymous reviews are often helpful and occasionally kind. The point is that, under circumstances in which social norms are removed and one is granted anonymity to be honest, the frankness can be devastating precisely because it contrasts so dramatically with the feedback one usually receives.

CONSTRUCTING THE SOCIAL ENVIRONMENT

Most of us construct our own social worlds so as to receive primarily positive self-assessments and avoid negative ones.[27] This careful construction is not always obvious, however. If we think about the process of finding a mate or developing friendships, it may seem rather haphazard and accidental. Your friends may be the people you happen to work with or the people who live next door. Your mate may be someone who happened to be in your high school history class or the person who helped you pick up the display of tabasco sauce that you knocked over in the grocery store. When people think about the relationships they have, they are often struck by how fortuitous or accidental the circumstances of meeting seem to be. If he had not rented the apartment across the street, or if she hadn't decided to go skiing at the last minute, we would never have met, is often the evaluation. Certainly these chance factors play an important role in relationships. But looked at another way, relationships are actively fashioned and constructed by the people who are in them. The world brings us into contact with many thousands of people, only a very few of whom become friends or lovers. From this perspective, it is easier to see how selective the friendship and mating process is.

Most of us pick as friends and lovers people who see us as we wish to see ourselves. We do not like to be perceived as having qualities we do not think are true of ourselves. Characterized by a friend as insensitive during a gruff or careless moment, a person may work hard to correct this misimpression in the future. Curiously, the desire not to be miscast extends to positive as well as negative qualities.[28] A man who thinks of himself as not very bright is unlikely to be interested in spending time with a partner who thinks he is bright. Rather, he would actively choose to be with someone who agrees that he is not very bright but who loves him nonetheless. When people have false impressions of us, even false positive ones, it puts pressure on us to continue to perform in ways that do not feel comfortable or natural, and it gives the relationship a tenuous quality, the potential to be terminated when the awful secret is revealed. Of course, it is also true that we want to be with people who think well of us. Ideally, the good friend or lover should be someone who values our positive qualities, is aware of our shortcomings, and loves us anyway.

There is a catch in this process of actively constructing the social world. People also seek out others they perceive to be similar to themselves; under these circumstances, one may be attracted to people who not only have the same talents but might actually be considered rivals.[29] How do people create their relationships in such a way that their valued qualities are acknowledged and highly regarded without creating potential rivals at the same time? Psychologist Abraham Tesser has studied this intriguing problem and drawn an interesting conclusion. People choose as friends those who are not quite as good as they are on attributes central to their own self-conceptions, but who excel on attributes they think are somewhat less important.[30] In this way, people can be friends, and the mutuality of friendship can be understood. For example, if Joan is a competent sales manager who is capable at tennis and cooking and her friend Donna is a real estate broker who is an able skier and gourmet, their talents may be complementary without inducing any competition. Joan may regard her occupation and avocations as somewhat more important than those of her friend Donna, and also perceive herself to be better than Donna at those activities. Nonetheless, she can value Donna's expertise, that is, her knowledge of food, her ability to sell real estate, and her skiing, knowing that they are important attributes, though perhaps not quite as important as her own. In cases where two friends are extremely close in the qualities that they value and are good at, one may actually see a negotiation process occurring whereby each person tries to figure out the attributes on which each excels, so they can reach a mutual understanding about what each of them is to be good at.

CONTROLLING SOCIAL SETTINGS

Choosing social companions is one way to construct the social world so as to create and maintain flattering portraits of ourselves. Another way is to choose the situations in which we function. The careful selection of settings that maximize our opportunities to display talents guarantees that positive self-conceptions can be reinforced.[31] Presumably we pick an occupation because it matches our talents and interests. We select social situations because they are ones that will bring us joy, as opposed to others that may be boring or threatening. We seek out settings that will demonstrate what we do and know well. In fact, the ability to control the situation may be one of the most powerful types of control there is. Consider dating as an example. The person who controls where the couple goes is in a great position to influence the perceptions that the dating partner forms. The date can be an opportunity to display a wealth of information and talents by picking Chinese food (over French food, about which one may be less knowledgeable), an art gallery (which may reflect the period of art with which one is familiar), or an athletic activity (such as sailing, at which one is very good, as opposed to skiing, which one has never tried before). By selecting a situation that enables one to display one's singular talents, one can actively manipulate and manage the impressions that the partner forms. Many a young woman may have been swept off her feet by a man who initially appeared to be multifaceted and multitalented, only to discover somewhat later in their relationship that he had exhausted his display of talents within a few well-orchestrated dates.

This account suggests that the control of situations is self-consciously undertaken in a calculating manner for the purpose of displaying one's talents. In fact, it can occur as a totally unselfconscious process, dictated only by personal preferences and interests. A person arranging a date with a new partner is unlikely to pick situations that he or she neither understands nor enjoys, but rather will select those that maximize the possibility of having a good time. Since people typically pick situations that are familiar and enjoyable, the selection of a setting for a date may inadvertently provide an opportunity to display one's talents. Selecting the social circumstances in which one comes off as most adept impresses not only others but oneself.

In these ways, then, we actively control both the players in our social environment and the scenes in which we perform.

What better way is there to be certain that things go as we like? As Russell Baker observed:

> Most of us are searching, if only subconsciously, for the medium that will best suit our peculiar requirements for creating the misunderstandings about ourselves we need to establish in order to make life's chaos seem sensible and, hence, tolerable.
>
> The luckiest are men like Homer and Shakespeare, who are known almost entirely through their poetry, which means that we understand about them almost precisely what they wanted us to understand, and little more, which means we probably misunderstand them extensively.
>
> Most of us, of course, don't realize that in looking for a way to call ourselves to the world's attention, a form of self-expression if you prefer, what we really seek is a device that will prevent our world, no matter how big or small, from belittling and humiliating us with its dreadful understanding.[32]

The ability to control the social companions with whom one interacts and the social settings in which one performs increases with age. One wonders whether the self-confidence that is usually associated with adulthood comes not from increasing maturity but from the fact that by controlling the choice of companions and social settings, one can construct one's world in a manner that enables one to display talents and avoid the betrayal of faults. By contrast, the adolescent, low in self-esteem and plagued by doubts, is presented involuntarily with an array of situations and companions from which there is no escape. Tested almost daily in every conceivable arena of life—music, art, athletics, mathematics, writing—the teenager is denied the adult's opportunity to avoid those situations that reinforce doubts and impede the development of a positive self-concept. Is maturity merely the process of learning how to construct the social world to one's best advantage?

SOCIAL SUPPORT

Social relationships may do more than passively permit the benign fictions of life to go undisturbed. In recent years, it has become evident to psychologists and health care providers that having a close family and good friends does more than make people simply feel good. There are important, often dramatic, physical and mental health consequences of having what has come to be known as social support.[33] Social support can be the love and comfort that one receives from one's immediate family, the social activity and camaraderie of good friends, the inspiration and sense of purpose that can result from belonging to a social or charitable organization, or even the affection and devotion of a pet. Numerous research studies now demonstrate that people who have social support are less likely to develop illnesses, both small ones and major ones, and to recover more quickly when they do become ill.[34] People with a lot of social support also show better mental health and are less likely to succumb to depression and other debilitating emotional problems, especially those that arise in response to stress.

The value of social support was dramatically illustrated in interviews we conducted some years ago with women who had been diagnosed with breast cancer.[35] Some of these women had strong, close families and were surrounded by the love of a husband, children, and close friends, whereas others lived alone, often divorced or widowed, separated geographically from children and restricted in social contacts. The impact of these different social situations was especially clear in one pair of women who were remarkably similar in ways other than the social support they received. Emily was the wife of a contractor and mother of three grown children, all of whom lived nearby. Interviewing her was difficult because the phone rang numerous times, children bounded in and out of the house, dropping things off and giving quick kisses as they raced to their activities. Two large dogs roamed the house, greeting every visitor enthusiastically. Even her husband called in from his busy office for a brief chat during the two hours we were there.

On her own, Emily was probably not a very good coper. She was not taking her medications on schedule, and she sometimes missed chemotherapy appointments. Although she had several personal goals, including writing a cookbook, most of them had not been realized. She had, nonetheless, successfully raised three children and was widely respected in the community for her charitable work.

One sometimes sees in cancer patients a fighting spirit and determination to overcome the disease, and neither was evident in Emily's makeup. She seemed more confused by the cancer, bewildered about how she had developed it initially, and puzzled over what, if anything, she could do to improve her chances for recovery now. Her family, on the other hand, seemed to have no such hesitation about what would keep her well. In a later interview, her husband admitted that he and his children had conspired to make her life as pleasurable and fun-filled as possible and, to all appearances, they had succeeded well. Despite her difficulties with the cancer, Emily seemed a serene and contented person, basking in the warmth of her family.

Some weeks later, we interviewed Linda, who coincidentally also lived in Los Angeles a few blocks away from Emily. Two years younger than Emily, she had been married to a commodities broker who had died suddenly in his early forties. Linda's children were scattered around the world. One son was traveling around Europe with his girlfriend, intending to relocate in Oregon upon his return. One daughter was living in Atlanta and the other, in Boston. According to Linda, the family had once been close-knit, but following the father's death and the children's relocations, the closeness had broken down and now consisted of brief phone calls every few weeks. When we interviewed her, Linda had lived alone for five years. She had become odd in ways that people sometimes do when they are isolated for too long. Having no one with whom to share her thoughts on a daily basis, she unloaded them somewhat inappropriately with strangers, including our interviewer. She felt that if she were able to find a male companion, her problems would be solved, but like many women in their early fifties who are divorced, separated, or widowed, she faced no easy task. Linda met many men, but some of them were married, and the others were often interested in a casual relationship.

The two women, Emily and Linda, had remarkably similar medical cases. Both had relatively large tumors located in the outer portion of the left breast. Although both had noticed lumps in their breasts, both had postponed going to the doctor for several months, so that by the time they were diagnosed, the tumors were quite advanced. Emily chose to have a lumpectomy (removal of the tumor only), and Linda chose a mastectomy (removal of the entire breast). Both then began a six-month course of chemotherapy, and at the time we interviewed them, both appeared to be symptom-free and were cautiously optimistic about the future.

Three years later, when we planned to reach the women for additional information, we learned that Linda had died two years before. Emily, on the other hand, was flourishing. Her family continued to provide her with the support she needed, and she and her husband had recently taken several exciting vacations. She seemed to be even happier than she had when we initially interviewed her.

The cases of Emily and Linda are remarkably similar in many respects except for the social support they received. The women were close in age, they had very similar medical profiles, they had roughly comparable financial situations, and they both had three children. To a psychologist's trained eye, both showed certain weaknesses and gaps in their coping abilities, yet one was enmeshed in a warm and supportive social network, while the other was trying unsuccessfully to create one.

It is impossible to say for certain that the difference in the outcome of these two cases was caused by the difference in the social support available to them. There may have been differences in their medical profiles that were undetectable to us and to the physician. Perhaps there was something in Linda's personality that led her children to move away from her; if so, it was difficult for the interviewer to ascertain what that quality might be. One is tempted to put some weight on the idea that the difference in the social support they received contributed to the different outcomes of their cancer.

Why is social support such an effective buffer against stressful events? Why is it associated with relative freedom from emotional problems and good prospects for recovery from illness? One answer is that family and friends are able to provide help. When Emily needed medications from the drugstore or food from the supermarket, there were at least four people in her life who could run those errands for her if she was tired or simply didn't feel like going. When Linda needed errands run, she either did without or she did them herself, regardless of how tired or disinclined she may have been. Friends and family can also provide useful information. When Emily was feeling low or just needed to talk, she had a built-in audience ready to hear her thoughts. When Linda needed to talk, the thoughts swirled round and round in her head, waiting for an opportunity to come out. If she needed advice, there were few people she could turn to.

Finally, and probably most important, is the emotional support that family and friends can provide. When people are asked what they find to be most supportive from others, love and affection are usually highest on the list. Emotional support can improve emotional functioning by creating warm and contented feelings.[36] Exactly how it exerts its effects on physical recovery from illness is not clear. A happy and contented mood may create a biochemical state in the body that is conducive to healing, and it may have direct effects on immune functioning. The mechanisms are not yet known. We do know, however, that there are often beneficial effects of emotional support on physical and mental health.

Of course, there are times when family and friends can actually make things worse.[37] One can imagine, for example, that a high school student trying to decide on a college would not perceive her family to be supportive if her parents, brothers and sisters, and aunts and uncles all had different opinions about where she should go. Or sometimes one may turn to a companion seeking emotional solace and get a lecture on what one should have done instead. Under these circumstances, social "support" can actually make a stressful situation worse. However, on the whole, these tend to be the exceptions rather than the rule, and despite the fact that well-intentioned friends and relatives can sometimes be intrusive or inappropriate, their presence, warmth, and efforts to be helpful are more commonly successful than unsuccessful.

During stressful times, then, when people's views of themselves, the world, and the future are challenged or threatened, the presence of social support can mute these experiences. Supportive close friends and family can bolster positive self-conceptions by actively denying the negative implications of the stressful circumstances and by making the person going through the stressful events feel loved and treasured. Supportive others can reinforce a sense of personal control by providing helpful suggestions, resources, and a sense of confidence in the person experiencing the stress, and support from others can foster optimism through expressions of encouragement and hope.

THE COGNITIVE CONTROL OF NEGATIVE INFORMATION

The self-reinforcing construction of the social environment is an important aspect of how people preserve their overly positive conceptions of the self, the world, and the future. But it still does not address the vital point, which is how people learn from negative information.

Not all negative information is useful. Some is gratuitous, relevant perhaps to only a single episode. The occasional caustic remark of a friend or a tiff with the drycleaner are the kinds of isolated negative events that we all encounter regularly and that, in themselves, have little or no meaning for future behavior. I will suggest that the cognitive strategies that are used to manage these small and ultimately insignificant setbacks or insults of life involve ignoring or forgetting the events, essentially putting them out of mind as quickly and completely as possible.

Other negative information is useful because it tells us something important about ourselves; that is, it is diagnostic. Most of us lack talent in at least a few domains of life, whether it be managing finances, playing tennis, or dancing the latest steps. Some of these faults and deficiencies are relatively minor in their consequences, whereas others pose more pervasive problems, representing a lack in a person's behavioral repertoire, such as debilitating shyness or grotesque obesity. Social and mental strategies for dealing with negative information differ, depending on these two characteristics: diagnosticity and pervasiveness. Diagnosticity is the degree to which negative information is indicative of some enduring quality of the self. Pervasiveness refers to whether the weakness or deficiency of the self is confined to a limited life domain (for example, playing volleyball) or whether it intrudes into many life domains (for example, shyness). I will suggest that negative information that is diagnostic or pervasive in its implications is represented faithfully in consciousness, but as benignly as possible.[38] As George Orwell noted in *1984*, "The secret of rulership is to combine a belief in one's own infallability with the power to learn from past mistakes."[39] This is the task that the healthy mind must accomplish, and which indeed it does with great capability.

SELECTIVE ATTENTION

It is impossible to live in the world without getting negative, hurtful, or unpleasant information. Some blows will be major ones, such as the death of a loved one or the diagnosis of a serious illness. Others, however, may be thought of as the flotsam and jetsam of everyday life, the tiny rebuffs that come our way on a daily or weekly basis. We can think of these as the small insults of life, unpleasant events that have no lasting significance or enduring implications, but which may cause one to feel bad temporarily nonetheless. All of us have had these kinds of experiences, but if pressed, most of us would have difficulty coming up with a lot of specific examples. We know the kinds of events involved—a snappy cab driver, an irritated clerk in a store, a neighbor angered by a careless dog—but to recall more than a couple of specific events in one's own life is difficult. This is precisely the point: the events are ignored because they have no lasting effects on our self-esteem and faith in ourselves. They are truly of no consequence.

What are the ways in which we are able to recognize that these small insults have occurred without their having any lasting effects? One method is by selectively attending to positive information and selectively ignoring negative information. An attractive woman in her mid-fifties is driving under the speed limit in the left lane. Behind her are a pair of angry boys in a pickup truck, honking the horn and gesturing for her to move over. As they finally succeed in passing her, they make uncomplimentary observations about her driving and then speed away. Throughout the event, she appears to be oblivious.

Not once does she turn to look at the boys or, as far as one can tell, even check her rear-view mirror to see what all the commotion is about. Has she noticed the event? Almost certainly. Is she aware that the angry and insulting behavior is directed at her? Again, the answer is almost certainly. Will she remember the event later in the day? Probably not, at least not as well as someone would who had engaged in a shouting match with the boys.

Selective attention is a wonderful filter for screening out negative information. It operates in a self-protective manner, scanning the environment for potential irritations or insults and then diverting full attention from them. We all employ selective attention to guard against upsetting or otherwise negative information in many ways. Some people look away from the scary or gruesome scenes in movies. People scan the headlines to censor stories they don't want to read. We avoid interacting with a highly successful friend who makes us feel bad about ourselves and our accomplishments. In many small ways, we isolate ourselves from bad news.

Psychologists refer to these biases as attentional and encoding biases, and have demonstrated in many research investigations that people deploy attention and take in information in highly selective ways.[40] Typically, these biases operate so as to admit, even welcome and seek out, positive information and avoid negative information, particularly when that information involves the self.

BENIGN FORGETTING

Another creative method by which people avoid unflattering information about themselves is to forget it.[41] Most of us have received unkind evaluations at one time or another. A past friendship may have ended with accusations of rudeness or insensitivity. A submission of an article to a magazine may meet with a one-line rejection. And, although this information can be dredged up from memory with prodding, it is rarely spontaneously recalled on its own. We try to forget about it, ignore it, and tuck it away in a part of memory where it will rarely come to the surface. D. R. Wixon and James Laird put it well: "As historians of our own lives we seem to be, on the one hand, very inattentive and, on the other, revisionists who will justify the present by changing the past."[42]

This is not as tricky a process as it might seem. Memory is organized by association. Similar events or beliefs are grouped together and linked to related groups of ideas and events.[43] When a very negative but uncommon event takes place, like an accusation of insensitivity, there is little in memory to attach itself to. People typically do not think of themselves as insensitive, but rather have myriad examples of their sensitive and thoughtful behavior, which are easily pulled out of memory. A single accusation of insensitivity wanders through memory looking for similar events with which to be placed. Finding no readily available home, it may perhaps group itself with "rude things people say when they are angry with you," or "the unpleasant consequences of friendship breakups." It is unlikely, however, to have much impact on one's perception of oneself as a sensitive, loyal, caring, thoughtful, and giving person. There is simply too much information and too many associations for these more heavily buttressed self-perceptions to be so easily undone. It is not that the memory of the rebuff is forgotten altogether; rather, it is stored in memory in a manner that makes it unlikely to be recalled and that renders its implications for the self generally inconsequential.[44]

Our amnesia for disappointment is often very dramatic. I recently experienced such a jarring confrontation with reality in preparing income tax records. In projecting our family's income for a particular year, I had estimated sales for a recently published book to be a certain figure, whereas the reality was less than one-quarter of what I had apparently expected. What startled me more than my abysmally low royalties was the fact that I had clearly once thought the figure would be so much larger. When the money came in, it was a welcome addition to the coffers, rather than the substantial disappointment it should have been.

How had I managed to forget it? To begin with, I must have grossly inflated my expected return to motivate myself to keep working. After all, who would write a book if he or she expected to be reimbursed at the rate of thirty-seven cents an hour? My vision of a lucrative future may have kept me motivated between bursts of writing and led me back to my desk on balmy days. But when did I let go of this fantasy? When did it conveniently slip from my mind, allowing me not to be disappointed when it failed to materialize? It must have happened gradually. The book departed for the publisher, I began another one, my dreams for the new one escalated, and my expectations for the old one passed from mind. The new one was so much more promising, so much better written, so much more appealing to a general audience, that I could now see that the old venture was merely a modest accomplishment on the way to a more distinguished future. It became practice, an exercise for the future, valuable experience for my soon-to-be-displayed accomplishments, and thus the means to a new end, no longer an end in itself. The illusions left their previous home and attached themselves to the new venture.

This process of benign forgetting is useful to many of us. The woman in her early forties with an empty nest who decides that she is going to open a clothing boutique may envision her shop as the busiest and most successful in town, not incidentally making her a wealthy woman at the same time. Who would undergo the trials and agonies of starting a small business in the belief that the response would be mediocre and the business would go under within three years, a fate that unhappily plagues the majority of small businesses? Rather, it may take the projection of a highly successful business venture to make the effort at all. Between the initial estimations and the actual results, benign forgetting may intervene. By the time the business has stabilized into a reliable, if modest, source of income, the proprietor may be so pleased with the results that she would be astonished to recall she had once thought it would bring success and fortune beyond her wildest dreams.

What this means is that, although soaring and unrealistic expectations about the success of a venture are very valuable, perhaps vital, to the creation of an enterprise initially, there may be little risk that the disconfirmation of these expectations will be devastating. As time goes on and a person's attention is diverted from the dream to the mundane tasks required to bring it about, the accomplishment of even small steps toward the initial goal may seem like successes. One both forgets the initial dream and forgets that one has forgotten. Again Orwell's *1984* offers insight through its fictional philosophy.

> The control of the past depends above all on the training of memory. . . . [It is] necessary to remember that events happened in the desired manner. And if it is necessary to rearrange one's memories or to tamper with written records, then it is necessary to forget that one has done so. The trick of doing this can be learned like any other mental technique. . . . It is called doublethink.[45]

Some might wonder whether the capacity to selectively attend to positive information and to selectively forget negative information represent truly healthy mental responses. Yet in a sense, we are only witnessing at the cognitive level what occurs quite adaptively though not so obviously at the social level. Consider two men, one of whom selects a career for which he is well suited and a set of companions who value his company, and the other of whom strives to succeed in a profession for which he clearly has little talent and who spends time with people who make him feel bad about himself. Which of the two would be judged to be mentally healthy? Few would have any hesitation in judging the first to be more mentally healthy. Yet by achieving this enviable situation, a great deal of selective attention and avoidance took place, as potential careers and unrewarding companions were jettisoned along the way. In many respects, the mind simply reinforces and perpetuates what the social self does very adaptively, augmenting and admitting positive information while making every effort to minimize or ignore the negative.

COGNITIVE DRIFT

Most of us think of our beliefs and attitudes as robust—if not actually etched in stone, then certainly resistant to change. Although certain beliefs have this permanence, many others, in fact, swing through a wide range of opinions without any apparent awareness on our part.[46] Many beliefs, including ones that would seem to be of great importance, actually change substantially in response to incoming information and environmental events, without people realizing that change has taken place.

Consider, for example, the change of opinions that many Americans experienced toward Fidel Castro following the Cuban revolution. While Castro and his followers were attempting to overthrow the dictator Batista, American public opinion was mildly and romantically on the side of the rebels. Once Castro won, his first understandable but shockingly ruthless act was to execute large numbers of Batista's supporters in the days following his rise to power. These executions received extended coverage by the American media, leading most Americans to be appalled by the inhumanity of the behavior. American public opinion shifted abruptly in an anti-Castro direction. More interesting is the fact that many people accomplished this reversal of their previous opinions by maintaining that they had held the revised opinion all along. The signs were there, they argued. They had always been suspicious of this savage upstart. This phenomenon, easily documented in normal thought, has been called "the rapid aging of new opinions."[47] When people make errors in judgment or are induced to change their opinions, they rapidly construct memories to support the view that they have always felt the same way. In so doing, they can learn from mistakes or change their opinions while simultaneously maintaining a view of their infallability, because the perception that they made a mistake in judgment or changed their opinion is fleeting, if present at all. Psychologist Baruch Fischhoff calls it the "knew it all along" effect.[48]

Sometimes, however, an assault on one's beliefs may be temporary, based on misinformation or on exposure to some deviant communication that will never be repeated. What happens to beliefs that shift in response to transitory but challenging feedback? Upon hearing a rumor that Joan is planning to divorce her husband, Tom, one may begin mentally to explain the event, dissecting the weaknesses in the marriage and the two partners. As the weeks go by and Tom and Joan are still together, seemingly happily so, one may unconsciously begin to put the marriage back together, mending the rifts one had mentally created in response to the apparently incorrect rumor. Typically, opinions shift in the direction of the new information, but then drift back to their original form if there is no additional information coming from the environment to suggest that the changed opinion is warranted.

Social psychologists who conduct laboratory research on attitude change frequently witness this phenomenon. People express their opinions on issues that would seem to be firmly held, such as their attitudes toward the risks of smoking or toward a particular political candidate. Faced with information that challenges this viewpoint, the opinions will show significant shift, yet the person may not perceive himself or herself to have been influenced by the communication at all. In some respects, this self-assessment is valid, insofar as several days later, the impact of the persuasive communication that once so dramatically shifted opinions is negligible, the opinion having drifted back to its initial level.[49]

ACKNOWLEDGED POCKETS OF INCOMPETENCE

Not all negative or contradictory information can be dismissed as inconsequential. Biases in attention to information, the interpretation of information, and the recall of information are successful only if the negative or challenging information itself is not ultimately useful or meaningful. Although there are many circumstances of everyday life in which precisely these conditions hold, there are other aspects of life in which negative feedback or unflattering information has diagnostic value—it says something important about oneself.

No one is adept at everything, simply because there is not enough time to develop every conceivable talent. Moreover, each of us has areas of life in which we have a total absence of talent. One person may be helpless at tennis, and another may be a disaster with finances. Some people resist all efforts to get them to dance at a party, as well they should, and others do not sing for good reason. No amount of selective attention, biased recall, or reinterpretation is going to turn a tone-deaf person into Luciano Pavarotti or someone with two left feet into Fred Astaire. Therefore, one must create a pocket of incompetence.

A pocket of incompetence is a domain of life in which a person readily acknowledges a lack of talent and consequently avoids the domain altogether.[50] If one is hopeless at financial tasks, one may delegate these responsibilities to someone else, such as one's spouse or a financial adviser. A miserable tennis player knows enough not to go on a summer vacation with tennis-playing friends. When negative information has validity and therefore must be dealt with in a way that acknowledges its existence, this must be accomplished without undermining positive conceptions of oneself. Once a person has recognized and come to terms with the lack of talent in a particular area, then the person may simply avoid getting himself or herself into circumstances in which the talent would be tested. The use of the term *pocket,* then, is not accidental. This method of controlling negative information about the self functions very much like a pocket in which one can place and hold an object without fear that it will get loose.

How is it possible to have an acknowledged pocket of incompetence without threatening self-esteem? First, by making the pocket of incompetence specific to a narrow area of life and then avoiding that domain, negative feedback is rare and therefore the threat to self-esteem may be minimal. Unathletic people who avoid athletic situations do not often have to confront the fact that they are unathletic. Moreover, once a person has acknowledged a particular area of incompetence, he or she may downgrade its importance or significance. A person who is unable to ski well may regard skiing as frivolous and a waste of money. To the unmusical, music may be something that plays in the background of hotel lobbies but that otherwise has little role in life. All of us have the creative capacity to prize the things that we are good at and to value less highly, if at all, those domains in which we lack talent.[51]

Sometimes creating a pocket of incompetence is not adaptive. The boss of a small company was frequently urged by his employees to join them at lunchtime, when most of them swam each day to stay fit. Each day he would invent a different excuse for needing to remain in his office or to have lunch out of the building. It was not until he realized that he was being perceived by his employees as standoffish and rude that he acknowledged his actual problem: he couldn't swim. Because the pocket of incompetence threatened to become a more pervasive and, in this case, inappropriate negative aspect of the self, he was forced to own up to it.

Acknowledged pockets of incompetence are not altogether threatening to the self most of us wish to create. Sometimes calling attention to or even exaggerating an acknowledged pocket of incompetence can be a successful social strategy for bolstering positive self-conceptions.[52] For example, a poor tennis player might exaggerate his incompetence so as to justify not participating in the sport at all. He will never have to show that, in fact, he has an unreliable serve, a mediocre forehand, and a nonexistent backhand—deficits that are, in some ways, more injurious to self-esteem and social functioning than simply not being able to play tennis. The person who has tried to learn a skill and is bad at it comes off less favorably than one who has never had the opportunity to learn. Moreover, people may readily acknowledge incompetence in one area of life in part to lend credibility to their positive self-assessments in some other domain. A woman who claims to be an expert on antiques but hopelessly lost with regard to modern painting is more likely to be believed than one who claims universal expertise. Thus, far from being a liability, a pocket of incompetence can actually be a humanizing aspect of the self.[53]

NEGATIVE SELF-SCHEMAS

Sometimes a flaw, weakness, or failing cannot be conveniently compartmentalized into a pocket of incompetence because the attribute in question is a more pervasive aspect of identity. The overweight person, for example, literally carries that fact into every situation, whether new or familiar, work-related or social. In chapter 1, the concept of self-schema was described as an organized set of beliefs about the self concerning some trait (such as being witty or kind) or life domain (such as being a musician or historian). People hold negative self-schemas, as well as positive ones, which permit them to recognize information as relevant to the self very quickly and efficiently.[54]

Like pockets of incompetence, negative self-schemas may enable a person to cordon off weaknesses from the rest of the self-concept. For example, by identifying one's self as simply "overweight" and actively managing that negative aspect of identity, one may avoid also thinking of the self as ugly or as a loser. Unlike pockets of incompetence, negative self-schemas do require active management and cannot be dealt with simply by avoiding situations that display the weakness. For example, short of joining a silent religious order, the shy person cannot avoid social settings altogether. Having a schema for a negative attribute enables people to identify schema-relevant situations quickly and then to prepare for them. Sociologist Erving Goffman, for example, describes the strategies employed by the handicapped, in this case a woman with a major hearing loss, to manage their interactions with "normals."

> Frances figured out elaborate techniques to cope with "dinner lulls," intermissions at concerts, football games, dances, and so on, in order to protect her secret. . . . [She] had it down pat that at a dinner party she should (1) sit next to someone with a strong voice; (2) choke, cough, or get hiccups, if someone asked her a direct question; (3) take hold of the conversation herself, ask someone to tell a story she had already heard, ask questions the answers to which she already knew.[55]

The five-year-old son of a friend has a well-developed self-schema of being "shy at first." This belief is so firm an aspect of his identity that he marches into new situations announcing that he is "shy at first," thereby thrusting onto others the responsibility of making him feel at ease. The ploy is quite successful, not only in helping him negotiate new settings, but in otherwise keeping his inflated little ego intact. Other than believing himself to be "shy at first," he appears to think well of himself, as a likable, outgoing, socially adept person, as, in fact, he is.

A negative self-schema, then, enables a person to put boundaries around some undesirable quality of the self, to decide what is relevant to it and what is not, and to anticipate and prepare for situations in which it will be relevant. Paradoxically, a negative self-schema may also protect the self-concept in certain ways. It may act as a convenient attribution for any failure ("I didn't get the job because of my weight") that miti-gates other, more threatening attributions ("I didn't get the job because I'm not good enough").

WHEN ILLUSIONS ABOUT THE SELF ARE EXPOSED

For most people, acknowledged pockets of incompetence and negative self-schemas apply to restricted domains of life rather than central ones. People typically do not launch themselves in careers where failure is highly likely or undertake central life activities that are almost certain not to succeed. Even so, there are circumstances in which one's talents may be shown up as less than one had hoped. A middle-level manager may experi-ence dawning awareness that she is not going to become her company's president. An athlete may begin to realize that he will always be second string. An actress may see that she is destined for minor parts in B films. What do people do when confronted with these threatening circumstances?

The gradual aspect of such awareness is its most important feature. When one does not have to confront a threatening assessment of one's self head-on, it is possible to begin a self-deceptive program of evasive action that effectively avoids re-ceiving that negative assessment in its blunt, unadulterated form. Withdrawing energy, time, and commitments from activ-ities that are increasingly unlikely to bring rewards and shifting these same resources to activities where at least some rewards are guaranteed both maintains self-esteem and avoids the need to acknowledge the threatening belief: I just wasn't good enough. The middle-level executive can view the fact that she will never be president, not as a personal failure, but as a sacri-fice she chose to make so that she could spend more time with her family. The athlete can avoid confronting his lack of talent by redirecting his energies toward building a business. After all, he can tell himself truthfully, athletics is only a temporary career.[56]

Even such self-destructive behaviors as drinking and taking

drugs can paradoxically be viewed as efforts to maintain illusions about the self.[57] In an intriguing analysis of these behaviors, psychologists Steven Berglas and Edward Jones concluded that they can often provide an excuse for failure that leaves beliefs about personal abilities intact.[58] For example, the writer whose productivity is severely hampered by his drinking can convince himself that, were it not for his drinking, he could be a Pulitzer Prize winner. The fledgling movie director who is hooked on cocaine can safely compare his talents with Huston, Bergman, or Fellini, knowing that his habit will protect him from ever having to demonstrate his grandiose self-assessments. This self-handicapping, as it is called, means that by guaranteeing present failure, one can preserve the illusion of intrinsic ability and potential future success.

THE PARADOX OF SELF-DECEPTION

How, then, do people maintain their positive views of themselves, the world, and the future in the face of negative information that challenges overly positive beliefs but would seem to be necessary for effective functioning in the world? The answer is that in order to maintain a positive yet adaptive view of the self, it is necessary to be self-deceptive. Negative information must be recognized for what it is and simultaneously kept from awareness as much as possible.[59] The mechanisms described in this chapter for dealing with negative information essentially outline a program of adaptive self-deception. What is begun in the construction of social life is perpetuated by the mind.

Self-deception has always presented philosophers with a logical paradox: How can a person know and not know information at the same time? What we have now learned about human cognition renders this puzzle more tractable. Through the twin mechanisms of selective attention and selective memory, it is possible to self-deceive not only successfully but adaptively.[60] People constantly monitor the environment for signs of what they should attend to and what they should avoid. A man interested in women can scan hundreds of faces and bodies in a few minutes, his glance resting only on the few who capture his attention. He may be virtually unaware of the hundreds rejected as inappropriate—too young, too old, unavailable, or not pretty—because the discriminations can be made in milliseconds, long before the mind can consciously respond, "She has a nice face, but she's pushing a stroller." So it is with positive and negative information more generally. Years of practice have enabled most adults to scan the environment for things it might be better not to know and then to avoid them even before their full nature can be identified. This "preprocessing" of information, as Greenwald terms it, is an efficient, effective, and ultimately self-deceptive mechanism because it recognizes negativity at some preconscious level and then shields it from view.

Memory is similarly selective. On the one hand, we have almost limitless capacity to recall what interests us. To appreciate the full implications of selective memory, consider the commonplace memorial feats almost any normal individual can perform. People with no special gifts except a fondness for music can identify who is singing a new song from the first note. We can pick out our dog's bark from many others. We can identify a close friend's footfall without even concentrating. The average adolescent may have the lyrics of several hundred or even several thousand rock songs cluttering his or her mind. But, say the memory experts, some of these events have the benefit of dozens or even hundreds of repetitions to reinforce the memory. Then how do we remember what we were wearing, where we were sitting, and what we had to eat on a particular date ten or twenty years ago? The mind actively chooses what is desirable to remember. With positive information stored through multiple pathways and associations for remembering and negative information stored with perhaps a few out-of-the-way associations, it is easy to see how memory actively fosters the self-aggrandizing self.

There are some not so obvious implications of viewing the accommodation of negative information as a self-deceptive process. The capacity for self-deception may be adaptive from a mental health standpoint. Sackeim and his colleagues developed a self-deception questionnaire, a measure of the degree to which people typically deny psychologically threatening but virtually universal feelings and behaviors. This scale asks people such questions as, "Do you ever feel guilty?" and "Have you ever made a fool of yourself?" questions that most of us would have to answer yes to, were we to be entirely honest, but which are often answered no as a self-deceptive maneuver. Sackeim and his colleagues found that people who were self-deceptive were in some respects actually mentally healthier than those who were not. People who scored high on the self-deception measure were less likely to be depressed than those who scored lower, and they showed fewer signs of mental disturbance.[61] Thus, rather than being associated with psychological malfunction, self-deception, at least in certain forms, may actually be healthy.

Illusion, then, may be an essential aspect of managing negative information. To all appearances, people do make adaptive use of information that tells them they are not quite as talented or successful as they would like to be, but they do so typically by taking from it what is useful and no more. Perhaps this inability to look at negative information squarely makes us a less mature species than the ideal one described by the neo-Freudians whose perspective opened this chapter. A. Bartlett Giamatti alluded to the matter in discussing his own decision to leave the presidency of Yale to become commissioner of baseball's National League:

There comes a time when every summer will have something of autumn about it. . . . There are others who were born with the wisdom to know that nothing lasts. These are the truly tough among us, the ones who can live without illusion, or without even the hope of illusion. I am not that grown up or up to date. I am a simpler creature, tied to more primitive patterns and cycles. I need to think something lasts forever, and it might as well be that state of being that is a game; it might as well be that, in a green field, in the sun.[62]

Yet, as Giamatti's comments also suggest, in our self-deceptions there is also self-knowledge to seek what we need to thrive and grow as healthy human beings.

CHAPTER 5

Confrontation with Tragedy

> Far away from the hospital experience, I can evaluate what I have learned. . . . I know my awareness of people has deepened and increased, that those who are close to me can want me to turn all my heart and mind and attention to their problems. I could not have learned *that* dashing all over the tennis court.
>
> —Polio victim[1]

ONE OF THE MOST impressive qualities of the human psyche is its ability to withstand personal tragedy. Despite serious setbacks, such as a life-threatening illness or the death of a family member, most people are able eventually to overcome the implications of the events and regain happiness and a sense of purpose. Not everyone readjusts, but most do; moreover, they often do so in surprising and moving ways. There are popular stereotypes of how people behave when they are faced with a severe threat, a loss, or the prospect of death. Many of us, perhaps, envision sudden and hedonistic changes—changing jobs, changing spouses, or squandering money on a series of self-indulgent adventures. In fact, these changes appear to be quite rare. Rather, the changes victims more commonly make in their lives involve growth and insight, leading those who have not been victimized almost to be embarrassed by their own lack of self-examination or sense of larger life purpose.[2]

When a person experiences personal setbacks or tragedies, the mind responds with cognitively adaptive efforts. Just as the need for control, a positive sense of self, and an optimistic view of the future are essential for normal functioning and for meeting the small rebuffs of everyday life, they appear to be essential to the readjustment process following more devastating victimizing events. The themes around which these adjustments occur include an attempt to restore self-esteem, an effort to regain a sense of mastery, and a search for meaning in the experience.[3]

Tragic events almost always involve loss. Victims of natural disasters such as floods or fires often lose their homes and personal possessions. Victims may also lose family or friends, or they may themselves be injured. The victim of illness loses the use of physical resources at least temporarily and may be permanently disabled, and chronic or life-threatening disease leads to an uncertain or deteriorating future. To be aware of one's victimization is to be aware of these losses.

But there are other, more subtle forms of victimization. Not only do tangible losses of family, friends, and property occur, but more insidious effects on valued beliefs about oneself and the world can take place. Psychologist Ronnie Janoff-Bulman argues that most people believe, whether explicitly or implicitly, that the world is a benevolent and meaningful place and that the self is a worthwhile person.[4] These assumptions are derived from knowledge and experience, often from early childhood events involving feelings of warmth and safety. From these early nurturing experiences, people come to believe that the world is a protective place that will shelter them from harm and evil and enable them to achieve their life goals. One aspect of these beliefs is the conviction that the self is relatively invulnerable to adverse events.

A victimizing event can shatter these perceptions of personal invulnerability and alter the assumptions about the world on which these beliefs are based. In particular, feelings of self-worth and beliefs that the world is benevolent and meaningful are often undermined. Long after victims have replaced their property and overcome their terror, their beliefs about the world and their own place in it may remain damaged, albeit nudged in a more realistic direction.[5]

The illusions on which mental health depends are especially vulnerable to victimizing events. Research on reactions to rape, illness, and other tragic or near-tragic events reveals that one of the most common reactions experienced by victims is a feeling of loss of control.[6] Feeling out of control can produce emotional problems such as depression and an inability to take action in other areas of life that remain controllable.[7] The assault on personal control is all the more threatening because research on reactions to stressful events so clearly indicates that beliefs in control promote successful adjustment.[8] The loss of control engendered in victimization, then, can have far-reaching consequences.

Loss of self-esteem is also often a consequence of victimization. Research on experiences as diverse as losing one's job, going on welfare, developing a malignancy, and being raped shows that these events lower self-esteem, even when the victim bears no conceivable responsibility for the victimizing event.[9] A man with epilepsy described his perceptions of himself before he realized how damaging they were:

> It took me quite a while to realize that there is nothing wrong with being an epileptic. I used to see other people that were mentally retarded, and I used to think I was like them. I discovered that it was not something to be ashamed of, and that my mind was as normal as anyone else's.[10]

The sense of optimism that normally pervades people's cognitions is also undermined by victimizing events. Victims no longer believe that the world has primarily good things in store for them. Rather, having been the victim of one disastrous or threatening event, they may perceive themselves as potential victims of future such events. Victimization leads to a cautiousness about the world and the future, a sense that one is no longer safe and protected, and that vigilance is essential for survival.[11]

Victimization is also aversive because it forces people to label themselves in negative ways or to categorize themselves with other people who are victimized.[12] People who have recently become victims have long experience with being "normal," and they know how they previously reacted to other victims. Now that they are themselves victims, they may react to themselves in part as they previously reacted to other victims, with aversion and perhaps some pity. For example, the cancer waiting room experience forces cancer patients to label themselves as such, to admit the full awareness of that status. As one patient said: "While I was going for the radiation treatments, I'd come in here and think, 'Gee, what am I doing here? I'm afraid in comparison with some of these people. I have something these people have?' and I'd realize that's why I was there."[13]

THE SOCIAL CONSEQUENCES OF VICTIMIZATION

In addition to personal devastation, victims often suffer unpleasant social consequences. Although Judeo-Christian ethics endorse a compassionate stance toward victims and although institutions for compensating victims exist, social reactions to victims are at best ambivalent and at worst hostile and rejecting. Sociologist William Ryan argues that nonvictims often "blame the victim."[14] People who have done well in life often attribute their success to their own efforts. When they perceive other people failing to achieve the same outcomes, they may attribute those failures to lack of effort, thereby blaming those trapped in adverse circumstances for their less desirable situations. Moreover, because people in advantaged social positions are implicitly allied with the institutions of society, to show compassion for, compensate, or otherwise materially or psychologically benefit victims would be tantamount to criticizing the social system that benefits themselves. Consequently, people are virtually compelled to derogate victims if they are to keep their perceptions of their own merit intact.

Psychologist Melvin Lerner similarly argues that people need to believe in a just world.[15] Victims are threatening to nonvictims because if the victimization seems to be due to random forces, it undermines beliefs in a stable, controllable, beneficent world. According to Lerner, random and severe victimization, such as that due to natural disasters or crime, raises the threatening possibility that the same thing could happen to oneself. People therefore try to derogate a victim's behavior as having brought on the victimizing event. "If she hadn't been out at night, she wouldn't have been raped." "If he hadn't eaten poorly all his life, he wouldn't have had a heart attack." These are the types of explanations we offer for victimization. It is safer to believe that a homeless person is there because he failed to hold a job than to believe that he is a random casualty of the work system. A random victimization could befall the self as well.

When a victim's behavior cannot be blamed, according to Lerner, derogation of the victim's character will result. One will see the victim as the sort of person who deserves to be victimized. The bigoted person may see victims of a ghetto fire as meriting their fate because they were probably all drug pushers and prostitutes anyway, or the victims of a flood may be seen as stupid for not having recognized the danger in the rising waters. Victims are aware of these social responses, either because they have had personal contact with such derogation, or because of their own experience in reacting to others as victims. Anticipating derogation from others is another negative aspect of becoming a victim.

Victimization, then, presents people with severe challenges to their ways of life and to their belief systems. Do victimizing events represent severe and permanent threats to the illusions that seem to bolster mental and physical health, or do people find ways of using their illusions and other psychologically adaptive mechanisms to overcome their perceptions of themselves as victims?

OVERCOMING VICTIMIZATION

> I never knew my neighbors before. It was never really what you could call a neighborhood, but in the last two days I've gotten to know everyone. We're all pulling together and taking care of each other. It's a nice feeling.
>
> —Flood victim[16]

> We were very lucky. He took only the stereo and the T.V. It could have been a lot worse.
>
> —Crime victim[17]

Watching victims interviewed on television news broadcasts can lead to the conclusion that there are no victims. Everyone seems to be lucky. Instead of bemoaning the loss of his home and car, the tornado victim is relieved, even jubilant, that he and his family so narrowly escaped death. The victim of fire expresses gratitude that her life was spared. Indeed, victims of life-threatening attacks, illness, and natural disaster sometimes seem from their accounts not only to have overcome the victimizing aspects of their situation but actually to have benefited from it. Psychological research on how people cope with tragedies suggests that people actively strive to overcome feeling like a victim. Studies of chronic illness or conditions, such as cancer, diabetes, severe burns, cystic fibrosis, or hemophilia, and investigations of coping with the loss of a child or spouse reveal that most people experiencing such events are able eventually to say that their lives are as good as or better than they were before the events.[18] This is not true of all victims, as some people are permanently scarred by these events.[19] Nonetheless, most victims report that after some time has transpired, their lives are at least back to normal or improved as a result of the events they have gone through.

Perhaps the most surprising aspect of these claims is that when victims are able to achieve this high quality of life following victimizing events, they typically do so on their own. That is, usually they do not turn to mental health professionals such as psychologists but rather cope with aversive events themselves either by drawing on their own internal resources or by using the social support of those around them.[20]

The brain is a remarkable organ and never more so than when it is actively seeking to turn a disastrous event into one that is less tragic or even beneficial. Victims have manifold ways of controlling their perceptions of themselves as victims. Viewed in one light, a situation may look to be quite dire and unenviable, yet viewed in another, one may appear to be quite fortunate. Systematic and selective perceptions and evaluations help victims to minimize their victimization by focusing on beneficial qualities of the situation.

IT COULD ALWAYS BE WORSE

A Jewish fable tells of a farmer who seeks a rabbi's counsel because his life is in an uproar. His wife nags him, his children fight, and everything around him is in chaos. The rabbi tells him to go home and move the chickens into the house. "Into the house!" cries the farmer. "But what good will that do?" The rabbi assures him that this is the right action and sends him home. But two days later the farmer is back, even more frantic than before. "Now my wife nags me, the children fight, and the chickens are everywhere, upsetting the furniture, laying eggs, dropping feathers, and pecking at our food. What am I to do?" The rabbi tells him to go back and bring the cow into the house. "The cow!" cries the distraught man. "That can only make things worse!" "Do as I say and come back to see me in a few days," responds the rabbi. A few days later, the farmer comes back in an even more harried state. "The chickens are getting into everything, the cow has knocked over the furniture, the children are fighting, and my wife is beside herself. You have made things worse. Nothing is helping." The rabbi sends him home with the advice to bring the horse into the house as well. The frantic man returns home and follows the rabbi's advice, but returns the next day beside himself with despair. "Rabbi, the horse and the cow have knocked everything over. There is no room for my family. The chickens are everywhere. Our lives are in shambles. What shall we do?" The rabbi says, "Go home and take out the horse and the cow and the chickens." The man does as he is told and comes back the next day smiling happily. "Rabbi, our lives are now so calm and peaceful. With the horse and the cow and the chickens gone, we are a family again. How can I thank you?" The rabbi smiles.

The point, of course, is that things can always be worse. Following natural disasters, illnesses, and other threatening events, victims commonly say that they are lucky because they could have been more severely victimized. The comparison of one's actual situation with what could have happened is a common response to serious events. Rape victims frequently note with relief that they could have been killed or subjected to greater violence or perversion than actually took place.[21] Cancer patients state that their experiences were not as bad as they could have been, considering that they could have died or had a long, drawn-out illness.[22] A tornado victim remarked, after his house was destroyed: "We were very lucky. God stopped that thing just before it got to us. If He hadn't, we would be dead right now."[23] A woman describes an automobile accident as follows: "I was very lucky. A split second later and the car would have hit my door and killed me. As it was, he hit the front end and totaled it."[24] Even a terminally ill cancer patient on the CBS documentary *A Time to Die* responded to his condition with the observation, "It's not the worst thing that could happen."[25]

The mental creation of how much worse things could have been shows up commonly in reactions to victimization, but why it occurs is not entirely known. There are at least two intriguing possibilities. One is that victims need to minimize their sense of themselves as victims. Imagining how things could have been much worse makes one seem better off. Indeed, compared with having died or being more severely affected by the event, one *is* better off. This is not to suggest that victims necessarily consciously create these worse situations in order to feel better about what actually happened. Rather, it may be an unconscious response of the mind to help the victim feel better.[26]

Another possibility is that victims imagine possible worse outcomes for some reason other than trying to minimize their sense as victims, but that this process has the beneficial side effect of making them feel better about their situation. Much of the terror associated with a victimizing event stems not from what is currently happening, but from the anticipation of how things may get worse. During the course of a victimizing event, victims often imagine what is likely to happen next and conjure up the worst possible outcome, perhaps as a way of preparing themselves mentally for it. Cancer patients usually report that they have contemplated their death during the cancer episode. Victims of natural disasters or accidents report that they were afraid of being killed or injured, rather than concerned about the damage that had already occurred. When later recalling the victimizing experience, impressions of what actually happened may be accompanied by these visions of worse events. When victims of disasters describe their situations by explaining how much worse things could have been, they may be reporting the fears and pictures that went through their minds during the events.[27]

COMPARISONS WITH LESS FORTUNATE OTHERS

Victims actively compare themselves with other people who have been more severely victimized. As a flood victim in Salt Lake City reported: "Guess we're pretty lucky. A lot of parts of the country have it a lot worse than this a lot of the time."[28] This process is known as social comparison. The idea that people evaluate themselves by comparing themselves with other people has been a cornerstone of social psychological theory for many years.[29] Usually people compare themselves with people who are somewhat better off. For example, when we think about our incomes, the ways we have furnished our homes, or the cars we drive, we may implicitly compare our assets with those of other people who may be somewhat more affluent, drive better cars, or have more beautifully decorated homes. By comparing ourselves with more fortunate others, we may get a sense of where we are headed and how we can improve our own situations.

When they are feeling threatened, however, people tend to evaluate themselves against people who are doing more poorly. These "downward" comparisons have the psychological advantage of making one feel better about one's own situation. Psychologist Thomas Wills argues that comparisons with less fortunate others are attempts to bolster and improve self-esteem.[30]

Part of the process of finding someone with whom one can compare one's own situation favorably involves the careful selection of the dimension in question. That is, someone who is trying to minimize her sense of victimization when she has lost her entire house in a devastating flood would not count the possessions she had lost. Rather, she might focus on the fact that, unlike her neighbors, she had not lost anyone in her family. Or a rape victim who had been badly beaten might think about other rape victims who had died or who were mutilated, whereas one who had been sexually assaulted but not beaten would likely compare herself favorably to a woman who had been beaten.[31]

The following statements illustrate creative comparisons made by cancer patients.

- From a woman whose breast cancer was treated with a lumpectomy (removal of the lump) rather than a mastectomy (which involves removal of the entire breast): "I had a comparatively small amount of surgery. How awful it must be for women who have had a mastectomy. I just can't imagine. It would seem to be so difficult."

- The remarks of a woman who had a mastectomy: "It was not tragic. It worked out okay. Now, if the thing had spread all over, I would have had a whole different story for you."

- An older woman with breast cancer stated: "The people I really feel sorry for are these young gals. To lose a breast when you're so young must be awful. I'm 73. What do I need a breast for?"

- A younger woman stated: "If I hadn't been married, I think this thing would have really gotten to me. I can't imagine dating or whatever knowing you have this thing and not knowing how to tell the man about it."[32]

The point, of course, is that one is always better off than someone as long as one picks the right dimension for evaluation. In the study of breast cancer patients just described, lumpectomy patients compared themselves favorably to mastectomy patients, but mastectomy patients never evaluated themselves against lumpectomy patients. Older women considered themselves better off than younger women but no younger woman ever expressed the wish that she were older. The women with the poorest prognoses consoled themselves with the fact that they were not yet dying or not in pain. Even the patients who were dying were able to achieve some solace from their state. Psychiatrist Elisabeth Kübler-Ross, who wrote extensively on death, reported the remarks of one dying man:

> The wife was upset, as she's never seen me like this, so I said, "We've all got to go, girl. I've had a good life—it doesn't worry me." Now those two honeymoon couples killed on the front page. They're the ones I'm sorry for, not me. I'm all right.[33]

Dying people often focus on the fact that they have achieved spiritual peace or lived a long and full life, compared with people who might never experience those things.

Clearly, the strategy of evaluating oneself favorably against others who are worse off can be a successful way of restoring self-esteem. However, what if no one else is worse off? Suppose there are no other victims. What if a victim of rape or assault has no personal contact with other women who have had similar experiences? Or a cancer patient may be the first among his family and friends ever to have had cancer. How do these people compare themselves favorably with others so as to boost their self-esteem? One answer is that comparisons with less fortunate others are created whole-cloth by the mind.[34] In other words, when people do not have less fortunate victims with whom to compare themselves, they make them up. The need to invent victims because they are not readily available may be somewhat more common than one might suppose. Victims typically heal their wounds in private. Consequently, there are many barriers to learning how fellow victims have coped.[35]

Moreover, the other victims people do encounter may, in fact, be doing poorly but appear to be doing well, simply because this is the way they present themselves.

The creation of imaginary people who are doing much worse than oneself is quite common. In studies with cancer patients, some of the following comments were noted:

I have never been like some of those people who have cancer and they feel that well, this is it, they can't do anything, they can't go anywhere. . . . I just keep right on going.

Some of these women just seem to be devastated, and with really less problems than I encountered. You know, smaller tumors.

You read about a few who handle it well, but it still seems like the majority feel sorry for themselves, and I don't think they cope with it that well. I don't understand it, because it doesn't bother me at all.

Where do these fantasy victims come from? In a sense, they are analogous to the imaginary worse situations described earlier. They are inventions of the mind based on people's ideas of what poor coping looks like. Reading articles or listening to news stories about people who have coped poorly gives one material for the mental construction of less fortunate victims. Descriptions of other victims by acquaintances may also provide such information. For example, for helping people deal with a victimizing event and regain self-esteem, counselors sometimes tell them how well they are doing compared with other people. If a physician tells a patient, "You're doing so much better than my other patients"—even if he gives this information to every one of his patients—the patient will feel good for having the information and believe it to be valid, sensing that there are a large number of others out there who are not doing as well.

The process of evaluating one's own situation in comparison to other victims is a highly creative one, involving active selection of the people in the environment who will make one appear to be most benefited. The primary, perhaps sole, purpose of these cognitive creations appears to be the restoration of self-esteem. If victims cannot altogether overcome the threats produced by victimizing events, at the very least they can regard themselves as having come out of the events as whole as possible and as coping with the events in admirable, even heroic, ways.

It might seem that reevaluating adverse circumstances simply by changing the people or situations with whom one compares oneself would be a weak way of restoring self-esteem following a victimizing event. After all, such perceptions have a flimsy quality, dependent upon what group or situation might happen to be available for comparison at any given time. Nonetheless, the self-evaluations that occur by readjusting one's frame of reference can often be very powerful. Consider the following surprising examples. Within weeks of their altered circumstances, lottery winners and victims of major automobile accidents evaluate their life situations in roughly equivalent ways. They report that they are about equally happy and satisfied with their lives.[36] The evaluations middle-class Americans make of their happiness and satisfaction with life are virtually the same as the happiness and satisfaction reported by rural peasants in India living in greatly reduced circumstances.[37] We evaluate our outcomes on the basis of other people in similar circumstances, not on the basis of some absolute scale of life circumstances. One might wish, on occasion, to be as beautiful as a movie star, as wealthy as a multi-millionaire, or as successful as a famed musician, but when we actually evaluate our own circumstances, we turn much closer to home. And when we do, virtually all of us regard our life situations to be fairly satisfying. While they are not the best they could be, we judge them to be satisfactory overall and better than most.

EFFORTS TO RESTORE LOST CONTROL

The sense of personal control that leads people to function so well under normal circumstances is often severely tested by victimizing events. Clearly, people do not plan to have disasters, at least under most normal circumstances; consequently, when some disaster or near-disaster strikes, it is a cruel reminder that many events in life are controlled by random factors and are not systematic outcomes of personal design. For a short time, the sense of personal control may be eliminated altogether. Research on victims of natural disasters, assault, and chronic illnesses reveals that often, immediately following the shock of the event, there is a period of inertia in which a victim can seem unable to perform even the most mundane of activities, such as making breakfast, getting dressed, or putting gas in the car.[38] It is as if the disaster has prompted the person to question the reason for virtually every activity, and actions as small as getting dressed may seem like the proverbial rearranging of deck chairs on the Titanic.

Another reason why efforts to control even the mundane activities of life will cease or exist at a low level for a while is that people's cognitive capacities may be overwhelmed by a victimizing event and its implications. The initial shock can give way to a period of numbness in which the gradual implications of the event start to sink in. As the unconscious and conscious mind is attempting to process the implications of the event for life in general, there may be relatively little capacity to deal with everyday matters.

For most people, this period passes fairly quickly, sometimes in a few days, other times after a few weeks; then the need for control can become insistent once more.[39] Many victims respond to the challenge by throwing themselves enthusiastically into their activities. Sometimes they will deliberately begin to make changes in their lives, deciding, for example, to go back to school or to change occupations, perhaps because self-consciously directing change tells them concretely that once again they have control over the activities of their lives.

Many victims attempt to exert control over the victimizing circumstances themselves. A rape victim may put bars on her windows and an extra lock on her doors. A fire victim may move to a one-story building with multiple exits. In this way, the victim is saying, "I may not be able to undo the event that just occurred, but I can certainly keep it from happening again."[40] Sometimes mastery needs can be satisfied by aspects of the disability itself. A polio victim describes his sense of accomplishment:

> Other children learn naturally and without conscious effort to move about and crawl and stand up. Not I. I had to achieve those things so deliberately, at the cost of so much pain and sweat and tears, that the attainment of each was a separate triumph. I stood almost in awe of my own power to accomplish. I was like a god.[41]

A blind man talks about his red-tipped cane:

> At street corners, it proved its worth. Car drivers saw it and stopped. I held it out before me and walked across the pavement with an assurance that I had never felt before. I was a worker of miracles. I was the Moses of the metropolis. I held out my staff over that roaring, honking sea, and lo! the traffic parted and I stepped up on the opposite curb sound as a dollar.[42]

One of the most intriguing examples of renewed efforts at control was uncovered some years ago in an investigation with cancer patients. Like other victims, cancer patients often find their feelings of control or mastery over their lives to be severely undermined by the cancer diagnosis. Not only does cancer lead to a host of immediate changes, such as the need for surgery or chemotherapy and management of the intense fear and depression that can result, it also creates uncertainty about the coming years. As a rule of thumb, oncologists maintain that a patient cannot be considered cancer-free until five years have passed without a recurrence. Consequently, for at least this five-year period, most patients are never certain whether the twinge of pain they experience in the morning is a pulled muscle or a new tumor, and whether their bodies are secretly harboring cancers that are as yet undetected.

Many cancer patients deal with this threat to mastery by believing that they personally can keep the cancer under control. In a study of breast cancer patients, two-thirds of the women interviewed believed that they personally could keep the cancer from coming back.[43] Many of the remainder believed that although they personally had no control over the cancer, it could be directly controlled by the physician or by continued treatments.

To begin the process of reasserting control, many of these women attempted to learn as much as they could about breast cancer. Myriad psychological research investigations ranging from studies of rats pressing levers in boxes to investigations of elderly people in nursing homes demonstrate that when people have information about the stressful circumstances they are going through, they adjust more successfully to those circumstances. They feel less upset, aroused, or depressed; they seem happier to others; their physiological state is more quiescent; and they are more active. Feeling knowledgeable about the event provides a semblance of control.

For cancer patients, information can lead to feelings of control for several reasons. For some, the value of information may lie primarily in being able to become actively involved in treatment decisions and cancer care. For others, the value of the information may simply lie in the ability to predict and understand what is happening to their bodies and what the likely future course will be. In either case, the desire for information can be intense. As one breast cancer patient put it: "I felt that I had lost control of my body somehow, and the way for me to get back some control was to find out as much as I could. It really became almost an obsession."[44] One man described his wife as follows: "She got books, she got pamphlets, she studied, she talked to cancer patients. She found out everything that was happening to her and she fought it. She went to war with it. She calls it 'taking in her covered wagons and surrounding it.' "[45]

Many of these women's efforts to control their cancer were mental. One of the most common methods was maintaining a positive attitude so that the cancer would not come back.

> My mental attitude, I think, is the biggest control over it that I have. I want to feel there is something I can do, that there is some way I can control it.

> I think that if you feel you are in control of it, you can control it up to a point. I absolutely refuse to have any more cancer.[46]

Other women who felt they could exert mental control over their cancers believed they could do so by practicing psychological techniques to reduce their cancers or to put their bodies into a healthier state. Most of these techniques involve inducing a state of total relaxation, as through meditation or conjuring up a peaceful scene. Through learning to progressively relax all of the muscles of the body, they were able to reduce heart rate and breathing, thereby controlling many of the adverse psychological and physical responses of anxiety, agitation, or depression. In other cases, these patients attempted to maintain a positive attitude, actively dispelling negative images and thoughts by exerting direct control over their cognitive processes. As one patient coping with chemotherapy put it: "It was kind of a game with me, depending on my mood. If I was peaceful and wanted to be peaceful, I would image a beautiful scene, or if I wanted to do battle with the enemy, I would mock up a battle and have my defenses ready."[47]

For some patients, the belief that they could now personally control the cancer stemmed from their perceptions concerning what had caused it in the first place. A causal explanation for a devastating event can contribute to a sense of control or mastery if the perceived cause is believed to be no longer in effect. One breast cancer patient, for example, characterized her first husband as a "boorish rapist" and believed that the stress produced by this destructive relationship had given rise to the cancer. Her involvement with her "wonderful" second husband, she felt, would keep her cancer-free, because the initial conditions producing the cancer were not only gone, but they had been replaced by conditions that might actually promote good health. Another woman believed her cancer had been due to a poor immune system, but felt that the cancer experience itself and the impetus it had given her to take control over her life more generally had "realigned the cells"; consequently, she believed that she was no longer vulnerable to a host of diseases, including cancer.

Other women were able to maintain their sense of control over the cancer by believing that the cancer had initially been due to some specific action, such as a single blow or recurring blows to the breast. A woman who had worked in a dress shop said that she always carried the dresses from the fitting room back to the racks over her left arm so that the hangers knocked against her left breast as she walked. As it happened, her tumor developed in precisely that part of the breast. She believed that the constant wear and tear had given rise to the lump that eventually proved to be malignant. Her solution and method of achieving mastery over the cancer was to put the clothes on a portable rack and wheel them from the dressing room back to the main body of the shop so that they no longer bounced against her. Another woman had worked in a fireworks assembly plant, and one of her tasks was to put the casings on the shells. As she was a short woman and not particularly strong, she used her rib cage and chest to push the casing onto the shell, as she held the end with both hands. Consequently, over and over again, the casing knocked up against her breasts. When she subsequently developed a breast tumor, she inferred that it was this activity that had led to the tumor. Since she retired shortly thereafter and was no longer exposed to what she perceived was the cause of the cancer, she felt confident that she would remain cancer-free in the future.

Those familiar with the causes of cancer will know that a blow to the breast is not regarded as a contributing factor. It is of no matter. The point is that these women *believed* that the blows had produced the cancer, and the belief was sufficiently powerful to help restore a sense of mastery and the confidence that the cancer could not recur. Many of these patients described a discontinuity between the precancer time and the postcancer time, the sense that things were different now. These beliefs promoted feelings of mastery by maintaining that the initial cause of the cancer was no longer in effect.

Other cancer patients went to battle with the cancer by making lifestyle changes that they believed would improve their health. Nearly half of the women interviewed said they had changed their diet since the cancer, usually by adding fresh fruit and vegetables and cutting down on red meats and fats. The National Cancer Institute and the American Cancer Society have published articles suggesting that certain dietary changes can lower one's risk for cancer. Although it is not clear that these factors will reduce the chances of recurrence once a cancer has developed, the women in the study believed that it would, or that at least it was worth a try. Moreover, diet is an aspect of life over which an individual has substantial control, and by actively making changes in diet, a feeling of mastery may be actively promoted. As one woman put it:

Where the cancer came from was an important question to me at first. The doctor's answer was that it was a multifaceted illness. I looked over the known causes of cancer, like viruses, radiation, genetic mutation, environmental carcinogens, and the one I focused in on very strongly was diet. I know now why I focused on it. It was the only one that was simple enough for me to understand and change. You eat something that's bad for you, you get sick.[48]

Sometimes the dietary changes made by these women involved fads suggested by magazine articles promoting untried cancer cures. One woman described in hilarious detail how she and her husband and another couple had gone on a lavish cruise during which she and her friend, also a breast cancer patient, had undertaken an anticancer diet of mashed asparagus that had been recommended in a pamphlet they had read. Consequently, while all the people around them were partaking of wonderful delicacies and extravagant desserts, these two women spent the entire week eating nothing but mashed asparagus until the last day, when they broke down and enthusiastically devoured everything they had so carefully avoided during the week.

Some women felt that drugs they had taken, such as birth control pills or estrogen replenishers for menopause, had contributed to their cancer, and so they stopped taking these medications altogether. As in the case of diet, the evidence relating these medications to the development of breast cancer is inconclusive. Nonetheless, it is belief rather than fact that promotes a sense of mastery, and the changes made by these women led them to feel that they were actively contributing to the cancer battle.

Exercise was another common strategy for maintaining a sense of control. Some of the women who had developed breast cancer had been out of shape and overweight at the time they were diagnosed with cancer, and several felt that these factors had contributed to the development of the malignancy. They believed that if they were to stand a chance of avoiding recurrences in the future, they must create a body that was in sufficiently good shape to battle an outside invader. By making themselves strong and taking off unnecessary weight, they believed that they would accomplish this goal.

Not all of the women who felt they could achieve control

over their cancer assumed that they could control the cancer itself directly. Many felt that successfully controlling the side effects of treatments could contribute directly to their cancer care and indirectly to the likelihood of a cancer remission. Most of the patients who had received chemotherapy, for example, undertook efforts to control its side effects. For some, this involved simply taking medications or sleeping, but half of the women used mental efforts at control, including imaging, self-hypnosis, distraction, and meditation. Similar kinds of efforts were made to control the less debilitating but still unpleasant side effects of radiation therapy. For example, one woman undergoing radiation therapy imagined that there was a protective shield that permitted the rays to enter the tumor but shielded the rest of her body from being burned. Another woman imagined her chemotherapy to be a powerful cannon that blasted away pieces of the dragon, cancer. One sixty-one-year-old woman simply focused her attention on healing the cancer with the instruction, "Body, cut this shit out."[49]

Whether or not people can directly affect cancer through mind control is an issue that has been hotly debated for centuries, never more than recently. We do know that patients who are in a state of total relaxation, whether through their own efforts or the intervention of a professional, are better able to withstand pain and discomfort of many kinds. Although there is evidence to suggest that these changes may also help put the body in a biochemical and immunologic state conducive to recovery, this evidence is still largely speculative. Moreover, the astute reader with some knowledge of cancer will know that many of the beliefs these women held concerning their ability to control cancer are fictitious. What, then, is the value of these beliefs if they are wrong?

The women in this study were given a battery of psychological tests to assess their adjustment to the cancer experience. Some tests consisted of rating scales to assess mood and depression. Others involved asking the women whether or not they found satisfaction and happiness in their daily life activities.

The patients' spouses, their physicians, and a trained psychological interviewer also provided information about the emotional distress these women were experiencing, how well they had adjusted to the cancer experience, and their abilities to get on with other aspects of their lives in ways that were both effective and rewarding. Those women who felt that they had direct control over their cancer were better adjusted than the women who believed that they did not have any control. Moreover, it mattered not what type of control the women believed they had. Any sense of mastery over the cancer experience, whether through mental efforts, behavior changes, or control over side effects—all led to better mental functioning. The women who believed they could exert direct control over the cancer were more satisfied with their lives, happier in their relationships, better adjusted to the cancer, and more likely to be free of the anxiety and depression that can intermittently affect the victim of any potentially devastating experience.[50] The illusion of control, then, was highly adaptive, permitting those who held it to enjoy their lives more fully than could those who were unable to achieve a sense of mastery.

The importance of mastery has been clearly demonstrated in this study with cancer patients, but it is by no means limited to this victimizing event. Mastery needs are important for many victims, and those who are able to achieve a sense of mastery over a victimizing event will likely be better adjusted.[51] For some serious diseases, it is easy to see how efforts to exert control may promote good mental and physical health. Cardiac patients, for example, exert direct control over their illnesses by stopping smoking, changing to a low-cholesterol diet, and engaging in exercise. Diabetics can exert control by maintaining blood sugar level, getting exercise, and controlling diet. These efforts are medically recommended to enhance physical functioning; but they also have beneficial effects on mental functioning, because they create tasks that people can undertake on their own behalf to enable them to achieve a sense of mastery over their adverse circumstances.

DISCONFIRMATION OF ILLUSIONS

The fact that people seek actively to restore their self-esteem and renew a sense of personal control is valuable evidence supporting both the existence of illusions and their adaptive role in the process of recovery from victimizing events. There is, however, at least one potential problem in arguing for the adaptive significance of these beliefs. To the extent that they are based on illusion, they are subject to disconfirmation. The belief that one has gained control over the course of a chronic or life-threatening disease, for example, can be abruptly disconfirmed by a recurrence. If adjustment to threatening circumstances depends upon the existence of false beliefs, what happens if those beliefs are challenged or disconfirmed?

These issues are important ones, for without a sense of how people will react when their falsely positive assessments of the future and their own role in it are challenged, it is difficult to know whether beliefs derived from illusions are truly adaptive. Should friends and family or professionals such as psychologists encourage these apparently adaptive but sometimes misguided beliefs, or should victims be induced to develop more realistic perceptions of themselves and the future which, though less pleasant, may ultimately be more accurate? One case for realism has been made drawing on a surprising source: research on learning conducted with rats. We will first consider the evidence and then evaluate whether or not the arguments can be applied meaningfully to human beings.

SELIGMAN'S RAT

One of the most important tasks psychologists have undertaken is the study of how people learn effectively. Often this research is conducted with lower animals, rather than with humans, and a favorite choice of species is the rat. Rats are exposed to various conditions to see what types of reinforcements are most effective for promoting learning. After engaging in a desired behavior, for example, a rat may be given a pellet of food in order to induce it to engage in the behavior again.

Whereas most research has focused on how rats and, by implication, people learn most effectively, more recent investigations have attempted to identify the conditions under which an organism will fail to learn. There are many circumstances in which people have opportunities to learn and yet fail to do so. They may experience frustration, a loss of hope, or low motivation, and without some understanding of these maladaptive learning patterns, our understanding of the learning process is incomplete. Therefore, psychologists have used the rat to develop models of the failure to learn.

Psychologist Martin Seligman of the University of Pennsylvania has been a leading figure in this endeavor. Seligman reasoned that one reason people fail to learn is because instead of receiving rewards for their efforts, they are punished for those otherwise adaptive responses, whether by design or accident. To mimic this circumstance, he put a rat in a cage and at random moments administered strong electric shock through the floor of the cage to the rat's feet. At first, the rat responded to these strong electric shocks by running around the cage, seeking a way out. It jumped up on the sides and made other efforts to escape the aversive situation. Over time, however, the rat learned that it was not possible to terminate the shocks; so when the shocks began, the rat simply cowered in the corner of the cage, making no effort to escape.

This is not in itself very surprising. Most animals and humans, when exposed to uncontrollable pain, will first make efforts to reduce it, which when unsuccessful give way to a passive acceptance of the discomfort. What Seligman did next revealed a more interesting process. He placed the rat in a new cage, similar to although not exactly like the cage in which it had previously received electric shock. In this cage was a bar that when pressed would terminate electric shock. Then, just as in the previous cage, the rat received electric shock. Instead of investigating the cage for ways to escape, which would eventually have led to pressing the bar, the rat again cowered in the corner, making no efforts on its behalf. Even when the electric shock was off, it failed to explore the cage; when the shock was on, it failed to learn the one response that would terminate the electric shock, namely the bar press. In effect, the rat had learned to be helpless. The inability to learn to control a new environment after having previously been in an uncontrollable environment is called *learned helplessness.* [52]

Seligman's rat became a model, even a parable, for many human situations. Psychologists argued that there are many circumstances in which people learn to be helpless. Prisoners, the mentally disabled, and other institutionalized populations may discover quickly that in a routinized institutional setting, there is limited opportunity for personal control. Efforts by an individual to alter his or her situation will meet with little success. Psychologists have argued that these institutional settings in effect promote helplessness and the more insidious consequence of learned helplessness. When institutionalized people attempt to reenter society, they may no longer have at their disposal the adaptive behaviors that will enable them to function effectively. They can function only in institutionalized settings where others exert control. Seligman's ideas concerning learned helplessness have also been applied to the ghetto child trapped in a racist educational system that promotes unfamiliar values. Initial efforts to learn in this alien environment may meet with prejudice, discrimination, and expectations of failure, so that eventually the child's fledgling efforts to learn give way to passive and helpless behavior. The child, in effect, learns to be helpless in new environments as well.

It is easy to see why learned helplessness prompts concerns about the potential maladaptiveness of illusions. People who have been through a threatening event in which they have lost control, experienced low self-esteem, and had their vision of the future severely taxed may be vulnerable to similar perceptions in the future. Having once responded to these victimizing circumstances with renewed efforts at control, efforts to raise self-esteem, and the vision of a more optimistic future, the victim could be ripe for learned helplessness, should those beliefs again be disconfirmed. Multiple experiences with loss of control have been so much a concern of psychologists that some have been hesitant to intervene to enhance people's feelings of control in stressful, victimizing circumstances. The fear has been that if people respond to victimizing circumstances with efforts to improve their lot and these efforts again meet with frustration, the results will be so devastating that the victim will be in a far worse psychological state than would have been the case if no efforts to restore control had been made. Thus, although there are clear benefits of control, there is also growing suspicion, drawing largely from learned helplessness, that when efforts at control are exerted in an environment in which no control exists, controlling efforts will lead to poorer, rather than more successful, adjustment. It is a realistic concern.

But the worlds of rats and people, though similar in some respects, are radically different in others. Perhaps people respond to disconfirmed expectations of control very differently. Some years ago, when we were working with cancer patients, we found ourselves with a patient in a situation analogous to Seligman's rat's. The patient was a woman named Anna, an attractive blonde in her mid-fifties. All her life, she had practiced a healthy lifestyle, long before it had become fashionable. She and her husband had self-consciously maintained a healthy diet and exercised regularly. Both were proud that they had rarely been sick, having missed a total of two days of work between them in nearly fifteen years. Accordingly, when Anna was diagnosed with breast cancer, both of them were surprised and upset. They could not imagine what could have given rise to the cancer. There was no breast cancer in Anna's family; she had felt that with her careful diet and regular exercise, she was not vulnerable to disease. The shock of her cancer was debilitating at first, but shortly after her surgery Anna began to fight back. Although her faith in her diet and exercise had been somewhat shaken by the cancer experience, she continued to believe that these were the best ways she had of fighting the cancer, and so she threw herself back into her health program with renewed vigor. She increased her running, cut red meat out of her diet altogether, and added cruciferous vegetables and fruits high in beta-carotene in an effort to fight the cancer.

When I interviewed her, she had just learned that the cancer had recurred. Her efforts to control her body had been disconfirmed dramatically, not once but twice. Essentially, then, she was in circumstances very similar to those of Seligman's rat. Recognizing the significance of her situation, I asked cautiously how she had responded when the recurrence developed in spite of her renewed efforts at good health. She shrugged and said she guessed she'd been wrong. She did not abandon her healthy lifestyle, but rather decided to redirect her energies in a new direction. She quit her dull job and used her remaining time to write short stories—something she had always wanted to do. Having lost control in one area of her life, she turned to another area, her work life, that was still controllable.

When Seligman's rat received electric shock, it responded by cowering in its cage, and when it was moved to a new environment, it did the same. Anna did not. In effect, she pressed the bar in the new cage. Was Anna unusual in her response to her repeatedly frustrating circumstances? This is a question that remains for science to answer definitively, but evidence to date suggests that she was not.[53]

MEDICAL DECISION MAKING AND SETBACKS

One of the ways in which people achieve control in threatening circumstances is by becoming actively involved in the decisions that are made concerning those circumstances. Nowhere is this clearer than in research with medical patients. Becoming actively involved in the selection of treatments, for example, is one way in which patients whose sense of control is otherwise threatened by the disease can retain some semblance of control over their lives. Despite this potential opportunity for control, there is the risk that the effort will fail, that the treatment will not cure the disease, or that it may backfire, leaving the patient with a sense of having been instrumental in his or her own demise. For this reason, psychologists and physicians have feared that if patients play an active role in treatment decisions and those decisions later fail, they may be put in a position of blaming themselves for their worsened circumstances. Patients might be better off, these critics argue, by being in a position to blame the medical establishment, their physicians, or even fate itself than to be placed in the unhappy position of wondering if they made the correct decision.[54]

These concerns take on added significance as legislation increasingly mandates that patients be actively involved in treatment choices. Informed consent is now a standard part of medical procedures. Even when patients do not actually choose the particular treatments they will undergo, they must be fully informed about potential negative side effects, so they can refuse treatment if they wish.[55] For some patients, particularly older ones, this can be a very stressful situation. They are used to having physicians and other medical authorities make decisions for them, and being informed about potential risks is stressful. They would rather the decisions be made for them without their active involvement. Despite these potential problems, the pressures for informed consent are increasing rather than decreasing. Some ethicists argue that any circumstances with a range of options for treatment should involve patients actively in the treatment process.[56] But these ethical concerns create an ethical issue of their own: When a treatment fails, who is worse off? The patient who had no role in selecting the treatment and is simply a victim of its adverse outcome? Or the patient who actively selected that treatment from an array of choices and therefore could be said to bear some responsibility for the choice?

Some years ago, a colleague and I became interested in this question concerning decisions regarding treatment for kidney disease. We interviewed a group of people who had been on dialysis for their kidney disorders and who were given the option of a kidney transplant.[57] When a person has kidney disease, it often means that the kidneys are operating at very low efficiency or have shut down altogether. Dialysis is a procedure for cleaning the blood of the wastes that build up because the kidneys, which normally perform this function, are unable to do so. The procedure is stressful and uncomfortable. It involves being hooked up to a machine several hours a day to drain and replenish the blood. Even when the patient is not actually on dialysis, he or she can experience fatigue, disorientation, and depression as a result of the toxins that gradually build up in the body. Most patients hope for an opportunity to get a transplant.

However, there are risks as well as benefits to this procedure. In order to receive a transplanted kidney from another body, the immune system must be suppressed in advance through drugs so that the kidney will not be rejected as foreign tissue when it is transplanted. This procedure makes the person vulnerable to other disorders governed by the immune system. Immunosuppression can, for example, lead to unchecked infectious disease or it can promote the growth of a malignancy. Transplant candidates are aware of these risks when they choose to undergo a transplant.

We interviewed twenty-six people who had been put in this position. We asked them how much of a role they felt they had had in the decision to undergo a transplant, and all of them said that they had been actively involved in the decision. Moreover, all of them were clearly aware of the risks they had incurred in agreeing to the transplant. Normally, there is about a 50 percent chance that a kidney transplant will succeed; in our group, as expected, half of the patients had successful transplants. The transplants had failed for the other patients, and they returned to dialysis. Interviews with this latter group revealed that concerns that a failed treatment decision would lead to self-blame and depression were misplaced. Virtually all of the patients whose transplants had failed believed they had made the right decision, despite the fact that several had developed diseases as a consequence. One woman was actually dying of an advanced malignancy that had developed rapidly when her immune functioning was suppressed by the pretransplant drugs. Despite the fact that she was losing her life as a result of the treatment failure, she told us: "I know I did the right thing. I really didn't have any other choice. On dialysis, we couldn't travel or anything. I know that, even though I am dying from this transplant, it was the only thing we could have done."[58]

How were the patients able to sustain such perceptions in the face of treatment failure? Their psychological responses are best expressed by comparing them with those whose transplants succeeded. Although the two groups had virtually identical medical situations prior to the transplant, their perceptions of the predecision circumstances differed dramatically in the context of the known outcome. When asked to reflect on the decision they had made regarding their treatment, successfully transplanted patients perceived that several options had existed and that they had clearly selected the best one. In contrast, patients with failed transplants perceived that they had little choice but to make the decision they had made. In fact, both groups had received the same options and had been involved to the same degree in the decision-making process. The perception of no choice among those whose transplants had failed, then, represented the way in which these patients had come to terms with their adverse circumstances. By arguing that they had had no choice in the matter, they could avoid blaming themselves or anyone else for the problems that resulted.

If we return to the haunting vision of Seligman's rat for a moment and compare it with what we see in humans who have been tried and tested in similar ways, there emerges a very different picture from that painted by learned helplessness. Instead of a frightened animal cowering in a corner, we see a person actively striving to exert control in circumstances that might seem uncontrollable from the outside. Instead of an apathetic reaction to a new environment, we see people struggling to reinterpret circumstances of failure and seeking new environments in which to exert control. In brief, we see triumph.

Why is there so little indication of helplessness and learned helplessness in people who would seem to be so vulnerable? Clearly, the circumstances of the rat and the human are different. The rat's world is simple, consisting of a cage, a bar, and the fact of electric shock. The rat has but one very low-level and limited goal, namely to escape the shock. Perhaps more important is that it has few opportunities to meet this goal. It can run around the cage and press the bar to no avail, or it can give up. The human, in contrast, lives in a rich environment and has many goals. Goals can be met in different ways, and if one response fails, another effort may be attempted. The world is not a cage; it is broader in its options and its implications. Possibilities may suggest themselves in even the most challenging circumstances. Because the human being has higher needs than the rat, it has many potential ways of achieving them. Any particular choice may be only one of many ways of achieving the goal. If one knows the overarching goal or need that a person has, one can look for its expression in different forms. People suffering from life-threatening illnesses have the goal of controlling their circumstances. Finding that one avenue to doing so is blocked, they might seek out another, and another, and continue seeking if the successive options are blocked. These examples are not intended to suggest that a person will respond to a failed transplant or other failed treatment with equanimity and a shrug of the shoulders. Setbacks are very upsetting, but the distress may not be permanent. In general, a person adjusts to setbacks by pursuing the same goal with whatever means remain.[59]

Behavior in complex environments, then, must be thought of as serving multiple goals through multiple means. Individual efforts, like efforts to exert control, must be thought of not as individual responses to be observed in isolation, but rather as elements of general themes that are themselves made up of many thoughts and behaviors. Consequently, when one choice is thwarted, it may not block the entire goal. Disconfirmation of some single effort at control, though experienced as a setback, does not remove the option of seeking other methods to achieve this same goal.

THE SEARCH FOR MEANING

Victimizing events present people with many losses and challenges. Some of these involve fundamental activities, such as the search for shelter, food, and clothing. Others involve restoring psychological needs, such as the sense of mastery and a belief in one's self-worth. Those who have been victimized will also often use their unfortunate circumstances not merely to restore and heal themselves but also to move beyond the event. Part of this search involves finding meaning in the experience, a need to understand why the event occurred, what its impact has been, and whether it signifies any value or purpose ultimately. In many respects, finding meaning in adverse circumstances is the most remarkable of the adaptive powers of the mind, for it is the process that often advances people not only beyond their victimizing circumstances, but beyond any point that they might have reached in their lives without their tragic experiences.[60]

Victims ask, "Why me?" and thus for some, the question of meaning centers on the factors that gave rise to the victimizing event. For example, a heart attack victim learns that he must change his diet, get more exercise, and stop smoking. But in addition, he may come to see the event as symbolic, a warning to him that the course of his life must change if it is to be a long and rewarding one. Thus, the heart attack becomes reinterpreted not as a frightening and stressful event, but as a benign, cautionary one designed to jolt him out of his feelings of complacency regarding his lifestyle.[61]

Meaning and needs for mastery may be intertwined. For example, the victim of a disease may search his or her past behavior not only to see why the disease developed but also to find a way to understand life more generally. In the case of the heart attack victim, altering diet, getting exercise, and stopping smoking are the means by which control can be asserted. Meaning is the construal of the event as the fortunate warning. In some cases, then, the search for meaning from the victimizing experience results in a reinterpretation of the event as a useful, even necessary part of life.[62]

Other events cannot be as easily construed as inherently meaningful.[63] Why an infant child died of Sudden Infant Death Syndrome or why an adolescent was struck down by a speeding car are not questions that can be easily answered in a meaningful way. In such cases, a search for meaning may center on what the implications of the event are for the future. For example, Norma Phillips may not have been able to find any meaning in the untimely death of her daughter, Sherry, who was killed by a drunk driver at the age of sixteen. The event, however, did give her life a valuable new direction as she founded the organization Mothers Against Drunk Driving (MADD), which seeks to impose stiffer penalties on those convicted of driving under the influence of alcohol. Similarly, the death of young Adam West, who was kidnapped from a shopping center and senselessly murdered, has no intrinsic solace to the family of the child or to anyone else familiar with the case. Yet John West, Adam's father, used this unwelcome event to develop a national network of child-finding services that identifies missing children and develops ways to locate them. Theresa Soldana, the young actress who was repeatedly stabbed by a deranged fan, used her experience to found the national group Victims for Victims, which develops legislation to protect victims' rights. In her article "Thanks for the Recession," Cynthia Hollander wrote about hard times:

Through our economic crisis we discovered that you can lower your standard of living and be happy—probably happier than we were before. We are better people than we were two years ago when we were crying over the loss of our home. Hard times have taught us a valuable lesson that we all recite idiotically but few of us really believe: material possessions do not make you happy. For every material thing we gave up, we gained something of greater value.[64]

Tragic events are not themselves beneficial, but victims are sometimes able to put their tragic experiences to the best possible use, working actively so that the same unfortunate outcome will not befall others.

Most commonly, a victimizing event does not itself provide meaning, but rather sets into gear a deliberate evaluation of one's self and circumstances in order to find better ways of living. In recent interviews with breast cancer patients, more than half of the women reported that the cancer experience had caused them to reappraise their lives. For example, one sixty-one-year-old woman stated:

You can take a picture of what someone has done, but when you frame it, it becomes significant. I feel as if I were, for the first time, really conscious. My life is framed in a certain amount of time. I always knew it, but I can see it, and it's made better by the knowledge.[65]

In some cases, the meaning derived from this life-threatening experience brought a new attitude toward life.

I have much more enjoyment of each day, each moment. I am not so worried about what is or isn't or what I wish I had. All those things you get entangled with don't seem to be part of my life right now.[66]

For others, the meaning gained from the experience was self-knowledge or self-change.

The ability to understand myself more fully is one of the greatest changes I have experienced. I have faced what I went through. It's a bit like holding up a mirror to one's face when one can't turn around. I think that is a very essential thing.[67]

When life seems to stretch out endlessly, a person may avoid taking an active role in structuring the use of every day. Such effort seems unnecessary because there is so much time. However, to those whose time on earth is threatened, each day seems valuable in its own right. Consequently, victimizing events often prompt people to reorder their priorities, giving low value to such mundane concerns as housework, petty quarrels, or involvement in other people's small problems, and high priority to relationships with spouse, children, and friends; to personal projects; or just to enjoying life. A cancer patient noted:

You take a long look at your life and realize that many things you thought were important before are totally insignificant. That's probably been the major change in my life. What you do is put things into perspective. You find out things like relationships are really the most important things you have—the people you know and your family—everything else is just way down the line. It's very strange that it takes something serious to make you realize that.[68]

By emphasizing the adaptive aspects of people's responses to victimizing events, one runs the risk of inadvertently representing tragedy primarily as an opportunity for personal growth. Not everyone who is a victim of a threatening event is able to find meaning in that event and derive benefit from it. Moreover, even when a person has been able to find meaning in a threatening event, it does not undo the suffering the event creates. Some events seem to be less conducive to finding meaning than others. Norma Phillips and John West are unhappily infrequent examples of the ability to turn the tragic loss of a child into a meaningful event. Many people who have lost a family member abruptly to a senseless personal tragedy are not able to do so. Rather, the most that they can achieve is to put the event behind them eventually, and get on with life.[69]

Those whose victimizations have occurred at the hands of others—victims of assault, rape, and incest, for example—also have difficulty finding meaning in the events.[70] Psychologist Roxanne Silver has for many years worked with victims of childhood incest experiences. These victims, many of whom had been molested by people they trusted—uncles, brothers, cousins, stepfathers, and even natural fathers—were sometimes more than fifty years from the experience, yet the poisonous residue of the incest remained. Years after the events, these women were still struggling to understand why they had been abused and whether there was anything to be understood from the experience. Although some of the victims had managed to put the events behind them, others struggled daily and unsuccessfully, trying to understand the meaning of the events.[71]

Victims of natural disasters and life-threatening illnesses, on the other hand, seem more able to find meaning, if not in the events themselves, then in their lives as a result of the victimizing experience. In one study of cancer patients, for example, nearly every person interviewed indicated there had been positive as well as negative changes in their lives as a consequence of the cancer.[72]

The search for meaning, then, seems to be a common outgrowth of a victimizing experience, and for many it is a successful search. In some cases, it centers on the question of why the events happened. For others, the challenge is to find a way to turn the event into something positive that can be accomplished for humanity. For a third group, the event prompts a close examination of the purpose of life, enabling them to structure their lives along more meaningful lines. Yet some who struggle with the question of meaning never find any. Exactly who these people are and which events are less likely to yield a successful search for meaning remain questions to be answered. What is clear is that many are able to find hope and benefit in events that others perceive to be tragedies in their pure and horrible form.

ILLUSIONS AND VICTIMIZATION

> An oyster, confronted with a grain of sand, creates a pearl.[73]
> —GEORGE VAILLANT

Biologists frequently note that the more they know about the human body, the more miraculous it becomes. The recuperative powers of the mind merit similar awe. The process of adjusting to threat, although often time consuming and not always successful, restores many people to happy and productive lives and inspires others to find new meaning and purpose. Meaning is addressed by finding a causal explanation for the experience and restructuring the purpose of one's life as a result of the setback. Mastery involves efforts to gain control over the threatening event in particular and over one's life more generally. Self-enhancement occurs by construing personal benefit from the experience, by comparing oneself with others who are less fortunate, and by focusing on aspects of one's own situation that make one appear to be well off. These active efforts to adapt are, in part, based on illusions—that is, beliefs that have no factual basis or that require looking at the facts in an optimistic way. Yet despite this unrealistic quality, illusions often help victims overcome adverse circumstances, and as such, they occupy a special place in the roster of human capabilities.

CHAPTER 6

Illusion, Mania, and Depression: A View from Mental Illness

> When you see through life's illusions, there lies the danger.
> —JACKSON BROWNE
> (paraphrased from "Fountain of Sorrow")

ALTHOUGH positive illusions have the risk of creating blind spots and gaps in perception and thought, in fact, the normal mind is highly responsive to threat in ways that make adaptive use of negative information while simultaneously preserving the benign integrity of the self and its positive view of the world. But what about the unhealthy mind? Do mentally ill people also hold adaptive positive illusions? Or do they lack these qualities that seem to promote mental health in others? No tidy generalizations can be made about the beliefs of the mentally ill, for the category includes a diverse assortment of unrelated disorders. However, two particular forms of mental illness—namely, mania and depression—provide useful comparisons for the healthy mind, because particular beliefs about the self, the world, and the future feature prominently in their symptomatology. In mania, the illusions of normal thought are magnified. Instead of mild self-aggrandizement, illusions of control, and overly optimistic visions of the future, there are extreme visions of prominence and power. By contrast, in depression, there is no self-aggrandizement, only a dismal view of the self, trapped in a hopeless world lacking in opportunity.

The comparisons with normal thought afforded by these extreme and opposite portraits are instructive in several ways. They help define the adaptive limits of positive illusions by illustrating the consequences of their excess in mania and their absence in depression. More important, they provide opportunities to examine the criteria usually associated with mental health in the context of very different views of the self, the world, and the future. If positive illusions are essential elements of mental health, then their absence or exaggeration in depression and mania, respectively, should lead to corresponding changes in mood, relations with others, motivation, and thought.

Before we embark upon this analysis, some cautions need to be raised regarding the limitations of drawing inferences about normal human functioning from studies of psychopathology. Mental illnesses such as depression and mania are characterized by biochemical and possibly even genetic underpinnings that contribute to their development and symptomatology; as a result, there is a certain discontinuity between these illnesses and the functioning of the normal human mind. As instructive exercises regarding the effects of illusions, depression and mania are useful comparison points only in their mild forms. At the extremes of the diseases, the parallels cease to be instructive, because beliefs about the self, the world, and the future become insignificant in the context of the disorientation and confusion of mania or the lethargic unresponsiveness of depression.

AN EXCURSION INTO MANIA

> There's a pleasure, sure in being mad, which none but madmen know.
>
> —JOHN DRYDEN

Mania is a mental illness marked by many of the perceptions that normal individuals hold in more restrained form: an exaggerated sense of one's talents and accomplishments, illusions about one's impact and ability to exert control, and unrealistic optimism. It is one of the rarer mental illnesses, and it usually occurs as part of a manic-depressive syndrome. Victims of this disease find their moods alternating over several weeks or months from extreme elation, energy, and activity to the depths of despair, without any seeming ability to control the mood swings. Some patients who have manic-depressive disease must be hospitalized for most of their lives, whereas others are able to function in the world, being maintained by drugs such as lithium, which control these aberrant mood swings.[1] Even so, there are some curious parallels between the experiences of the normal human mind and those with this particular madness.

Of the two extremes, depression has occasioned more research interest than mania because it is potentially more dangerous. Victims of manic-depressive disease are vulnerable to suicide in the depressive state; when not suicidal, they are intensely unhappy. The manic phase of this illness has been considered somewhat less important because, although it can be debilitating and disorientating in the extreme, it can produce pleasure for its victims in its early or mild form. Indeed, many manic-depressive patients cannot be induced to take their mood-controlling drugs on a regular basis, because the lithium not only protects them from depression but mutes the pleasurable elation that accompanies mania as well. Treatment raises the fear that the wonderful enthusiasm and excitement, the sleepless nights of fanciful creations, the thrilling sexual encounters, and the feeling that one's capabilities are boundless will all disappear. A sixty-two-year-old lawyer described his manic periods: "I literally enjoyed the manic phases. I was a big shot, on top of the world. I spent not only my own money, but everyone else's I could get my hands on—I bought six suits at a time, a lot of stupid unnecessary things."[2]

Mania is an enticing madness, an excursion into a world in which all one's fantasies of power, accomplishment, and sexual prowess can seem true. In its early or mild stages, mania is marked by good will toward others, self-reliance, high self-esteem, unflappable happiness, and no apparent problems. The manic person is playful, even festive, in ways that can be infectious. Manic people are often more quick witted than others and can consequently draw others into the fun because they are so sociable and entertaining. The manic person has boundless energy and seemingly limitless ability to accomplish things. Accompanying this is a supreme confidence that any undertaking will be successful.

Indeed, mania seems to change the personality altogether. Some years ago, I worked in a large mental hospital and encountered an unforgettable manic episode. On a back ward lived a stooped little man in his mid-fifties who kept to himself, rarely talked, and never smiled. Overshadowed by the more colorful paranoid schizophrenics and psychopaths, he never participated in ward activities and games. The aides and student volunteers hardly knew that he was there.

One day he began to grow more active. At first he joined activities, and then he began to organize them. His previous withdrawal turned to sociability, then garrulousness. At one ward picnic, he had the staff and students spellbound with witty banter and fascinating stories of his colorful prehospitalization exploits, which centered around him as a hero. He became increasingly self-confident and likable, and even seemed to grow more physically attractive as he flirted outrageously with the nurses and female volunteers.

His energy grew with each day. He developed a complex plan for world peace and an elaborate scheme to secure his discharge from the hospital. He began to wander the halls at night, having imaginary conversations with world leaders and television heroes. When the aides tried to subdue him, he became physically and verbally abusive. Soon he could not be managed on the ward at all. No ward activity could be undertaken, for soon he would literally leap into the middle of it, dancing and laughing and so dominating the activity that nothing could be carried on unless it centered around him. Finally, one afternoon he was removed from the ward and was not seen for several weeks. When he returned, he was once again the withdrawn, stooped little man he had been before the manic episode.

Most of us have had enough experience with manic-like states to know how attractive they can be. A sudden burst of insight that brings a solution to a difficult problem, an unexpected accomplishment, or the admiring esteem of others is addictive. When an undertaking is new and promising, one may forsake sleep, food, and all social activity for the singleminded pursuit of it. This kind of exhilarating and promising involvement often characterizes the early stages of mania. As psychologist Kay Jamison, an expert on mania, has written, "Who would not want an illness that numbers among its symptoms elevated and expansive mood, inflated self-esteem, more energy than usual, decreased need for help, hypersexuality, sharpened and unusually creative thinking, and increased productivity?"[3]

Even this cursory look at mania reveals some suggestive parallels with normal thought. The normal person's positive beliefs about the self, the world, and the future are associated with happiness, sociability, motivation, and heightened activity. In the manic person, these same beliefs taken to an extreme foster an extraordinarily good mood, unrelenting sociable behavior, and boundless energy and enthusiasm. Moreover, just as normal illusions may contribute to creative intellectual functioning, so there may also be parallels in mania. As scientific attention has focused on manic episodes, it has become evident that mania may actually facilitate the creative process, at least in some individuals. That is, mania may not merely lend energy and enthusiasm to projects that would otherwise languish from inattention, it may actually promote them.

MANIA AND CREATIVITY

> One must harbor chaos within oneself to give birth to a dancing star.
>
> —NIETZSCHE

> There is no great genius without some touch of madness.
>
> —SENECA

The idea of a connection between madness and creativity has been in existence for centuries. Pre-Grecian myths represented the artist as possessed by madness, and philosophers from Aristotle to William James have mused on the role that insanity may play in genius.[4] Emil Kraepelin, the German psychiatrist who first identified the manic syndrome in the 1800s, noted that the excitement that accompanies mania may actually "set free powers that otherwise would be constrained by inhibitions."[5] Mania is not, he argued, sufficient to produce genius, but coupled with latent ability, it can make those talents explicit and give voice to gifts that would otherwise be silent.

Anecdotal evidence for the prevalence of mania and manic-depressive illness among creative geniuses is plentiful. Composers George Frederick Handel, Hector Berlioz, and Robert Schumann are all reputed to have suffered from manic-depressive illness. Handel is said to have written *The Messiah* in twenty-four days during a manic episode. Writers and poets are also prominently featured among the ranks of manic-depressives, and include Eugene O'Neill, Honoré Balzac, Virginia Woolf, Ernest Hemingway, F. Scott Fitzgerald, Lord Byron, Percy Bysshe Shelley, Samuel Taylor Coleridge, Edgar

Allen Poe, Thomas Chatterton, Hart Crane, Robert Lowell, Anne Sexton, and Sylvia Plath. In a close examination of the creative processes of these geniuses, psychologists Kay Jamison and Steven Goodwin culled available biographies and autobiographies for clues about the concomitants of this disease. From those accounts, it appears that many of the finest accomplishments of these geniuses were accomplished during the early stages of their manic episodes.[6]

The prevalence of manic-depressive illness among documented geniuses is more than five times the rate in the normal population; thus, manic-depressive illness appears to be an element in creative genius. As the list of its victims implies, it may be especially prevalent among poets. Indeed, the number of mad poets is astonishing and has been the topic of both literary volumes and musings by poets themselves for decades. Literary critic Anatole Broyard described the later years of poet Delmore Schwartz: "Delmore talked like a man whose life passes in review before his eyes at an awful speed. His nervous system became his typewriter. He was under siege, bombarded by stimuli."[7] The nineteenth-century French poet Baudelaire wrote, "I cultivate my hysteria with joy and terror."[8] Pulitzer Prize–winning poet Robert Lowell wrote to another Pulitzer Prize–winning poet, Theodore Roethke:

How wierdly our lives have often gone the same way. Let's say we are brothers, have gone the same journey and know far more about each other than we have ever said or will say. That's a strange fact about poets of roughly our age. It's this, that to write, we seem to have to go at it with such a single-minded intensity that we are always on the point of drowning. I have seen this so many times, and year after year with students that I feel it's something almost unavoidable, some flaw in the motor.[9]

Exactly how does mania enhance the creative enterprise? One possibility is that mania speeds up thought in a way that fosters creativity.[10] To take an extreme example, it may be difficult to be creative if good ideas come every hour or so, but when good ideas or insights come in rapid succession, a momentum is created which itself may further the creative process. Moreover, since mania increases the number of ideas and associations an individual has, it may also increase the likelihood that at least some of those ideas or associations will be good ones. Assuming that the manic individual has the insight to jettison the poor ideas and to cultivate the good ones, then the apparent benefit of mania may lie in the likelihood that at least some ideas generated will be worth pursuing.

Another possibility is that mania does not speed up thought as much as it loosens it up. Whereas normally people think in a relatively linear and orderly fashion, mania may have the effect of freeing associations, permitting a person to combine and recombine ideas in unusual ways. In this context, Jamison and Goodwin speculate that, more than is true for the other arts, poetry is closely tied to primitive thought processes. As a result, mania may actually facilitate creativity among poets by putting them in touch with their more primitive perceptions. Manic thought may be characterized by more novelty and flexibility than is usually true, which can ultimately lead to creative poetic combinations.

Others have argued that the role of mania in the creative processes is intrinsic to the disease itself and not some by-product of its impact on thought processes. In its extreme forms, mania alters sensory experiences. A common symptom of mania is hyperacusis, the heightening of sensory experiences. Individuals in the manic phase are often unable to block out the vast amounts of stimulation they experience, or they may be unable to tone down these stimuli, which is a function of the normal mind. In the extreme, this experience may disrupt functioning altogether, but in a less extreme form, it can produce novel and creative ideas and associations. For example, the delusions and hallucinations that Martin Luther, the religious leader, suffered during his manic episodes may have contributed to the development of the Protestant religion.[11] Alternatively, the experience of mania coupled with depression may create a sheer range and depth of emotion that produces insight. By providing the artist with depths of untapped and irrational resources and experience, it may produce material for creativity.[12]

MANIA AND LEADERSHIP

The apparent benefits of mania are not limited to artistic creativity. There is mounting evidence that manic-depressive illness is also unusually common among the great leaders of the world. Winston Churchill, Robert E. Lee, Abraham Lincoln, Napoleon Bonaparte, Benito Mussolini, Oliver Cromwell, and Lord Nelson are all believed to have suffered from manic-depressive illness.[13] Historians have argued that the euphoria of mania and the confidence it produces can be a major asset for the manic leader in the face of real or potential adversity. For example, in his biography of Winston Churchill, Anthony Storr notes that Churchill's mania, with its accompanying unrealistic optimism, may have helped him to inspire the British people during the dark days of the Second World War. A more sober man, Storr noted, might have concluded that all was lost.[14] Anthropologist Lionel Tiger has speculated on the adaptive value of the manic leader for communities more generally:

> Perhaps the strident exuberance of the manic phase is an energizing and unsettling stimulus to communities otherwise too complacent and unchanging. Certainly there are indications of this in the religious field, where certain individuals with improbably grandiose ideas, coupled with very imperious attitudes toward others, may produce charismatic religions or political groups which often have extraordinary effects on formerly settled social systems.[15]

One need not look at the biographies and autobiographies of great leaders and creative geniuses to see the positive impact that mania can exert. Mania is unique among the mental illnesses in an important respect: it is the only mental disorder that is associated with upward social mobility. Usually the costs of mental disorder are substantial. The mentally ill may be committed to institutions or left to wander the streets in search of food and shelter. In contrast, manic-depressive illness is disproportionately a disorder of the upper social classes, and those who develop it, at least in its mild form, are more rather than less likely to rise in social status.[16]

THE DARKER SIDE OF MANIA

Lest mania be thought a disorder worth having, its dark side must be revealed. Since mania in isolation is relatively rare, existing instead as part of the manic-depressive syndrome, one of the chief risks is depression. The person who enjoys aspects of the manic episode must also experience the alternating despair of depression. Thomas Chatterton, Virginia Woolf, Ernest Hemingway, Anne Sexton, and Sylvia Plath may have had their creative visions facilitated and enriched by their manic episodes, but each died by his or her own hand during a period of depression.

Mania itself also has drawbacks. The point at which it facilitates creative genius or leadership may be in the hypomanic stage, that is, just as mania is coming on, before it has reached its extremes. In the early stages of mania, people may be highly productive, but as the mania becomes more extreme, productivity becomes more apparent than real. A person in the extremes of the manic phase is highly distractable and may move from project to project with little ability to devote attention to any one project in depth. Manic individuals may suffer delusions of persecution or grandeur and may even develop hallucinations. Experiencing sensations intensely can become so extreme that the manic person is overwhelmed by every smell, feels each breeze as a touch, and hears even the smallest sound as a clang-ing distraction. The disorientation of mania may be so complete that the person cannot even recognize familiar environments. This in itself can lead to panic.

Mania can also have devastating social consequences. Al-though a manic individual can be highly entertaining and witty, he or she will also often engage in silly and extreme behavior that can embarrass or upset others. For example, a college stu-dent who was later hospitalized for mania attempted to woo back his increasingly terrified girlfriend by engaging in a num-ber of extravagant gestures, including having an enormous bou-quet of flowers delivered to her in the middle of a lecture class of three hundred students. Many victims of mania feel in-tensely sexual during their manic episodes and will move from partner to partner with abandon and concomitant risk. Mania can give rise to extraordinary spending sprees, in which people shop uncontrollably for items they neither want nor need. A manic entrepreneur can be highly manipulative, pulling others into fanciful and often risky projects, only to thrust the blame on his companions when the ventures ultimately fail. Thus, while the manic person can be socially engaging in the early stages of mania, eventually the extreme behavior prompted by this syndrome will drive away those initially attracted to the exuberant person.

Moreover, although mania in its early stages can produce charismatic leadership and witty, entertaining banter, at its ex-treme it can lead to abusive anger and hostility. When thwarted, a manic person can become very angry and easily upset by seemingly harmless comments or observations that anyone else would ignore. The manic person is highly sensitive to criticism and can turn quickly from expansive friendship to abusive hostility. A common gambit of the manic individual is to single out one acquaintance for abuse and entertain the other friends in the social circle by picking on the one designated target. Mania, then, is not a desirable mental state. Although its early phases can be exhilarating, producing inspired work with the accompanying thrill of accomplishment, as it progresses the individual feels out of control, with no ability to tone down the extreme emotions.

There is, nonetheless, valuable information in analyses of the manic experience. The potential lessons of mania are several. First, even in their unbridled form, unrealistic optimism, exaggerated perceptions of one's own powers and abilities, and a heightened sense of control can be temporarily adaptive. Moreover, in mania, these beliefs appear to be adaptive in many of the same ways as normal illusions. Self-aggrandizing beliefs in mania are associated with positive mood, sociability, high levels of motivation, and creative thought processes, just as their less extreme forms are associated with these adaptive outcomes in the mentally healthy person. In two areas, mania appears to confer extreme benefits, at least in those with latent talents and at least during the early phases. Mania may facilitate the ability to attract and to lead others and promote creative genius, both by enhancing motivation and possibly by modifying creative thought processes as well.

Is there any reason to believe that people who hold the positive illusions of normal thought could become manic as a result of their self-aggrandizing beliefs? It is easy to see why this might be a concern. Even normal people have experiences that are reminiscent of manic episodes. In the first excitement of a new idea, a writer or artist may work furiously, forgetting to eat or sleep. When nudged into a more controlled state of mind, the distraction may be so irritating that manic-like symptoms such as the paranoid belief that people are trying to stop one's endeavors may result. Entrepreneurs beginning new businesses sometimes experience a manic-like phase in the early days when they and their associates plan a new project at a frenzied pace. The infectious enthusiasm and charismatic leadership of the entrepreneur can sound very much like the qualities associated with leaders suffering from mania. But merely because we resonate to the experience of the manic individual through occasional isolated episodes of our own does not mean either that normal people are prone to mania or that mild illusions could catapult a person into full-blown mania. Mania is not a disease that results from beliefs. Though its causes are not fully known, genetic links and chemical imbalances are clearly implicated. Moreover, its clinical rarity in itself belies the fear that it is somehow intrinsically connected to the positive illusions that most people hold. The illusions that people have about themselves, the world, and the future are mild ones, and the evidence indicates that there is little danger of their lurching into more sinister distortions of reality.[17]

DEPRESSION AND THE LOSS OF ILLUSION

In its mild form, mania provides a useful counterpoint to the normal illusions of everyday life by showing that, even when carried to extremes, positive self-regard, faith in personal control, and unrealistic optimism can have certain adaptive consequences, at least for a time. Depression provides another useful point of reference, for similar reasons. Much of the research that has documented the prevalence and adaptiveness of positive illusions in normal people has implicitly or explicitly compared them with mildly depressed people or people in a sad mood to show the maladaptive impact of the loss or absence of illusions.

Depression is primarily an aberration of mood, a determined gloominess that pervades perception.[18] The depressed person regards the self, the world, and the future through mud-colored glasses. Nothing holds joy or promise. A depressed person typically sees work and leisure activities as trivial and without value, and the past life as worthless and full of little but failure. Moreover, there seems little prospect for improvement. Activities that may have been satisfying prior to the onset of depression seem to lose their attraction altogether, and if the depressed person is able to work at all, it is usually at the lowest level. Indeed, many depressed people stop going to work and lose interest in other activities. The severely depressed person is unable even to get out of bed and fulfill the basic tasks of survival.[19]

Maggie Scarf, the author of *The Sorrowful Sex,* describes one of the depressed women she interviewed.

> She told me . . . that she felt as if she were "litter." She was, she said, like a piece of drifting newspaper, "something that's just floating around, being blown around the sidewalk, underfoot, you know, being kicked aside. . . ." She was excess matter in the universe, unwanted and without value. . . . She'd come home after successfully playing in a tennis tournament and suddenly felt "as if the bottom were dropping out of my life, and that I was a nothing, that I'd promised to do too many things I didn't care about for too many people I didn't give a damn about. I was on all these committees, and running like crazy, but it was stupid and meaningless. And I wanted out—to quit trying—to be dead." While her children were at school, she had emptied the medicine cabinet and swallowed everything in sight.[20]

Indeed, suicide is the biggest risk of depression. About 5 percent of the people who are chronically depressed actually kill themselves.[21] Others consider it and think how nice it would be to fall asleep and not wake up, or to have a sudden accident. Civil War general Robert E. Lee, who was plagued by bouts of depression throughout his life, was said to believe that death would be a welcome release from the world.[22]

DEPRESSIVE REALISM

Clearly, the depressed person is lacking in the positive illusions that most people hold. The self, the world, and the future are seen negatively. For the past hundred years or so, psychologists and psychiatrists have assumed that these negative perceptions involved distortions of reality. In recent years, however, evidence has accumulated to suggest that, rather than having a negatively biased view of the world, mildly depressed people may see at least some things quite realistically. In fact, the mildly depressed appear to have more accurate views of themselves, the world, and the future than do normal people.

It is hard to spend much time with someone who is depressed. For one thing, it is painful to see anyone in misery. But a more subtle reason is that the musings of a depressed person begin to gnaw at you. The unhappy pronouncements begin to sound like insights rather than distortions, and you begin to catch not only the depressed person's mood but the depressed person's way of thinking. When the depressed person tells you that he or she has done nothing truly worthwhile in life, quite unconsciously one may begin a search for what has been worthwhile in one's own life, and as the mind scampers through the past, searching for a true accomplishment, it may be difficult to find one. Since the depressed person willingly dismisses his or her own modest successes as trivial, it is hard to do otherwise with one's own. Will anything any of us has done matter in a hundred years? The depressed person leads us down this unhappy path, forcing us to set our accomplishments in the context of centuries of achievement, inducing us to compare ourselves with Mozart, Leonardo da Vinci, or Newton. Depression can be contagious.

Freud was the first to note the kernel of truth that may reside in depressive thought. Writing about the depressed person, he stated:

> In certain self-accusations [the depressed person] seems to us justified, only that he has a keener eye for the truth than others who are not melancholic. When in his exacerbation of self-criticism, he describes himself as petty, egoistic, dishonest, lacking in independence, one whose sole aim

has been to hide the weaknesses of his own nature, for all we know it may be that he has come very near to self knowledge; we only wonder why a man must become ill before he can discover truth of this kind.[23]

Freud's observation slipped from view for several decades as psychological writings on depression emphasized the irrationality of depressive beliefs. Depressed people were regarded as filtering out positive experiences in their lives and amplifying negative ones. Recently, however, Freud's observation has come into relief as research evidence has mounted to suggest that it is in some respects true. Psychologists have coined the term "depressive realism" to refer to the observation that mildly depressed people actually have a somewhat more accurate view of reality, at least about certain things, than do people who are not depressed.[24]

Normal people exaggerate how competent and well liked they are. Depressed people do not. Normal people remember their past behavior with a rosy glow. Depressed people are more evenhanded in recalling their successes and failures. Normal people describe themselves primarily positively. Depressed people describe both their positive and negative qualities. Normal people take credit for successful outcomes and tend to deny responsibility for failure. Depressed people accept responsibility for both success and failure. Normal people exaggerate the control they have over what goes on around them. Depressed people are less vulnerable to the illusion of control. Normal people believe to an unrealistic degree that the future holds a bounty of good things and few bad things. Depressed people are more realistic in their perceptions of the future. In fact, on virtually every point on which normal people show enhanced self-regard, illusions of control, and unrealistic visions of the future, depressed people fail to show the same biases. "Sadder but wiser" does indeed appear to apply to depression.[25]

The discovery of depressive realism requires a major shift in thinking about this mental disorder. In the past, depression was thought to be characterized by negative biases in the processing of information. It must now be considered that depression itself may not engender biases, but rather may result from a lack of or loss of the positive biases that normally shelter people from the harsher side of reality. The depressed person may have a deficit, not a surfeit, of biases.

Lest depression be thought of primarily as a result of accurate conversance with the world, it must be noted that although realism can be a characteristic of depression, depression is not always realistic. In some of their perceptions, depressed people are not more accurate, they are just more negative; this is more true, the more severe the depression. Their vision of the future is often too gloomy for reality to sustain. They are sometimes haunted by feelings of guilt without any sense of what they may have done to make themselves feel guilty. Depressed people castigate themselves for imaginary flaws and oversights. Thus, depression, especially in its severe form, is characterized by unrealistic pessimism.[26] For that reason, it is the mild forms of depression that are instructive regarding the relationship of realistic perceptions and mood.

Depression functions as a useful counterpoint to normal thought for two reasons. First, depressive cognition, in its early or mild form, seems to be marked by a certain amount of realism, in contrast to the illusions that are present in the thinking of normal people. More important, as a circumstance in which normal illusion is lacking, depression provides the opportunity to see how the absence of these biases is associated with other attributes of mental health. That is, if positive views of the self, personal control, and the future lead to happiness, improved social relationships, and creative and productive work, would we not expect to see that the depressed person who lacks these illusions is unhappy, difficult to get along with socially, unproductive, and less prone to creative enterprise?

DEPRESSION AND THE ATTRIBUTES OF MENTAL HEALTH

Asking if depression is associated with unhappiness is like asking if salt is found in a salt mine. Unhappiness is one of the disorder's main characteristics. Just as positive illusions seem to foster self-confidence and high self-esteem, depressed people suffer from feelings of worthlessness and helplessness. At best, their lives are emotionally flat, without feeling; at worst, they deteriorate into a morass of pessimism and despair.

In terms of social relationships, one of the most problematic aspects of depression is that depressed people often drive away others who could be supportive and helpful to them. Depressed people may have deficient social skills to begin with.[27] To the extent that they have had a history of depression, they may have been oriented inward toward their own flaws and faults rather than outward, and consequently failed to learn the social skills that normal people acquire as a matter of course. Depression itself exerts a negative effect on social relationships. Typically, when a person becomes depressed, someone close, such as a spouse or other family member, will attempt to provide support. Depression is so persistent, however, that the depressed person effectively disparages many of these supportive efforts and the unrelenting negativity eventually drives other people away. Indeed, marital disturbance, separation, and divorce are some of the most common social consequences of depression.[28]

Whereas mentally healthy people are active, the depressed person's activity level is extremely low. As Sir Joshua Billings wrote, "I never knew a man troubled with melancholy who had plenty to do and did it." Everything is an effort. Depressed people tire easily, feel exhausted, and are typically unable to make concerted efforts to achieve goals. They have little motivation to undertake tasks and often lose their appetites for food and sex altogether. They have difficulty falling asleep but they are chronically tired.

In severe cases, there is often complete paralysis of the will. The patient has no desire to do anything, even those things that are essential to life. Consequently, he may be relatively immobile unless prodded or pushed into activity by others. It is sometimes necessary to push the patient out of bed, wash, dress and feed him. In extreme cases, even communication may be blocked by the patient's inertia.[29]

Depressed people have long been recognized as less competent than people who are not depressed, but until recently their poor functioning was thought to be due to their low motivation and consequent inability to achieve their goals. There is now evidence that depressed people may actually be less capable of creative, insightful thought than nondepressed people. In particular, the thought processes of depressed people are disturbed in ways exactly opposite to those fostered by positive illusions. Depressed people show less complex thought processes than nondepressed people. They use fewer categories to make sense of information than nondepressed people, and the categories they do use tend to be quite simple ones, such as good and bad, black and white.[30]

The tendency to organize information very simply and into diametrically opposite categories extends to the self, and moreover, may actually exacerbate depression. Work by psychologist Patricia Linville and her associates finds that people who think of themselves in complex ways may be buffered against a setback in one domain of life because they have other life domains that continue to be satisfying. For example, although having a difficult adolescent in the home may be a trying experience, it may be less so for a parent who has other interests and rewarding activities than it is for one whose entire energies are invested in nurturing. By thinking of themselves in simple terms, people prone to depression may actually set themselves up for depression because a stressful event in one life domain will have a more major impact when it is unbuffered by other positive self-perceptions and roles.[31]

Depressed people also seem to have more difficulty learning and grasping complex ideas than do nondepressed people. When complex ideas are explained to them, they understand them as well as nondepressed people, but left to grasp the ideas on their own, they take longer. Just as positive illusions foster multiple associations among ideas and more creative thought as a consequence, depressed people think in very narrow, inflexible ways, often ignoring and even filtering out the multiple possible ways of looking at a situation.[32] Asked to come up with as many uses for a brick as one can imagine (an odd but commonly used test of creativity), the depressed person may think of one, namely hitting someone over the head with it. In the same amount of time, the nondepressed person may have thought of using the brick for building, as a paperweight, as a hammer, for drawing, as a wedge, and as a fence for bugs. In extreme depression, the ability to process information and to retrieve it from memory may be severely impaired.

IS THE LOSS OF ILLUSION A CAUSE OF DEPRESSION?

Why do depressed people fail to show the illusions that buffer most people against reality; or if they once had them, why do depressed people come to lose these illusions? In essence, these questions are part of the larger question of why people become depressed. This is a difficult question to answer, first, because depression is a very common disease, and second, because there are many different types of depression. Unlike mania, which is rare and relatively homogeneous, at least with respect to its onset, depression is an umbrella term for a set of disorders that may result from different sets of factors but that share a negative mood and pessimistic perceptions. Studies of depressed people have made some points clear regarding the causes of depression. At least some forms of depression seem to result from a mix of stressful experiences and vulnerabilities in personality.[33] People who have gone through stressful events that they were unable to control, such as a marital separation, an unwanted pregnancy, or the loss of a job, are more vulnerable to depression. When a person must face an uncontrollable event without a partner or when multiple stressful events occur at the same time, depression is more likely. But not everyone who faces such events becomes depressed. Some people seem to be more prone to depression than others. Depression runs in families, and depressed mothers are likely to have depressed children. Because of this fact, some experts have speculated that some forms of depression may be, in part, genetically determined.[34] It is also possible, however, that children learn from a parent that depression is a way of reacting to stress. Psychologist Christopher Layne suggests that depression-prone people may have suffered a variety of stressful events in their childhood that prevented them from forming the normal positive illusions that buffer most people against the painful side of reality.[35]

It is possible, then, that childhood is an important time for the development and nurturance of illusions about oneself, the world, and the future. Indeed, as already noted, psychologists who have studied self-aggrandizing illusions in children typically find that they have even more grandiose conceptions of their abilities than adults do. The usual process of socialization may consist of teaching children to tone down these exaggerated views of themselves, the world, and the future without losing them altogether. Among children who will later become depression prone, however, these illusions may be undermined by stressful events and their accompanying lack of control.

The discovery of depressive realism and the fact that depressed people do not hold or are unable to use the positive illusions that are so advantageous to normal people suggests that positive illusions—more particularly, their absence—may figure into the onset and progression of at least some forms of depression. The prominent depression researcher Aaron Beck alludes to this possibility in his description of the role of negative cognitions in depression. He argues that depression results from a combination of stress and a propensity to develop depression which, in turn, produce negative evaluations of the self, the world, and the future. These beliefs seem to develop early in depressive episodes and may cause other symptoms such as reduced motivation and lack of effort. Arguing that these cognitions are central to depression, Beck targets them for modification through cognitive therapy designed to induce depressed people to think more positively about themselves and the world. In one important respect, however, Beck's perspective departs from the recent work on depressive realism. Beck argues that the goal of cognitive therapy for depression is to help people form more realistic judgments about themselves, the world, and the future. In contrast, the research on depressive realism suggests that the goal of therapy might better be to help people develop cognitive illusions so that they can think more positively about themselves, the world, and the future, employing the mildly inflated biases that normal people characteristically use.[36]

Martin Seligman, Lyn Abramson, and their associates represent another group of depression researchers who have targeted a more narrow illusion for modification in the treatment of depression, namely the causal explanatory style that depressed people use to explain positive and negative events. Abramson and Alloy argue that one function of self-enhancing biases may be to act as a buffer against stressful events that might trigger depression. When illusions are absent or access to them is blocked, depressed people have a tendency to interpret the causes of negative events as internal, stable, and pervasive. Instead of seeing a setback at work as temporary, a depressed person may regard it as an indication of having reached a level of incompetence that cannot be surpassed. The most severe depression results, they argue, when people attribute negative events to stable and pervasive aspects of themselves.[37] For example, the person who attributes the breakup of a relationship to his own unlovable qualities would develop more severe depression than someone who regarded the breakup as simply a result of a mismatch of personalities and interests.

Like Beck, Seligman targets these cognitions for therapeutic intervention, inducing depressed people to interpret positive and negative events in a more ego-enhancing manner. In essence, depressed people are taught to make self-serving causal attributions as a form of therapy, the kind of attributional explanations that normal people typically offer for success and failure. Consistent with the idea that this explanatory style figures into the development of depression, research suggests that the style of explaining bad events as due to pervasive, stable negative qualities about the self appears to develop early in depression and to precede the development of other depressive symptoms, at least in some cases.[38] Other researchers have suggested, however, that a focus on causal attributions may be too narrow and that depressive thinking reveals a host of negative ways of thinking about the self, the world, and the future, none of which can be conclusively identified as the central causal element of depression.[39]

Other researchers have suggested that the problem may lie less in the content of the self-concept than in its accessibility. Both depressed and nondepressed people seem to have positive and negative beliefs about themselves, but for nondepressed people the positive material is easily accessed, whereas for depressed people negative information is more easily brought to mind.[40] One of the factors that is most striking about depression is its seeming determination to maintain itself. Depressed people are able to counter almost every effort to cheer them up with reasons why they should stay in their gloomy mood. A therapist provided the following example.

One woman patient went to a movie and felt very depressed afterwards. When I asked her why, she said, "Oh, it was a terrible movie and I saw myself in it, so it made me very unhappy." . . . Psychiatrists don't always give very profound advice, so I said to this patient, "Next time you go to the movies, go see a happy movie." She went to see a very upbeat movie and then she came to me, "Oh, I'm so depressed, I'm so depressed. I went to this movie, a very happy movie, and I saw how wonderful life could be. It was so different from my life that I left feeling more depressed than ever."[41]

Psychologists are now realizing that it is not simply depressed people's negativity but their inability to make use of positive associations that marks them. Earlier we noted (chapter 2) that when normal people find themselves temporarily in a bad mood, they often make active efforts to get themselves out of those moods. They will try to think happy thoughts, distract themselves with pleasurable activities, help a person in need, or perform other activities that are likely to restore positive emotions. Depressed people seem not to have these same skills at their disposal. Although positive information and strategies for alleviating a bad mood may exist in their minds in some latent form, access to those associations and strategies appears to be blocked. Depression is associated with some chronic deficits in neurotransmitters, the chemicals that permit transmission through the brain. These neurotransmitters include epinephrine, which can produce a mild euphoria, heightened activity and motivation, and fluency in thought processes. The inability to access positive information and the corresponding deficits that are observed in depression may result from deficits or imbalances in neurotransmitters.[42]

Whereas some theories have focused on the importance of depressive cognitions in the development of depression, such as the belief that one is worthless, others have focused on the affective or emotional experience itself. This theory essentially argues that emotion plays a pivotal role in the ability to sustain normal human illusions about the self, the world, and the future. Emotions clearly influence thought processes. When otherwise cheerful people are temporarily put in a state of mild depression by concentrating on sad things that have happened or that might happen in their lives, the illusion of control and unrealistic optimism virtually disappear. Under such circum-

stances, people also become more balanced in their self-perceptions, acknowledging that they have faults and limitations as
well as talents. Inducing happiness has exactly the opposite
effects. When normal people are led to feel elated by focusing
on happy aspects of their past or exciting prospects for the
future, they become even more susceptible to an illusion of
control, they see themselves as even more responsible for successful outcomes than usual, they evaluate themselves more
favorably, and they become more optimistic. The irresistible
conclusion is that emotion helps to confer a positive or negative
vision of the self and the world (see chapter 2).

There is an obvious rebuttal to the argument that depressed
people simply lack high self-esteem, optimism, and the sense of
control that buffer normal people against setbacks. Maybe depressed people really do have more miserable lives. Perhaps
they *are* unable to control what goes on around them or have
little reason to be optimistic about the future. Depressed people
may simply be more inadequate and have fewer resources, and
their low self-esteem may consequently be justified. This
"schmuck" theory of depression, as one prominent depression
researcher has called it, would also account for realistic perceptions of little control, low self-esteem, and a realistic vision of
the future.[43] This alternative explanation must be ruled out to
make the argument that depression is marked by a loss of
illusion.

Most depression researchers have by now rejected the viewpoint that depressed people are simply more inadequate than
others and that depression merely gives voice to these
inadequacies.[44] When depressed people are no longer depressed, they show the same self-enhancing biases and illusions
as nondepressed people. Thus, whether or not they are more
inadequate as people than nondepressed individuals is moot.
They show the same misperceptions of reality when they cease
to be depressed.[45] What we see, then, in the depressed person
is the antithesis of what is characteristic of the person whose
illusions are intact: an often dramatically reduced activity level,

pessimism, a negative view of the self, feelings of helplessness rather than a sense of control, and an inability to pursue goals in a concerted fashion. Moreover, this sad profile appears to be directly tied to an absence of normal positive illusions, and at least some forms of depression may even be caused by it.

CAN DEPRESSION BE USEFUL?

Evolutionary theorist Charles Darwin has had a profound effect not only on biology but on all the sciences. This pervasive influence prompts us to ask functional questions of many phenomena, and so we may ask them of depression. Does depression have any adaptive value? That is, is it useful in any way? Depression may have significance for society in general. Although depression can be a response to many different conditions, it is especially a response to uncontrollable stressful events. As such, depression can act as a cultural pointer that draws attention to those elements of a society that are chronically exposed to adverse events over which they can have no control. Two groups that are at high risk for depression are women at home with three or more children and women with young children who have to work for economic reasons. Depression is even more likely if the woman has no husband or partner. These high rates of depression should tell us something about the demands that society places on women who must occupy too many social roles.[46] They are overwhelmed, feel little control, maintain a hectic pace, achieve little rest, and perform repetitive and sometimes thankless tasks throughout seemingly endless stress-filled days. As Gerald Klerman, former head of the National Institute of Mental Health, has noted, depression should serve a signal function by alerting a social group that some of its members are in danger.[47]

Does depression have any adaptive value for an individual? Investigators of manic-depressive illness suggest that depression may serve as a counterveiling force for mania.[48] During mania, when energies are at their peak, the person expends physical and psychological resources at a staggering rate. The alternating period of depression, while devastating and risky, may be necessary to slow the person down, enabling him or her to rest and restore resources. For normal people, an occasional period of depression may serve an analogous but milder function. Nearly everyone has temporary bouts of mild depression. Some of these are reactions to specific unpleasant events, whereas at other times melancholy may hang over a person for no particular reason. In either case, during these times, perceptions appear to become more realistic and illusions may temporarily give way to more accurate appraisals of the self, the world, and the future. Possibly, this temporary depression acts as a window on the world, an opportunity to take realistic stock of what one is and where one is going. It may provide an opportunity for a person to slow down and brood long enough to make an accurate assessment of his or her capabilities in relation to the demands of the world. As one sufferer of intermittent depression put it, "It's the vacuum cleaner in my head."[49] Indeed, most depression is short-term, and the person spontaneously recovers within six months. For students, the prognosis is even better: the average bout of depression lasts approximately three weeks.[50] Intermittent doses of realistic feedback provided by these occasional periods of melancholy may act as one force that keeps illusions within reasonable bounds at other times.

The idea that depression is functional, both for an individual and for society more generally, is speculative. It may be that bouts of melancholy serve no useful function, and instead merely make people feel miserable. From the standpoint of normal illusion, however, if occasional depression serves any useful function, it may be to enable people to garner a more realistic perspective on their abilities, talents, and future life than their otherwise more optimistic and self-aggrandizing vision can provide.

Whether depression will be found to have any adaptive significance or not, there are clear lessons from depression that illuminate the positive illusions of normal people. Depressed people clearly lack the illusions that in normal people promote mental health and buffer them against setbacks. In addition, there is now considerable evidence that depression is marked not by unrealistic pessimism but by depressive realism and the absence of illusion, lending credence to the idea that it is the falsely positive aspects of normal illusions that gives them their adaptive qualities. More intriguing still is the amassing evidence to suggest that the loss or absence of illusion may actually be causal in the development of depression. At this point, several different aspects of normal illusions have been suggested as central in the development of depression. Whether evidence supporting any of these theories will accumulate remains unclear. But it is intriguing to think that positive illusions about the self, the world, and the future may not merely promote mental health, but may actually be essential to it, and that their absence can lead to the mental illness of depression.

CHAPTER 7

Illusions in
Perspective

> I refuse to be intimidated by reality
> anymore. After all, what is reality
> anyway? Nothin' but a collective
> hunch. . . . I made some studies,
> and reality is the leading cause of
> stress amongst those in touch with
> it. . . . Now, since I put reality on a
> back burner, my days are jam-
> packed and fun-filled. . . . When I
> think of the fun I missed, I try not
> to be bitter.
> —JANE WAGNER, writing for
> Lily Tomlin as Trudy,
> the Bag Lady[1]

EVERY THEORY of mental health considers a positive
self-concept to be the cornerstone of the healthy ego. Self-
confidence, self-esteem, and self-respect are undeniably important elements of mental health. The debate is now over how
best to achieve this state. Traditional concepts of mental health
promote the idea that an accurate or correct view of the self is

critical to the healthy self-concept. But decades of empirical research suggest that a quite different conclusion is merited. Increasingly, we must view the psychologically healthy person not as someone who sees things as they are but as someone who sees things as he or she would like them to be. Effective functioning in everyday life appears to depend upon interrelated positive illusions, systematic small distortions of reality that make things appear better than they are.

The evidence for this perspective is rich, perhaps richer than has ever been the case for a theory of mental health. It draws upon hundreds of research investigations, each of which includes dozens, in some cases hundreds, of ostensibly normal well-functioning children, adolescents, and adults, presumably the most logical sources for a perspective on mental health. Another, more easily ignored, asset of the evidence is the fact that these hundreds of studies were designed to address many different aspects of social and cognitive functioning. Their investigators did not set out to confirm the role of self-aggrandizing illusion in mental health, but rather sought to clarify more local questions concerning how the mind organizes information or how social life proceeds. Yet the studies provide a vision of mental health.[2]

Nonetheless, certain questions remain. Why are we not more aware of our illusions? Or phrased another way, if we're so happy, how come we're not happier? Why do some people hold positive illusions more than others? What factors promote or undermine illusions? And finally, are illusions ever maladaptive? What keeps them in check?

ILLUSIONS AND AWARENESS

If illusion were so essential to human functioning, skeptics ask, wouldn't we already know it? Wouldn't we simply make a collective, amused shrug at our petty self-aggrandizements and go about our business? Why aren't we more aware of illusion?

One reason why illusion is not generally recognized as a feature of normal human functioning is that our theories of mental health are, ironically enough, derived largely from studies of mental illness. Psychiatrists and psychologists have portrayed the mentally healthy person, at least in part, as one who avoids the distortions so obviously present among the disturbed. In this context, small positive distortions among the healthy may go unobserved, compared with the large negative distortions so often present in the thinking of the mentally ill.

A more compelling reason why we are not more aware of our own illusions is that they typically work so well that we do not become aware of their falsely positive nature. Often, by leading people to attempt more ambitious undertakings than they might otherwise, illusions become self-fulfilling, and thus the lack of realism that gave rise to the undertakings initially becomes inconsequential and hence unrecognized. Moreover, as stressed repeatedly, people avoid engaging in distortions that can be easily, frequently, or dramatically disconfirmed. Disconfirmation with its accompanying disappointment are the conditions most likely to produce awareness of the self-aggrandizing nature of perception, and we construct our self-deceptions carefully so as to avoid precisely these circumstances.

Illusions are mild, not extreme. It is easy to miss them. And this feature helps explain why people do not seem to be as happy as they might. Many of the world's sources of misery and distress have little to do with illusions. Many organizations ask too much time and energy of their employees. Others pay too little. Some people must combine several roles at once, like those who work full time and are rearing young children, a situation conducive to conflict and distress. Random accidents produce death and loss. Illusions may help people cope most effectively with the stresses of life or construe negative events as positively as possible, but they will not remove distress and pain altogether. Hence, the world holds many sources of distress that are not amenable to change through illusion. Were our illusions to be systematically stripped away, we might well become more aware of them, as we attempted to cope with a bleaker reality still.

ILLUSIONS TEMPERED OR LOST

There are circumstances that undermine illusion. We have already considered two sets of conditions under which people's positive illusions are at least challenged and at worst destroyed. The first of these is victimizing events, those involving tragic loss or threat. Ronnie Janoff-Bulman, the psychologist who documented the positive assumptions that people typically hold about the self and the world, also discovered that those who had been victimized at an early age are less likely than those who have never experienced a victimizing event to feel that the world is a benign and protective place and the self is a worthwhile person. In one such study, college students were asked whether they had ever experienced any of several victimizing events, including the death of a parent, a serious illness, a fire, and child abuse. Those students who had undergone a victimizing event before college were less likely to have high self-esteem and were more likely to regard the world as at least somewhat threatening and dangerous.[3]

At first, these conclusions might appear to be in conflict with the findings that victims are often able to overcome their tragic experiences and not only regain but actually exceed their previous quality of life. In fact, victims of tragic events may hold both sets of perceptions simultaneously. While on the one hand believing that they have been tried and tested in ways that have made them stronger and better people, they may also clearly recognize that the world and their future hold certain threats over which they may not have complete control.[4]

A second set of conditions under which illusions are lost are the circumstances that produce depression. As was noted in chapter 6, many depression researchers now believe that a combination of stressful experiences in early childhood, coupled perhaps with some preexisting propensity for depression, produce the conditions conducive to long-term depression. Whether this predisposition to depression is genetically based or learned, as by observing parents who have also experienced depression, remains unknown.

Cultural beliefs also influence the degree to which people hold positive illusions. In recent years, I have had a number of European and Asian scientists in my laboratory. When I have shared my ideas on mental health with them, some have smiled tolerantly, asking whether the ideas have been examined cross-culturally. As one particularly skeptical but polite visitor put it, "Is the mentally healthy person an American, then?" There is no question that self-esteem, control, and optimism have been critically important themes in American life. Although some of the research on illusions has been conducted with non-Americans, the overwhelming body of evidence does indeed come from studies of Americans or Canadians. Moreover, it would be fatuous to assume that intermittent bits of cross-cultural support could demonstrate the universality of these ideas.

There are clear cultural differences in the degree to which positive illusions are expressions of cultural values. Societies and religious groups that have been persecuted over hundreds, perhaps thousands, of years may recognize that unbridled optimism and belief in personal control may be neither very descriptive of their own experiences nor very functional ways of anticipating the future. Tempering an inclination toward high self-esteem, a sense of mastery, and optimism with a culturally instilled cautiousness and vigilance may ultimately be more adaptive for such groups as the Jews, Armenians, and American blacks, who have been repeated victims of prejudice, discrimination, and in some cases, efforts at extermination.

But a culture need not have a history of oppression to exhibit more muted expressions of optimism, self-esteem, and mastery than can be identified in the United States. Does this mean that the illusions demonstrated in research investigations are culturally bounded, evident only in American culture and ones similar to our own? Not necessarily. It may be that the needs for self-esteem, mastery, and optimism are cross-cultural themes, but that their relative importance and the forms for meeting them vary from culture to culture in ways that sometimes obscure commonalities. For example, among Americans, optimism is typically expressed in the belief that good things will happen to people in general and the self in particular over the coming years. The history of the American economy indicates that this belief is not altogether unrealistic. Such a belief, however, might be unrealistic among the rural poor of India. Faith in reincarnation and a belief that if one has led a good life, one's soul may return in a more advantaged form, would appear to be profoundly optimistic but appropriately cognizant of the likelihood that one's current life will not improve appreciably.

In an article entitled "Standing Out and Standing In: The Psychology of Control in America and Japan," authors John Weisz, Fred Rothbaum, and Thomas Blackburn make a similar point regarding expressions of the need for control in the two societies. They argue that people can achieve control in the characteristically American way by attempting to bend and shape circumstances to meet personal needs and goals (what they term "primary control"). Or one can modify one's own attributes and needs so as to fit in with existing realities and maximize satisfaction with them ("secondary control"). The Japanese appear to see primary control as both unlikely and undesirable. Their focus on secondary control may be a logical outcome of socialization practices that emphasize the interconnectedness of family members and the subordination of individual will to duty. The Japanese ideal is to "stand in," so identified with the cultural group as not to be noticed as an individual. Weisz and his colleagues argue that this secondary control fosters exactly the values that Japanese culture promotes: "self-discipline, politeness, attentiveness to others, a strong sense of personal and group identity, and confidence as to appropriate behavior in a variety of situations,"[5] thereby achieving that "intricate serenity that comes to a people who know exactly what to expect from each other."[6]

Weisz and his associates also argue that both primary and secondary control have potential disadvantages. Among the Japanese, the emphasis on secondary control and accommodation to the group and the larger society "makes them excessively conforming, overly sensitive to disapproval, prone to read failure not only as a personal humiliation but also as a disgrace to family and [the wider social group], and even inclined to atone by acts of self-destruction."[7] In essence, they argue that too much emphasis on social accommodation threatens individual autonomy. The reverse may be true of the American emphasis on primary control, which, they maintain, can promote self-absorption, alienation, loneliness, and vacuity. This point is important not only because it suggests potential liabilities of both primary and secondary control, but also because it suggests that the criteria of mental health and their relation to each other may ebb and flow culturally just as the expressions of themes related to mental health may do so. To the extent that there is risk in the American embodiments of self-esteem, control, and optimism, Weisz and his associates suggest, it may be in undermining the capacity to forge strong social relationships and ties. To the extent that there is risk in the Japanese resolution of these themes, it may lie in the capacity for individual achievement, autonomy, and creativity. Weisz and his colleagues make these arguments primarily to suggest that a balance between primary and secondary control may ultimately be the best integration for the healthy personality. While their arguments are provocative, their analysis more convincingly demonstrates that different cultural expressions of a basic need, such as the need for control, fit and adapt better in different cultural niches.

ILLUSIONS AND CHILD REARING

Earlier we noted that positive illusions tend to foster and be linked to each other. Those who are overly optimistic about the future also tend to be high in self-esteem. Those with an exaggerated sense of their own mastery tend to have inflated views of their self-worth and likelihood of future success. It is unusual to find a person who is overly optimistic about the future but lacking in self-esteem or mastery, beliefs that would seem to be essential to the implementation of a rewarding future.[8] The fact that positive illusions are linked is given additional credence by the fact that child-rearing practices that tend to foster one set of beliefs, such as optimism about the future, have also been related to the others, namely a sense of mastery and high self-esteem.

Most of the research on children's sense of mastery, self-esteem, and optimism has focused on three general types of behaviors that children demonstrate early in their classroom experiences at school.[9] One of these is called "self-regulation," a general term that refers to the degree to which a child initiates achievement-related activities and follows through on them. Important to self-regulation is the idea that the child initiates these activities out of an intrinsic desire to learn and master the situation, rather than out of feelings of pressure, anxiety, or coercion. Competence is another attribute that has been studied in depth; the term refers to the acquisition of knowledge and skills that lead a child to cope effectively with the school situation. Competence includes not only the actual skills and knowledge that produce learning but the perception of the self as competent as well—that is, the belief and understanding that one can produce a successful outcome. Finally, classroom behavior has been identified as a criterion of adjustment to the school setting. Children who act out or who are shy and withdrawn are judged to be performing in a manner that does not reflect adjustment, while those children who are outgoing, cheerful, and controlled in the school setting may be said to be adjusted to it.

The parents' attitudes and behaviors regarding control appear to be critically implicated in the development of competence and self-regulatory skills. In particular, a style of parenting in which the child, even the very young child, is encouraged to express opinions and make choices, usually on the basis of information provided by parents, has been related to higher grades in school and more effective self-regulatory behavior.[10] Either extreme in parental control, whether in the strict or permissive direction, appears to undermine the development of esteem- and mastery-related skills. A highly authoritarian parental style, in which parents permit children little control and are highly restrictive of their activities and participation, leads to more discontent and more withdrawal from new situations. Similarly, a highly permissive parental style, in which children are expected to make their own decisions, but without the guidance and structure that a parent can provide, appears to undermine school-related competence. One might characterize the effective parenting style, at least in terms of the development of a sense of competence and self-regulation, as democratic, involving parent and child in an informed mutual decision-making process.

In a similar vein, psychologists Wendy Grolnick and Richard Ryan have emphasized the importance of what they call "autonomy support" in the development of competence and self-regulation.[11] Autonomy support is the degree to which adults encourage independent problem-solving, choice, and participation in decisions, as opposed to simply dictating choice and motivating achievement through discipline, pressure, or controlling rewards. Studies have found that teachers who promote this kind of autonomy had students who were more intrinsically motivated and who showed greater competence and higher self-esteem than students of teachers who exerted greater control.[12]

Despite the fact that democracy appears to be important in

the development of children's sense of autonomy and competence, it is evident from research that providing a clear structure and explicit guidelines for behavior in the home also facilitates the development of school-related competence. It is difficult for children to make capable decisions and choices in a home environment that has few guidelines for action or consistent rewards and punishments for behavior. For example, if a child is permitted to choose his or her own dinner but has received no guidelines concerning the nutritional value of different foods, it would be unrealistic to expect that a child could select an appropriate meal. The existence of clear standards of what is right and wrong and guidelines for what constitutes appropriate behavior means that when children are put in a position of expressing choices or making decisions, they can do so in a context that provides them with information useful for making those choices and decisions.[13]

Finally, involvement in a child's life also promotes competence and self-regulation. A parent who is interested in and knowledgeable about a child's life and who takes an active role in it conveys to the child that what he or she does is valuable, thereby enhancing a child's self-esteem. It also gives a child a sense of confidence that what he or she is doing is correct.[14]

ARE POSITIVE ILLUSIONS ALWAYS BENEFICIAL?

The fact that positive illusions are often distortions of reality leads many people to reject the idea that such illusions are always and inevitably positive in their consequences. Might there not be long-term limitations of positive illusions? On the surface, each of the positive illusions that most people demonstrate would seem to have inherent risks. A falsely positive sense of one's accomplishments might lead people to pursue careers and interests for which they are ill suited. Faith in one's capacity to master situations might lead people to persevere at tasks that might be uncontrollable; knowing when to abandon a task may be as important as knowing when to pursue it. Unrealistic optimism might lead people to ignore legitimate risks in their environment and to fail to take measures to offset those risks. False optimism, for example, might lead people to ignore important health habits or to fail to prepare adequately for a likely catastrophic event, such as a flood or earthquake. As we saw in chapter 4, most of these obvious concerns appear to be misplaced, for the healthy mind is not without means for accommodating negative information in a manner that enables people to modify their behavior and make decisions that are appropriately responsive to realistic contingencies.

Another version of the argument that positive illusions may have some maladaptive consequences stems from a quite logical though not well tested suggestion that, whereas a little illusion may be very useful in helping people to adapt successfully to life, a large amount of illusion might produce distortions that would interfere with negotiating life successfully. This argument maintains that there is an optimal margin of illusion and that deviations in either direction are maladaptive.[15] It is easy to find apparent examples of illusions run to excess, both in history and in current events. The children's crusade of the Middle Ages can be thought of as optimism and overconfidence gone awry. The downfall of Gary Hart's 1988 candidacy for president at the hands of the media can be construed as over-confidence in the ability to manage sexual and political desires simultaneously. The downfall of Ivan Boesky and others in the securities industry can be seen as cautionary tales, symbols of optimism and self-confidence turned to greed, lawlessness, and delusions of invulnerability.

But there are risks in overgeneralizing from such readily available examples. Merely because a person can be character-ized as high in self-esteem, a sense of mastery, and unrealistic optimism does not mean that any failure can automatically and appropriately be ascribed to these features of thought. The dilemma with individual case studies is that one can never conclusively demonstrate that a particular factor, such as an illusion, led to a particular error or problem.

One also cannot judge the adequacy of a process solely on the basis of its outcome. This is an issue that frequently arises in studies of decision making. People can make quite capable decisions and yet the outcome of the decisions can sometimes be bad ones for a variety of reasons. Chance, incomplete information, or an unexpected development in the environment can all undermine a decision that was made according to the highest standards. One would not then judge the decision-making process to be a faulty one solely because the decision turned out to be incorrect. Likewise, one cannot assume that merely because many people with high self-esteem, an exaggerated perception of control, and unrealistic optimism about the future sometimes fail to bring off their visions, unrealistic illusions produced the failure. Illusions are, in essence, the fuel that drives creativity, motivation, and high aspirations, but they are not themselves the contents of those dreams and aspirations, which may be flawed. Just as one would not typically fault gasoline for a breakdown in an automobile's engine, so one cannot fault self-aggrandizing illusions for sometimes being used in the service of flawed ideas and dreams.

Does this mean that positive illusions are without liabilities? Are there no disadvantages to falsely positive construals of one's own attributes, the world, and the future? The concept of an optimal margin of illusion is logically a reasonable one. But does the phenomenon exist? In other words, can one identify people in whom illusions exceed the optimal margin and whose lives suffer as a result? As already noted, it is logically inappropriate to use anecdotes to address this question, since one can never demonstrate in a particular instance that a specific illusion produced a specific outcome. Consequently, we must look to research evidence and clinical records.

To begin with, research evidence suggests that most people do not distort reality to a very substantial degree. Almost to a person, the positive distortions of personal attributes, mastery, and assessment of the future that one witnesses in research investigations are quite mild. Statistically, what one sees is a skewed distribution, with some people holding negative self-perceptions and the majority holding slightly positive ones.[16] There is little evidence for the existence of a group of people with substantially exaggerated positive self-impressions.

One would further expect that if there are people who distort reality in so falsely positive a manner that it interferes with their ability to function effectively in the world, there would be clinical evidence for such a group. But therapists typically do not see people who have overly high self-esteem, too much faith in their capacity to bring about desired events, and unbridled optimism. They see people who are miserable and whose self-perceptions and perceptions of the world are negative. If there are people whose grandiose assessments of the self, the world, and the future put them sufficiently out of touch with reality to interfere with the ability to live life effectively, then it does not seem to bother them very much.[17]

The preceding arguments are not intended to suggest that illusions have no liabilities. There may indeed be some; what is required is a research program explicitly designed to examine such a possibility. The absence of clinical or research evidence in support of such an obvious hypothesis, however, gives one pause. If the idea of an optimal margin of illusion is so inherently persuasive and yet there is no research evidence to support it, this suggests that there are internal or environmental forces that keep illusions within bounds, at least on the positive side, preventing them from running to excess.

ILLUSIONS TAMED

What are the factors that might conspire to keep illusions within mildly positive bounds? A partial answer was provided by the arguments and evidence in chapter 4. Two main points are of particular importance in this context. Illusions could be shown to be excessive and maladaptive if there were evidence that information concerning one's weaknesses, frailties, and faults were distorted into positive attributes. The fact that inconsequential negative information is ignored or forgotten but that diagnostic or pervasive negative information is simply represented in a more benign manner than might be justified indicates that this concern is not realistic. Useful negative information is typically represented in a way that retains its usefulness without its full nature being devastating. The second point concerns the interaction of illusions with threat. If positive illusions prevented people from accurately perceiving threatening situations, then we could argue that they run to excess. There are psychological mechanisms that have this quality, and they have been described and documented by clinicians as repression and denial. Illusions, in contrast, can be clearly differentiated from defense mechanisms because they are realistically responsive to the threat value of information.

Beyond these points, there may be somewhat less obvious ways in which illusions are kept in check so that they do not exceed an optimal positive margin. People's positive beliefs about themselves, the world, and the future are only one type of belief that they hold. There may be information inherent in situations that can offset what might otherwise be maladaptive effects of self-aggrandizing illusions.[18] Consider, for example, a man who does poorly at his job, but who fails to interpret negative feedback correctly as evidence that he is doing a poor job. Although his perceptions of himself as a capable worker may persist, it cannot have escaped his attention that his work situation is not the most desirable one possible. He may come to feel that he does not like the job very much or that he does not particularly enjoy interacting with his boss or his co-workers. Consequently, he may leave his position, even though he has failed to correctly interpret the negative feedback as evidence that he is doing a poor job. One can argue that he has made the right decision for the wrong reasons, but ultimately it may not matter. Moreover, if he can leave this job with his self-esteem relatively intact, his remaining self-confidence may lay the groundwork for greater success in a new occupation, at least more than would be the case than if he perceived himself to be a failure.[19]

Positive illusions are also not etched in stone, unresponsive to feedback from the world. People converse and interact with others in ways that may correct blatantly inflated perceptions of the self, the world, and the future. Although there is an implicitly agreed upon social conspiracy to provide people primarily with positive feedback, there are boundaries within which this social positivity operates. When a person's self-assessments stray too much in a positive direction, the social environment may mute them by providing gentle but clear feedback to suggest that the grandiosity has exceeded appropriate limits.[20] A worker who assumes most of the credit from some jointly undertaken venture, for example, would no doubt be rapidly corrected by irate co-workers, thereby knocking her grandiose self-assessment back within reasonable bounds.

Certain beliefs about oneself may be more subject to illusions than others, specifically, those with few objective standards for evaluation. Most of us are at least intuitively aware of the fact that our grandiose self-conceptions are better held about attributes that cannot be directly tested than about attributes that can be readily held to a standard. Some years ago, I made the mistake of representing myself at a party as a fairly decent pool player. I felt confident that I would not be called upon to display this talent in the middle of the party, and that I probably would not find myself in a pool room at some later date with this particular group of people. My confidence was soon shattered, because one of my companions responded: "Good. There's a table downstairs. Let's go shoot a couple of games." The results were predictably disastrous.

Most of the time we are savvy enough to avoid these situations. We may exaggerate both in our own minds and to others our social qualities but are less likely to distort our knowledge of certain accounting procedures, for example, particularly in the company of accountants. As psychologist Jonathon Brown put it:

> Insofar as personality characteristics are inherently subjective in nature, it may be the case that individuals are relatively free to assume, for instance, that they are more interesting, friendly, and humorous than the average other person, and precisely because social attributes lack objective referents, such beliefs may be harbored with psychological impunity.[21]

For personal qualities with more objective referents, such as the ability to play the piano or to shoot pool, our assessments may usually stay closer to the truth. When the environment provides objective standards against which our self-assessments can be directly compared, or those self-assessments concern abilities that can be relatively easily confirmed or disconfirmed, we may show a more appropriate degree of modesty than may be the case concerning our attributes that are unlikely to be challenged or that lack objective standards of evaluation.

Illusions may also provide experiences that enable people to use them with ever-increasing success. Consider, for example, the illusion of control and the oft-noted potential risk that people may attempt to control situations that are actually uncontrollable. According to this argument, people with an exaggerated sense of their personal mastery may persist inappropriately at tasks that cannot be mastered. If this were true, it would constitute a clear limitation of the illusion of control. It does not, however, appear to be true. The available evidence suggests, instead, that people with high needs for mastery may be better able to discriminate controllable from uncontrollable situations, a very different and quite adaptive outgrowth of control needs.[22]

Friends who recently traveled to India inadvertently illustrated this point. The wife, a very controlling person, was warned in advance that she would have difficulty getting along in this culture, which does not respond well to characteristic American assertiveness. The husband, more laid back than his wife, was judged by his friends to have a nature more in tune with the frustrations of Indian society. In fact, the opposite turned out to be the case. The wife quickly learned what worked in India and also learned when it was best to sit back and wait for the train. The husband, in contrast, spent the trip railing against the corruption and inefficiency he observed around him.

Why might people with a high need for control be better able to discriminate the situations when it can be used successfully? People who have a high need to master or control situations almost certainly avail themselves of more opportunities to exert control than people with a low need for control. In so doing, they expose themselves to more opportunities to learn what things can be controlled and what cues in situations signal opportunities for control or its absence. Learning about control is unlikely to be different from learning about any other kind of contingent situation: people get better with practice. So it may be that people with a high need to control learn more about how to exert it successfully.

Finally, the idea that positive illusions are in the service of self-esteem virtually requires that they stay in check. If one develops substantially unrealistic expectations regarding the future that greatly exceed what one is actually able to accomplish, then one is set up for failure and disappointment, leading to lower self-esteem.[23] There appears to be a natural feedback loop for keeping illusions in check. Except for those rare and unfortunate few who actively court failure and humiliation, most of us derive no comfort or satisfaction from such situations. Consequently, one would expect our illusions to operate within a narrow band, to nudge us into attempting slightly more but not excessively more ambitious undertakings than we otherwise might. Our illusions both work and are held in check, then, in part because they are self-fulfilling, creating the world that we already believe exists. Illusions produce adaptive behaviors, action, and persistence, which are certainly more likely to pay off than lack of persistence and inactivity. Should the goal be set too high and the efforts fail, then the goal may be readjusted so that failure will not occur again.

ILLUSIONS AS EVOLUTIONARY ACCOMMODATIONS

> Cannot [mental] health merely be a form of madness that goes unrecognized because it happens to be a good adaptation to reality?
> —George Vaillant[24]

For most of this chapter, we have focused attention primarily on illusions as variants in human nature: why some people have them while others do not and why some people come to lose their illusions. Yet this emphasis threatens to obscure the central point. Mild positive illusions appear to be characteristic of the majority of people under a broad array of circumstances. It is hard to resist the conclusion that the mind may be intrinsically structured so as to be healthy. It almost seems that good mental health is not something that a few fortunate people achieve on their own, but something intrinsic to human nature, at least for the majority. The evidence from studies with children suggests that positive illusions may actually be wired in, inherent in how the mind processes and ascribes meaning to information. The fact that positive illusions are typically so much stronger in children than in adults argues against the idea that they are learned adaptations to life. This does not mean that certain forms of positive illusions cannot be learned. Certainly, as people become older and more sophisticated, they develop more complex cognitive structures for dealing with information of all kinds.[25] Sophisticated self-deception is unlikely to be very different. Rather, the basic form of positive illusions—seeing the self, one's potency, and the future in a falsely positive manner—may not have to be learned. In fact, the opposite appears to be true. Positive illusions may actually have to be unlearned, at least to a degree, for people to function effectively in the adult world.

The fact that positive illusions are stronger in children than adults has significance beyond what it may say about their intrinsic nature. It may alert us to the value of extreme illusion and its limited responsiveness to negative feedback in the first six years of life. Young infants and children amass an unprecedented amount of difficult knowledge and acquire extraordinary skills in their first six years. Indeed, there is no other period of learning like it throughout the lifetime. It is, therefore, essential that learning take place and that the organism not give up during this critical time. From studies with older children and adults, we know that the belief that one may fail leads not only to poor performance but to the unwillingness even to try. The perception that one is not very able leads older children and adults to withdraw from challenges and to feel bad about themselves. The unrealistic and unresponsive optimism and positive views of the self that are evident in very young children virtually guarantee that children will persist at learning, at least for the first few years of their lives, thus benefiting both themselves and the species.

Positive illusions, then, may be evolutionary accommodations. Others who have studied illusions in children and adults have also been drawn reluctantly but persuasively to this conclusion.[26] The apparent adaptiveness of illusions for mental and physical health inspires such speculation, for it is difficult to imagine how these adaptive psychological forms could otherwise have become so much a part of human nature.

At the beginning of this undertaking, I had some trepidations concerning where it might take me. It is like going to a summer cottage, finding a blank box filled with jigsaw puzzle pieces and not being certain that all the pieces are there or even that all the pieces in the box are actually parts of the same puzzle. But in the same lighthearted and hopeful spirit that one sets out on the puzzle, one seeks answers from the myriad small bits of data provided by individual investigations.

With the jigsaw puzzle, there is always the danger that what you think is a house with blue sky overhead is actually a mountain overlooking a lake, upside down. So in science, a set of observations may apparently hang together, but someone else may come along, give the data a good whack, and show them to mean something altogether different. That is the risk of being in a field that advances.

Science is a cumulative process and any discovery or insight is not an end in its own right, but a means of opening up new directions for exploration. I offer these observations, not in the expectation of having provided answers, but in the hopes of having moved us a little closer to the right questions.

NOTES

Preface

1. Maslow, 1950, 1954.
2. Kohut, 1966; Beck, Rush, Shaw, and Emery, 1979; Thoresen and Mahoney, 1974.
3. Recounted by Lionel Tiger (1979), p. 78.

Chapter 1

1. Jahoda, 1958, p. 6.
2. Jahoda, 1953, p. 349.
3. The importance of contact with reality was first established in Freud's writings about the functions of the ego. The neo-Freudians, especially Sullivan (1953, 1956), Erikson (1976), G. Allport (1955), Hartmann (1958), Fromm (1955), and Carl Rogers (1942, 1951), established contact with reality as a central criterion of mental health.
4. Jourard and Landsman, 1980. See also Schulz, 1977; Worchel and Goethals, 1985.
5. Kuhn (1970) writes about this issue in the context of changing scientific paradigms more generally.
6. Snyder, 1988.
7. Lazarus, 1983, p. 1.
8. See Fiske and Taylor, 1984; Greenwald, 1980; Nisbett and Ross, 1980; Sackeim, 1983; Taylor, 1983; Taylor and Brown, 1988, for reviews. Such claims put us on the perilous brink of philosophical debate concerning whether one can ever know reality. Fortunately, at least to some degree, the research methods employed by psychologists spare us this frustrating conundrum. Science affords us methods of measuring whether people's self-perceptions and beliefs about the world and the future are accurate. In some cases, a person is given information about his or her performance, such as whether he or she succeeded or failed on a test. Some time later, the person's perceptions or recall of that feedback may be assessed. By using such a method, one can not only measure the individual's accuracy at remembering the feedback, but also identify the directions of any distortions, whether positive or negative. As will be seen, people typically distort feedback about themselves and their performance in a self-serving manner.

More subjective self-evaluations, such as how happy one is or how well-adjusted one is, do not have these kinds of objective standards of comparison. In such cases, a bias is implied if the majority of people report that they are more (or less) likely than the majority of other people to hold a particular belief. If most people believe that they are happier or better adjusted or more skilled on a variety of attributes than most other people, such perceptions provide evidence that is suggestive of systematic bias in a positive direction.

Biases in the perception of the future are difficult to establish, because no one knows for certain what the future will bring. If one can show, however, that most people believe their future is more positive than that of most other people, evidence suggestive of bias is provided. More compelling still, if there is objective information about the likelihood that certain future events will happen and people's estimates of those future events are considerably off base, then evidence suggestive of bias about the future is also provided. In this very limited sense, then, we do know what reality is and we can compare it directly to what people think it may be. When we do so, we typically find that people's perceptions of reality are often what they want it to be rather than what it is.

9. For a clinical perspective on the importance of illusions about the self, the reader is referred to Kohut (1966, 1978); a brief summary and perspective on this viewpoint is provided by Ornstein (1980).

10. See, for example, Kelley (1967); Jones and Davis (1965) for discussions of this issue in the context of causal attributions. See Fischhoff (1976) for a discussion of the general question.

11. See, for example, Nisbett and Ross, 1980; Fiske and Taylor, 1984; Hogarth, 1980.

12. Stipek, 1984; Harter, 1981; Greenwald, 1980.

13. See Stipek, 1984; Stipek and MacIver, in press; Harter, 1981, for reviews.

14. Harari and Covington, 1981, p. 25.

15. Stipek, 1984.

16. Alicke, 1985; Brown, 1986; Campbell, 1986; Larwood and Whittaker, 1977; see also Shrauger and Kelly, in press.

17. Campbell, 1986; Marks, 1984; Harackiewicz, Sansone, and Manderlink, 1985; Lewicki, 1984.

18. Campbell, 1986; Marks, 1984.

19. See Greenwald, 1980; Taylor and Brown, 1988, for reviews. One might argue that overly positive self-descriptions reflect public posturing rather than privately held beliefs. Several factors, however, argue against the plausibility of a strict self-presentational interpretation of this phenomenon. For example, Greenwald and Breckler (1985) reviewed evidence indicating that (a) self-evaluations are at least as favorable under private conditions as they are under public conditions; (b) favorable self-evaluations occur even when strong constraints to be honest are present; (c) favorable self-referent judgments are made very rapidly, suggesting that people are not engaging in deliberate (time-consuming) fabrication; and (d) self-enhancing judgments are acted on. For these as well as other reasons, a consensus is emerging at the theoretical level that individuals offer flattering self-evaluations not merely as a means of managing a public impression of competency but also as a means of managing impressions of themselves for themselves (see Schlenker, 1980; Tesser and Moore, 1986; Tetlock and Manstead, 1985).

20. Brown, 1986; Lewinsohn, Mischel, Chaplin, and Barton, 1980; Forsyth and Schlenker, 1977; Green and Gross, 1979; Mirels, 1980; Schlenker and Miller, 1977; Brown, 1985; Campbell, 1986; Rosenberg, 1979; Sachs, 1982.

21. Svenson, 1981.

22. E.g., Lewinsohn et al., 1980; see Shrauger 1975, 1982, for a review.
23. Greenwald, 1980, p. 64.
24. Markus, 1977.
25. Greenwald, 1980.
26. Markus, 1977
27. Greenwald, 1980.
28. Kuiper and Derry, 1982; Kuiper and MacDonald, 1982; Kuiper, Olinger, MacDonald, and Shaw, 1985.
29. Schlenker, 1980; Snyder and Wicklund, 1981.
30. Fuentes, 1964, p. 58.
31. See Bradley, 1978; Miller and Ross, 1975; Ross and Fletcher, 1985; Zuckerman, 1979, for reviews.
32. *San Francisco Sunday Examiner and Chronicle,* April 22, 1979, cited in Greenwald, 1980.
33. Greenwald, 1980, p. 605.
34. Miller and Ross, 1975.
35. Ross, 1981; Ross and Sicoly, 1979.
36. Thompson and Kelley, 1981
37. Harris, 1946, recounted in Ross, 1981.
38. Ross, 1981; Thompson and Kelley, 1981; Ross and Sicoly, 1979.
39. Thompson and Kelley, 1981.
40. See Ross, 1981.
41. Erikson, 1950; Alper, 1952; Sherif and Cantril, 1947.
42. Miller and Ross, 1975; Snyder, Stephan, and Rosenfield, 1978.
43. Lefcourt, 1973, p. 417.
44. White, 1959.
45. Berlyne, 1960; Fowler, 1965; White, 1959.
46. Donaldson, 1978; Harter 1981; White, 1959.
47. White, 1959.
48. Berlyne, 1960.
49. Piaget, 1954; White, 1959.
50. White, 1959.
51. Diener and Dweck, 1978, 1980; Weisz, 1986.
52. Piaget, 1954.
53. E.g., Lindsay and McCarthy, 1974.
54. Diener and Dweck, 1978, 1980.
55. Stipek, 1984.
56. Ryan, 1971.
57. Jones and Davis, 1965; Jones and Harris, 1967.
58. Miller and Ross, 1975.
59. Crocker, 1981; Smedslund, 1963; Ward and Jenkins, 1965; Arkes and Harkness, 1980; Bower, Black, and Turner, 1979; Franks and Bransford, 1971; Owens, Bower, and Black, 1979; Harris, Teske, and Ginns, 1975; Jennings, Amabile, and Ross, 1982.
60. Janis, 1982.
61. Langer, 1975; Langer and Roth, 1975.
62. Goffman, 1967.
63. Henslin, 1967.
64. Langer, 1975; Langer and Roth, 1975; see also Gilovich, 1983.
65. Langer, 1975.
66. See Thompson, 1981; Averill, 1973; Miller, 1979, for reviews.
67. Geer, Davison, and Gatchel, 1970; Geer and Maisel, 1972.

68. Laudenslager, Ryan, Drugan, Hyson, and Maier, 1983; Hanson, Larson, and Snowden, 1976.

69. Gonzales and Zimbardo, 1985. In this study, 57 percent of the people interviewed said that they thought primarily about the present and the future, and another 33 percent were oriented primarily toward the future. Only 1 percent spent most of their time thinking about the past.

70. Tiger, 1979.

71. Free and Cantril, 1968; Brickman, Coates, and Janoff-Bulman, 1978.

72. Markus and Nurius, 1986; Weinstein, 1980, 1982, 1984; see Perloff, 1983, for a review.

73. Crandall, Solomon, and Kelleway, 1955; Irwin, 1944, 1953; Marks, 1951; Robertson, 1977; Perloff and Fetzer, 1986; Weinstein, 1980; Kuiper, Mac-Donald, and Derry, 1983.

74. Frank, 1953; Pruitt and Hoge, 1965.

75. Hayes-Roth and Hayes-Roth, 1979.

76. Stipek, 1984; Marks, 1951; Irwin, 1953.

77. Stipek, 1984, p. 53.

78. Kirscht, Haefner, Kegeles, and Rosenstock, 1966; Lund, 1975.

79. Weinstein, 1980, 1982.

80. Weinstein, 1980, 1982.

81. Weinstein, 1980, 1982, 1984.

82. Seligman, 1975; Tiger, 1979.

83. Weinstein and Lachendro, 1982.

84. Kunda, 1987.

85. Kunda, 1987.

86. Conway and Ross, 1984.

87. Aronson and Linder, 1965.

88. Conway and Ross, 1984.

89. Gibbs, 1981.

90. Johnson and Tversky, 1983.

91. Kulik and Mahler, 1987.

92. See Clark and Isen, 1982.

93. Erikson, 1976, p. 234.

94. See Tiger, 1979, for a discussion of these issues.

95. *Random House Dictionary, the English Language,* ed. J. Stein, New York: Random House, p. 662.

96. E.g., Nicholls, 1975; Miller, 1976; Snyder et al., 1978; see Greenwald, 1980, for a review and discussion of this issue.

Chapter 2

1. For reviews, see Jahoda, 1958; Schulz, 1977; Jourard and Landsman, 1980; see also Diener, 1984. As noted earlier, many formal definitions of mental health incorporate accurate self-perceptions as one criterion. In establishing criteria for mental health, then, one must subtract this particular one.

2. Jourard and Landsman, 1980, p. 14.

3. Diener, 1984.

4. Freedman, 1978.

5. Beck, 1967; Kuiper and Derry, 1982; Kuiper and MacDonald, 1982; Kuiper et al., 1985; Lewinsohn et al., 1980; Shrauger and Terbovic, 1976; Kuiper, 1978;

Rizley, 1978; Abramson and Alloy, 1981; Golin, Terrell, and Johnson, 1977; Golin, Terrell, Weitz, and Drost, 1979; Greenberg and Alloy, in press; Alloy and Ahrens, 1987.

6. See Isen, 1984, for a review.

7. *The Short Stories of Katherine Mansfield.* New York: Knopf, 1937. p. 342 This passage was cited by Clark and Isen (1982).

8. Clark and Isen, 1982.

9. Velten, 1968; Isen and Daubman, 1984; Isen, Johnson, Mertz, and Robinson, 1985; Laird, Wagener, Halal, and Szegda, 1982.

10. Velten, 1968.

11. Isen, Shalker, Clark, and Karp, 1978.

12. Mischel, Coates, and Raskoff, 1968; Wright and Mischel, 1982.

13. See Fiske and Taylor, 1984.

14. MacFarland and Ross, 1982; Gibbons, 1986.

15. Ringer, 1977.

16. E.g., Rogers, 1951.

17. Coopersmith, 1967; Shrauger, 1975; Stipek, 1984; Bohrnstedt and Felson, 1983; Felson, 1981.

18. Strack and Coyne, 1983; Coyne, 1976a, 1976b.

19. Cutrona, 1982.

20. Isen, 1984, p. 189; see Isen, 1984, Diener, 1984; Salovey and Rosenhan, in press, for reviews; Batson, Coke, Chard, Smith, and Taliaferro, 1979; Cialdini, Kenrick, and Baumann, 1982; Moore, Underwood, and Rosenhan, 1973; Isen, 1970; Gouaux, 1971; Griffith, 1970; Veitch and Griffith, 1976; Carnevale and Isen, 1986. Evidence linking positive affect to better social relationships is not in itself evidence for the positive impact of illusions on relations with others. The argument here is an indirect one, suggesting that to the extent that illusions foster positive mood, a relationship that is well established, mood constitutes a secondary or indirect causal route by which illusions may lead to good relations with others.

21. Gouaux, 1971; Griffith, 1970; Veitch and Griffith, 1976.

22. Isen, in press; Salovey and Rosenhan, in press.

23. Strack and Coyne, 1983; Coyne, 1976a, 1976b.

24. Tiger, 1979, p. 96.

25. Coopersmith, 1967; Kiesler and Baral, 1970; Shrauger, 1972; Brockner, 1979; Felson, 1984; Bandura, 1977; Baumeister, Hamilton, and Tice, 1985; Feather, 1966, 1968, 1969; Vasta and Brockner, 1979; Shrauger and Terbovic, 1976; McFarlin and Blascovich, 1981.

26. Novack and Iacocca, 1984.

27. Berges, 1977.

28. Miller, 1977.

29. Greenwald, 1984, p. 5.

30. Kamen and Seligman, 1986. Similar findings have been uncovered with children (e.g., Dweck & Licht, 1980). Children who explain performance setbacks and failures through negative emotions, explanations for the setback, and thoughts irrelevant to finding solutions had poor expectations for future success and less adaptive behaviors regarding future similar tasks. In contrast, those who responded to setbacks with self-instruction and solution-oriented thinking and with relatively few causal explanations for the failures showed more adaptive behaviors and less interfering negative emotions (see also Diener & Dweck, 1980; Brunstein & Olbrich, 1985).

31. Life Insurance Marketing Research Association, 1983.

32. Seligman and Schulman, 1986.

33. Zullow and Seligman, 1988. They also give the candidates' statements that follow.

34. Zullow and Seligman, 1988; see also Zullow, Oettingen, Peterson, and Seligman, 1988.

35. Bandura, 1977; Brunstein and Olbrich, 1985; Dweck and Licht, 1980; Diener and Dweck, 1978, 1980; Burger, 1985; Atkinson, 1964; Mischel, 1973; Weiner, 1979.

36. Carsrud and Olm, 1986. Additional attributes identified as characteristic of successful entrepreneurs were work orientation, reflected in such statements as, "I like to work hard," and interpersonal competitiveness, reflected by such sentiments as, "I feel that winning is important in both work and games." A somewhat puzzling qualification, however, was that these factors were most important when the entrepreneurs were minority owners in their firms and not in the case where they held the majority of the equity.

37. Gonzales and Zimbardo, 1985.

38. Scheier and Carver, 1985.

39. Beck, 1967, Seligman, 1975.

40. Trump with Schwartz, 1988.

41. Brown, 1984; Mischel, Coates, and Raskoff, 1968; Wright and Mischel, 1982; Weinstein, 1982.

42. Diener, 1984.

43. Greenwald, 1980.

44. Cited in Greenwald, 1980.

45. Greenwald, 1980; see also Brim, 1976; Epstein, 1973; Kelly, 1955; Sarbin, 1962.

46. Greenwald, 1980, p. 614.

47. Brim, 1976, p. 242.

48. Epstein, 1973, p. 407; see also Lynch, 1981.

49. Greenwald, 1980.

50. See Mayer and Salovey, in press, for a review.

51. Mayer and Salovey, in press; Isen, 1984; Bower, 1981.

52. Mayer and Salovey, in press.

53. Mayer and Salovey, in press; Isen, 1984.

54. Isen, Shalker, Clark, and Karp, 1978; Isen and Means, 1983; Isen and Daubman, 1984; Isen, Daubman, and Nowicki, 1987; Isen, Johnson, Mertz, and Robinson, 1985.

55. Isen et al., 1985; Isen et al., 1987.

56. Isen et al., 1978; Isen and Means, 1983; Isen and Daubman, 1984; Isen et al., 1987; Isen et al., 1985.

57. Epstein, 1988.

58. Bandura, 1977; Brunstein and Olbrich, 1985; Dweck and Licht, 1980; Diener and Dweck, 1978, 1980; Burger, 1985; Atkinson, 1964; Mischel, 1973; Weiner, 1979.

59. Isen and Patrick, 1983.

60. Berkowitz, 1972; Mischel, Ebbesen, and Zeiss, 1976; Seeman and Schwarz, 1974; Schwarz and Pollack, 1977.

61. Diener and Dweck, 1978, 1980.

62. Jahoda, 1958.

63. Cannon, 1932.

64. Lazarus, 1966; Lazarus and Folkman, 1984.

65. Taylor, 1986.

66. Thompson, 1981; Averill, 1973.
67. Cohen, Glass, and Singer, 1973.
68. Glass and Singer, 1972.
69. Thompson, 1981.
70. Johnson and Leventhal, 1974.
71. See Taylor, 1986 for a review.
72. Bandura, in press, (manuscript pp. 23–24).
73. Taylor, 1986; Thompson, 1981; cf. Suls and Fletcher, 1985.
74. Taylor and Clark, 1986; Langer, 1975; see Thompson, 1981, for a review.
75. Cohen and Edwards, in press; Pearlin and Schooler, 1978; Hobfoll and London, 1986; Hobfoll and Walfisch, 1984.
76. Scheier and Carver, 1985; Scheier, Weintraub, and Carver, 1986.
77. Kobasa, 1979.
78. Kobasa, Maddi, and Covington, 1981; Kobasa, Maddi, and Kahn, 1982; Kobasa, Maddi, and Puccetti, 1982; Kobasa and Puccetti, 1983.
79. Salvatore Maddi, cited in Brodoff, 1985, p. 235
80. Frederic Flach, cited in Brodoff, 1985, p. 239.
81. Markus and Nurius, 1986.
82. Markus and Nurius, 1986; Taylor and Schneider, 1989; Wurf and Markus, in press. People regard future situations that they can readily envision as much more likely to occur than future situations for which they have less clear images (see Taylor & Schneider, 1989, for a review). Once a person has a future possible self in his or her head, the person is more likely to think about it, and if it is a desirable one, think about ways to achieve it. Such concrete, goal-directed activity can be facilitated by beliefs in personal control.

Chapter 3

1. Konner, 1988.
2. S. Taylor, confidential research material.
3. The National Center for Health Statistics is one source of information on this topic. See also reports by the surgeons general, such as Harris (1980).
4. American Cancer Society, 1982; *Oncology Times*, 1984.
5. Ashley and Kannel, 1974.
6. See Matarazzo, 1982; Harris, 1980.
7. Strickland, 1978; Wallston and Wallston, 1980.
8. Bandura, 1977, 1986.
9. Beck and Lund, 1981; Strecher, McEvoy De Vellis, Becker, and Rosenstock, 1986; Bandura, Taylor, Williams, Mefford, and Barchas, 1985; Bandura, 1986.
10. Taylor, Bandura, Ewart, Miller, and DeBusk, 1985.
11. Kobasa and Puccetti, 1983.
12. Langer and Rodin, 1976.
13. Rodin and Langer, 1977.
14. Schulz, 1976.
15. Horowitz and Schulz, 1983; Schulz and Aderman, 1973; Horowitz and Schulz, 1985. Not all studies find clear-cut negative effects, and consequently, this has been an area of some controversy. Nonetheless, on balance, the evidence does seem to suggest adverse effects. It is significant that no studies have found positive effects from involuntary relocation.

16. Lemoine and Mougne, 1983.
17. Lefcourt, 1973, p. 422.
18. Engel, 1971, p. 774.
19. Cottington, Matthews, Talbott, and Kuller, 1980; Engel, 1971.
20. Engel, 1971.
21. Epidemiologic data on the incidence, prevalence, and factors associated with cancer are available from the National Cancer Institute and from the World Health Organization.
22. E.g., Blumberg, West, and Ellis, 1954.
23. Fox, 1983.
24. E.g., Shekelle et al., 1981.
25. Cassileth, Lusk, Miller, Brown, and Miller, 1985; Derogatis, Abeloff, and Melisaratos, 1979; Greer, Morris, and Pettingale, 1979; Pettingale, Morris, Greer, and Haybittle, 1985; Pettingale, Philalithis, Tee, and Greer, 1981; Jensen, 1987; Levy, Herberman, Maluish, Schlien, and Lippman, 1985; Rogentine et al., 1979; DiClemente and Temoshok, 1985; Temoshok et al., 1985.
26. Kavetskii, 1958; Amkraut and Solomon, 1977.
27. Sklar and Anisman, 1981.
28. Sklar and Anisman, 1981; Bartrop, Lockhurst, Lazarus, Kiloh, and Penny, 1977; Tache, Selye, and Day, 1979.
29. Visintainer, Seligman, and Volpicelli, 1983. Although some of the studies that have attempted to relate uncontrollable stressful events to cancer have methodological flaws that lead scientists to question their results, the fact that studies of both humans and animals have uncovered fairly consistent evidence relating lack of control or loss of control to cancer suggests that this relationship may, in fact, exist.
30. Schmale and Iker, 1971. In one study designed to examine these ideas, Schmale and his associates interviewed women who were awaiting biopsies for cervical cancer. They found that the women who expressed a lot of hopelessness in the interviews were more likely to have diagnoses of malignancies than were the women who expressed few feelings of hopelessness.
31. Sklar and Anisman, 1981; Thomas and Duszynski, 1974; Thomas, Duszynski, and Shaffer, 1979; Shaffer, Duszynski, and Thomas, 1982; Weisman and Worden, 1975. A potential concern regarding the relationship of psychological variables (e.g., depression, social support) to cancer concerns direction of causality. Might not cancer itself produce lack of social support or depression, for example? Alternatively, both cancer and certain psychological variables may be caused by some third variable. There is clear evidence that cancer can produce difficulties with social support and/or depression (e.g., Wortman & Dunkel-Schetter, 1979; Kübler-Ross, 1969). In longitudinal studies, however, it can be conclusively established that, as the temporally prior variable, the psychological factor (e.g., lack of social support or depression) contributes to cancer; the reverse direction of causality is not tenable in such data. More troublesome is the possibility that some third variable, such as gender or exposure to a carcinogen, may produce both the psychological state (e.g., depression or lack of support) and cancer. The studies demonstrating the apparent causal relationship between these variables have, for the most part, controlled for potential third factors as causal variables and ruled out the most likely ones. This does not mean that some other third variable that causes both cancer and the psychological state will not be identified at a later date. At present, however, the data strongly imply a causal relationship between depression and cancer (Shekelle

et al., 1981) and between lack of social support and cancer (Sklar & Anisman, 1981).

32. Taylor, Lichtman, and Wood, 1984a.

33. Levy, 1983a, 1983b; Rogers, Dubey, and Reich, 1979; Solomon, Amkraut, and Kasper, 1974.

34. For current reviews, the reader is referred to Stein, Keller, and Schleifer, 1985; Calabrese, Kling, and Gold, 1987; Kiecolt-Glaser and Glaser, in press.

35. Borysenko and Borysenko, 1982; Monjan and Collector, 1977; Keller, Weiss, Schleifer, Miller, and Stein, 1981; Laudenslager, Reite, and Harbeck, 1982; Reite, Harbeck, and Hoffman, 1981.

Stein and his colleagues suggested that immune functioning may be enhanced by stress under two circumstances. Specifically, low-level exposure to stress, such as that provided by low-voltage electric shock, may enhance immune functioning (Solomon, 1969; Hirata-Hibi, 1967). Similarly, while acute exposure to certain stressful events can suppress immune functioning, repeated exposure can sometimes produce an apparent adaptation of the animal to the stressors and in some cases enhance immune functioning. (Gisler, 1974; Monjan & Collector, 1977; Joasoo & McKenzie, 1976)

36. Hinkle, 1974; Meyer and Haggerty, 1962; Boyce et al., 1977; Glaser et al., 1987; see Jemmott and Locke, 1984.

37. Fischer et al., 1972; Kimzey, 1975; Leach and Rambaut, 1974.

38. Bartrop et al., 1977; Schleifer, Keller, McKegney, and Stein, 1979; see Jemmott and Locke, 1984.

39. Hanson et al., 1976; Laudenslager et al., 1983; Bandura et al., 1985.

40. Weinstein, 1980, 1982, 1984, 1987.

41. Weinstein, 1984.

42. Weinstein, 1982, 1984.

43. Scheier et al., 1986. Positive mood is also associated with fewer somatic symptoms, although it is not clear exactly why this effect occurs (Persson & Sjoberg, 1987).

44. Scheier et al., 1988.

45. Strack and Coyne, 1983.

46. Peterson, Seligman, and Vaillant, 1988.

47. Friedman and Booth-Kewley, 1988. To reach these conclusions, Friedman and Booth-Kewley employed the statistical technique of meta-analysis, which provides a well-controlled method for inferring relationships from multiple research investigations. The use of these kinds of controlled analytic procedures provides considerably greater confidence for the results than would be furnished by merely reviewing all of the appropriate studies.

One can legitimately question, of course, whether emotions are causing disease or whether disease is causing negative emotions. Some of the studies analyzed by these investigators were ones in which mental states were measured before there were any signs of a disease, and these studies found evidence for the role of depression, anger, hostility, and anxiety in the development of illness as well.

48. Schmale, 1958; Imboden, Canter, Cluff, Leighton, and Trevor, 1959; Imboden, Canter, and Cluff, 1961. It should be noted that studies examining the effects of particular stressful events and psychological states such as depression on immunologic functioning have not directly tied reductions in immunologic functioning to disease states or increased rates of infection. Indeed, in some cases, the adverse effects on the immune system are small, making it question-

able whether such declines could actually increase susceptibility to disease states. However, evidence is mounting to tie both depression and uncontrollable stressful events to both immunologic changes and to increased risk for diseases independently, thereby lending credence to the idea that gaps in immune functioning may have at least some direct relationship to the likelihood of illness (Calabrese et al., 1987).

49. Kronfol et al., 1983. The studies relating depression to compromised immunologic functioning were conducted primarily with clinical samples of depressed people. It is not clear whether the mild depressions to which people are often exposed during the course of their everyday lives would actually compromise the immune system to any significant or reliable degree.

50. Findley, 1953; Shapiro, 1960.

51. Liberman, 1962, p. 761.

52. Beecher, 1959.

53. Shapiro, 1964, p. 74.

54. Siegel, 1986, p. 35.

55. See Taylor, 1986, for a discussion.

56. Levine, Gordon, and Fields, 1978.

57. Shapiro, 1964.

58. Liberman, 1962; Shapiro, 1964.

59. Broskowski, 1981.

60. Shapiro, 1964.

Chapter 4

1. Freud, 1930/1961, p. 28.

2. Horney, 1950; Erikson, 1950; Sullivan, 1953; Maslow, 1954.

3. Maslow, 1950, cited in Jahoda, 1958, p. 28.

4. Kübler-Ross, 1969; Lazarus, 1983.

5. E.g., Kübler-Ross, 1969.

6. Goleman, 1985.

7. Horney, 1950.

8. Freud, 1915/1957; A. Freud, 1966.

9. Weinberger, personal communication, October 23, 1988.

10. Weinberger, personal communication, October 23, 1988.

11. Sackeim, 1983.

12. Sackeim, 1983, p. 114.

13. Sackeim, 1983, p. 114.

14. Weinberger, in press. Weinberger distinguishes repressors from those who do not engage in the repressive style using a combination of the Taylor Manifest Anxiety Scale and the Marlowe-Crowne Social Desirability Scale. Those who are low on manifest anxiety but high on social desirability, he argues, represent the repressive style.

As Weinberger indicated in his review, repressors show less negative affect than people who are actually low in anxiety, but assessments of their reactions to stress—as through psychophysiological measures, analysis of vocal speech, facial characteristics, and other nonverbal cues—suggest that they are at least as anxious or more anxious than people who report chronic distress (p. 52). He goes on to distinguish them from George Vaillant's "well-adjusted suppressors, who when appropriate, decide to postpone but not avoid dealing with conflictual issues" (p. 52). In essence, then, Vaillant's well-adjusted suppressors appear to be very close to those people who employ the normal illusions of life as we have described them.

15. Doster, 1975.

16. Nielsen and Fleck, 1981. Repressors seem to have difficulty recognizing and dealing with several aspects of negative emotions, compared to people who are truly low in anxiety. For example, when asked how they would feel if their spouse died, repressors recognized that they would feel sad but failed to recognize some of the more subtle emotions they might experience, such as anger.

17. Wilkins, Epting, and Van De Reit, 1972.

18. Weinberger, in press, p. 36.

19. Weinberger, in press. Although they report low levels of anxiety, repressors have substantial physiological responses to threatening information, much more so that people who are truly low in anxiety.

20. Weinberger, in press.

21. Jensen, 1987; see also Viney, 1986.

22. Weinberger, in press.

23. Taylor, in press. See chapter 3 for a discussion of this issue.

24. Lehman and Taylor, 1987.

25. Weinberger, in press, p. 51.

26. Blumberg, 1972; Parducci, 1968; Tesser and Rosen, 1975; Goffman, 1955.

27. See Swann, 1983, 1984, for reviews.

28. Swann and Hill, 1982; Swann and Read, 1981a, 1981b; see Swann, 1983, 1984 for reviews.

29. Eckland, 1968; Hill, Rubin, and Peplau, 1976; Richardson, 1939; Spuhler, 1968; see Swann, 1984 for a review; Secord and Backman, 1965; Swann, 1983.

30. Tesser, 1980; Tesser and Campbell, 1980, 1982; Tesser, Campbell, and Smith, 1984; Tesser and Paulhus, 1983.

31. See Swann, 1983, 1984 for reviews.

32. Baker, 1986, p. 26.

33. Pinneau, 1975; Cobb, 1976; House, 1981; Schaefer, Coyne, and Lazarus, 1981.

34. See Wallston and Wallston, 1982, for a review. Psychologists maintain that social support is valuable for everybody, whether they are under stress or not. When things are going well, they seem to be going just a bit better when one can celebrate them and enjoy them with close friends and family. Researchers have suggested, however, that social support may be especially valuable in muting the effects of stressful events. That is, although social support can make people happy all of the time, it may exert some of its strongest effects on emotional and physical health when a person is confronted with a threatening situation. In this sense, social support buffers the effects of stress (e.g., Cohen & Hoberman, 1983).

35. Confidential research data. In the context of the case histories about to be described, it is useful to know that married people appear to be more likely to survive cancers once they are diagnosed than people who are not married (American Cancer Society, 1982). Compared with people who are divorced, widowed or never married, married people are more likely to be alive after five years of cancer, with divorced people facing the greatest risk of mortality due to cancer.

36. Taxonomies of social support have been many and varied, but there is now some convergence on the chief benefits as tangible support, information, and emotional support (e.g., Pinneau, 1975; House, 1981; Schaefer et al., 1981).

37. Lieberman, 1983; Suls, 1982; Coyne, 1976a, 1976b.

38. See Taylor, Collins, Skokan, and Aspinwall, in press.

39. Orwell, 1949, p. 177.

40. See Fiske and Taylor, 1984; Nisbett and Ross, 1980; Greenwald, 1980 for reviews.

41. See Fiske and Taylor, 1984; Nisbett and Ross, 1980; Greenwald, 1980 for reviews.

42. Wixon and Laird, 1976; p. 384.

43. See, for example, Klatzky, 1975, for a description of this process.

44. See Greenwald, 1980.

45. Orwell, 1949, p. 176.

46. Greenwald, 1980; Walster and Berscheid, 1968; cf. Swann, 1983; Markus and Nurius, 1986.

47. Greenwald, 1980.

48. Fischhoff, 1976.

49. See, for example, Zimbardo, Ebbesen, and Maslach, 1977, for a review.

50. Taylor and Brown, 1988.

51. Campbell, 1986; Harackiewicz, Manderlink, and Sansone, 1984; Lewicki, 1984, 1985; Rosenberg, 1979.

52. See Taylor and Brown, 1988; cf. Wurf and Markus, 1983.

53. Taylor and Brown, 1988.

54. Markus, 1977; Wurf and Markus, 1983.

55. Warfield, 1957, p. 36, cited in Goffman, 1963.

56. See, for example, Brim's (1988) discussion of ongoing studies of American Telephone and Telegraph executives.

57. Baumeister and Scher, 1988. It should be noted that not all self-destructive behavior should be considered in ultimate service of the ego. Clearly, there is a trade-off. Self-handicapping behaviors do not make people happy. Quite the contrary. They often make people miserable, but somewhat less miserable than would be the case if a more damaging self-attribution for failure were made.

58. Berglas and Jones, 1978; Jones and Berglas, 1978.

59. See Sackeim, 1983; Fingarette, 1969; Sackeim and Gur, 1978, 1979; Greenwald, 1980, for discussions of this issue. Sackheim and Gur argue that there are four criteria necessary and sufficient for ascribing self-deception to some observed phenomenon. First, the individual must hold two contradictory beliefs and do so simultaneously. He or she must be unaware of holding one of the beliefs and the act that determines which belief is and which belief is not subject to awareness must be a motivated act.

Although the methodology used to demonstrate self-deception has been hotly debated (e.g., Douglas & Gibbons, 1983; Rubin, 1985; Smith & Richardson, 1985), the existence of the phenomenon has been generally acknowledged.

60. Greenwald, 1980.

61. Gur and Sackheim, 1979; see also Viney, 1986. Lettieri (1983) found that self-deception and self-consciousness were positively associated, but that self-consciousness was unassociated with mental health. Self-deception was modestly associated with mental health. Similarly, research using the MMPI (Minnesota Multiphasic Personality Inventory) finds that elevated scores on the K scale, which assesses defensiveness, are indicative of good adjustment, cheerfulness, and optimism (Welsh & Dahlstrom, 1956; Butcher, 1969; Dahlstrom, Welsh, & Dahlstrom, 1975).

62. A. Bartlett Giamatti, quoted in *Time,* June 23, 1986, p. 94.

Chapter 5

1. Heinrich and Kriefel cited in Goffman, 1963.
2. For studies documenting recovery from traumatic events, the reader is referred to Taylor (1983), Antonovsky (1979), Andreason and Norris (1972), Brickman et al. (1978), Chodoff, Friedman, and Hamburg (1964), Frankl (1963), Myers, Friedman, and Weiner (1970), Visotsky, Hamburg, Goss, and Lebovits (1961), Thompson (1985). For references describing conditions under which full emotional recovery may not occur, the reader is referred to Silver and Wortman (1980), Silver (1980), Wortman and Silver (1987), Berglas (1985).
3. Taylor, 1983.
4. Janoff-Bulman and Frieze, 1983.
5. Janoff-Bulman, in press.
6. E.g., Burgess and Holstrom, 1979; Leventhal, 1975; see Taylor, Wood and Lichtman, 1983.
7. Seligman, 1975; Brehm, 1966; Wortman and Brehm, 1975.
8. Chapters 2 and 3 discuss this issue. See also Thompson, 1981; Fiske and Taylor, 1984, for reviews.
9. Briar, 1966; Scholzman and Verba, 1979; Abrams and Finesinger, 1953; Burgess and Holmstrom, 1979.
10. Kleck, 1968, p. 1245.
11. Erikson, 1976; Janoff-Bulman and Frieze, 1983.
12. Davis, 1961.
13. This and other accounts of cancer patients are Taylor, Lichtman, and Wood, confidential research data, unless otherwise noted.
14. Ryan, 1971.
15. Lerner, 1965, 1970; Lerner and Lichtman, 1968; Lerner and Matthews, 1967; Lerner and Simmons, 1966.
16. *CBS Evening News,* March 15, 1982.
17. Confidential research data.
18. See Silver and Wortman, 1980; Turk, 1979; Thompson, 1985; Keyes, 1985.
19. Silver and Wortman, 1980.
20. Gurin, Veroff, and Feld, 1960; Wills, 1983.
21. Burgess and Holmstrom, 1979.
22. Wood, Taylor, and Lichtman, 1985.
23. *CBS Evening News,* May 31, 1982.
24. Confidential research data.
25. CBS, *A Time to Die,* July 1982.
26. Taylor et al., 1983.
27. Taylor et al., 1983.
28. *CBS Evening News,* May 31, 1983.
29. Festinger, 1954; see Suls and Miller, 1977, for a review.
30. Wills, 1981.
31. Taylor et al., 1983.
32. Taylor et al., 1983, p. 29.
33. Kübler-Ross, 1969, p. 99.
34. Taylor et al., 1983.
35. Wortman and Dunkel-Schetter, 1979.
36. Easterlin, 1974; Silver, 1980; Gallup, 1976–1977; Brickman et al., 1978; Diener, 1984; Watson, 1930; Tellegan, 1979.

37. Diener, 1984.
38. E.g., Leventhal, 1975; see Taylor, 1983.
39. Kübler-Ross, 1969; Lazarus, 1983.
40. Taylor, 1983.
41. Goldman, 1947, p. 38.
42. Ohnstad, 1942, p. 69.
43. Taylor et al., 1984a.
44. Taylor, 1983, p. 1164.
45. Taylor, 1983, p. 1164.
46. Taylor, 1983, p. 1163.
47. Taylor et al., 1984b.
48. Taylor, 1983, p. 1164.
49. Taylor, 1983.
50. Taylor et al., 1984b; see also Marks, Richardson, Graham, and Levine, 1986.
51. Affleck, Tennen, Pfeiffer, and Fifield, 1987.
52. Seligman, 1975.
53. Affleck et al., 1987.
54. Clements and Sider, 1983; Crile, 1972; Lyman, Wurtele, and Shannon, 1980.
55. Greenfield, Kaplan, and Ware, in press.
56. E.g., Crile, 1972; Clements and Sider, 1983.
57. Wagener and Taylor, 1986.
58. Wagener and Taylor, 1986, p. 491.
59. See Taylor, 1983, for a discussion of this issue; Showers and Cantor, 1985. The point of this discussion is not to suggest that learned helplessness effects are absent in humans. There may well be such effects, particularly among institutionalized populations subject to external control (see Taylor, 1979; Seligman, 1975; Wortman & Brehm, 1975). Rather, the point is that, in contrast to animal species like the rat, the human has symbolic capacities, and the potential for multiple goals and multiple pathways to them. Consequently, in situations in which one might expect to see learned helplessness in humans, one may instead see active striving for a goal using varied, inventive networks.
60. Taylor, 1983; Chodoff et al., 1964; Frankl, 1963; Mechanic, 1977; Visotsky et al., 1961; Weisman and Worden, 1975; Thompson, 1988, 1985.
61. Taylor, 1983.
62. Taylor, 1983.
63. Lehman, Wortman, and Williams, 1987.
64. Hollander, 1983.
65. Taylor, 1983, p. 1183.
66. Taylor, 1983, p. 1183.
67. Taylor, 1983, p. 1183.
68. Taylor, 1983, p. 1183.
69. Silver and Wortman, 1980; Wortman and Silver, 1982; Lehman, Ellard, and Wortman, 1986; Silver, 1980.
70. Janoff-Bulman, 1979, in press.
71. Silver, Boon, and Stones, 1983.
72. Collins, Taylor, and Skokan, 1988.
73. Vaillant, 1977, p. 7.

Chapter 6

1. The general descriptions of mania derive from Tyler and Shopsin, 1982; American Psychiatric Association, 1980.
2. *Time,* January 8, 1973.
3. Goodwin and Jamison, in press, Chapter 18 (manuscript p. 24).
4. See Goodwin and Jamison, in press, for a review. The accounts of composers, novelists, and poets in this section are also derived from this source, unless otherwise noted.
5. Kraepelin, 1921.
6. Goodwin and Jamison, in press.
7. Broyard, 1985, p. 9.
8. Broyard, 1985, p. 9.
9. Letter from Robert Lowell to Theodore Roethke, 1963; cited in Goodwin and Jamison, in press.
10. Goodwin and Jamison, in press, list the possible relationships between mania and creativity that follow.
11. Erikson, 1960.
12. Andreason, 1980.
13. Goodwin and Jamison, in press.
14. Storr, 1968.
15. Tiger, 1979, p. 162.
16. Goodwin and Jamison, in press.
17. Some have argued that the self-aggrandizement of mania may actually be defensive in nature, possibly representing a camouflaged depression (Zigler & Glick, 1988) or a mask for low self-esteem (Winters & Neale, 1985). It may represent a qualitatively quite different psychological state from the self-aggrandizement observed in normal individuals.
18. It should be noted that there are several different forms of depression that share common symptoms but may derive from different conditions. Reactive depression is typically a normal and temporary response to some loss or stressful event such as the death of a parent or the diagnosis of a serious disease. Bipolar depression is part of the manic-depressive syndrome. Unipolar depression, by far the most common, is a chronic, dysphoric reaction usually considered to be out of proportion to and more enduring than objective conditions would dictate as normal. In most of this chapter, we will be referring to unipolar depression, although most of the points regarding the symptoms and manifestations of depression refer to the other types as well.
19. American Psychiatric Association, 1980, gives the symptoms of depression described in this chapter.
20. Scarf, 1979, p. 47.
21. Minkoff, Bergman, Beck, and Beck, 1973.
22. Goodwin and Jamison, in press.
23. Freud, 1950, p. 156.
24. Abramson and Alloy, 1981.
25. Abramson and Alloy, 1981; Alloy, Abramson, and Viscusi, 1981; Alloy and Ahrens, 1987; Brown, 1985, 1986; Campbell and Fairey, 1985; Derry and Kuiper, 1981; Golin et al., 1977; Golin et al., 1979; Greenberg and Alloy, in press; Kuiper, 1978; Kuiper and Derry, 1982; Kuiper and MacDonald, 1982; Kuiper et al., 1985; Lewinsohn et al., 1980; MacDonald and Kuiper, 1984; Nelson and Craighead, 1977; Pietromonaco and Markus, 1985; Pyszczynski,

Holt, and Greenberg, 1987; Rizley, 1978; Sweeney, Shaeffer, and Golin, 1982. See Coyne and Gotlib, 1983; Ruehlman, West, and Pasahow, 1985; Watson and Clark, 1984; for reviews. It should be noted that people low in self-esteem but otherwise not depressed nonetheless show many of the effects demonstrated by depressed people with respect to processing information about the self (Shrauger & Terbovic, 1976). Chapter 1 introduced the concept of self-schemas, which involve the organization of information about the self. Depressed people have more negative self-schemas than those who are not depressed, so they make themselves ready for unflattering interpretations of situations. In any circumstance that is seen as relevant to the self, the depressed person is poised to interpret his or her behavior disparagingly. This negative self is rigidly applied to new information, and the depressed person becomes unable to develop alternative and more positive self-perceptions (MacDonald & Kuiper, 1984).

26. Abramson, Alloy, and Rosoff, 1981; Benassi and Mahler, 1985; DeMonbreun and Craighead, 1977; Gotlib, 1983; see Beck, 1967; see also Dykman, Abramson, Alloy, and Hartlage, in press.

27. Lewinsohn et al., 1980.

28. Coyne, in press; Coyne, 1976a, 1976b; Coyne et al., 1987; Strack and Coyne, 1983.

29. Beck, quoted in Seligman, 1975, p. 83.

30. Abramson et al., 1981.

31. Linville, 1982, 1987.

32. Abramson et al., 1981; see also Bargh and Tota, 1988; Ellis, Thomas, and Rodriguez, 1984; Ellis, Thomas, McFarland, and Lane, 1985.

33. Brown and Harris, 1978; Kuiper and Olinger, 1988.

34. Paykel, 1982.

35. Layne, 1983.

36. Beck, 1967; Beck, Rush, Shaw, and Emery, 1979; Beck, 1974.

37. Abramson and Alloy, 1981; Abramson, Seligman, and Teasdale, 1978; Peterson and Seligman, 1984; see also Andersen and Lyon, 1987.

38. Brewin, 1985; Coyne and Gotlib, 1983; Sweeney, Anderson, and Bailey, 1986; Peterson and Seligman, 1984; Nolen-Hoeksema, Girgus, and Seligman, 1986; see also Brown and Siegel, in press. Abramson, Alloy, and Metalsky, in press; Abramson, Metalsky, and Alloy, in press, suggest that attributions for negative events may be important for some kinds of depression but not others.

39. Brewin (1985) for example, concludes after a review of the evidence that there is no basis to conclude that explanatory style causes or creates a vulnerability to depression, only that it is characteristic of depression (see also Cochran & Hammen, 1985). Rholes, Riskind, and Neville (1985) and Anderson and Arnoult (1985) suggest that feelings of loss of control may lead to the onset of depression. Kuiper and Olinger (1988), for example, suggest that people prone to depression have defective cognitive mechanisms for evaluating their self-worth. In particular, they may be more prone to anxiety under stress and develop an acute sensitivity to the evaluations of others, which sometimes leads them to isolate themselves socially during stressful times.

Swallow and Kuiper (1988) suggest that people prone to depression may make poor choices of others with whom to compare themselves. Whereas normal people may compare themselves to others who are worse off and/or to others who have a better situation that is within reach, depressed people may compare themselves to more fortunate others whose attributes and outcomes they can never hope to reach.

Pyszczynski and Greenberg (1987) suggest that depression may be triggered by a stressful event that threatens self-worth. The person may then become locked in a state of chronic self-focus which leads to negative affect, self-derogation, and more experiences that threaten self-worth.

Others (e.g., Hammen, Miklowitz, & Dyck, 1986; Dance & Kuiper, 1987) point to the importance of negative self-schemas in the symptomatology but not necessarily the onset of depression.

40. Bargh and Tota, 1988
41. *Psychology Today,* April 1979, p. 58.
42. Zis and Goodwin, 1982.
43. Hammen, personal communication.
44. Coyne, 1976a, 1976b.
45. Hammen et al., 1986; Kuiper et al., 1985. Interestingly, depressed people fail to hold positive illusions about themselves, but they do hold them regarding others. Thus, for example, they distort the degree of control that another person might have in a situation in a positive direction, but they do not distort the degree of control that they themselves have (Martin, Abramson, & Alloy, 1984; Golin et al., 1977; Alloy & Ahrens, 1987; Tabachnik, Crocker, & Alloy, 1983).
46. For discussions of social roles and sex and their relations to depression, see Brown and Harris, 1978; Oatley and Bolton, 1985.
47. Klerman, 1979, 1986.
48. Goodwin and Jamison, in press.
49. S. Taylor, confidential research data.
50. Paykel, 1982; Gotlib, 1984.

Chapter 7

1. Wagner, 1986, p. 14.
2. I do not wish to imply that the scientists on whose work this analysis is based were concerned exclusively with low-level scientific issues, and that a larger picture somehow eluded them. This would be nonsense. Many other scientists in my field have seen this picture taking shape, including Anthony Greenwald, Richard Lazarus, George Vaillant (albeit using very different evidence), and Richard Nisbett, to name a few, as well as many others who may have envisioned it but felt there was little reason to state what may have seemed to be a quite obvious extension of the literature.
3. Janoff-Bulman, in press.
4. Collins et al., 1988.
5. Weisz, Rothbaum, and Blackburn, 1984, p. 965.
6. Morrow, 1983, p. 22.
7. Weisz et al., 1984, p. 965.
8. Seligman, 1975.
9. For reviews, see Harter, 1983; Maccoby and Martin, 1983; Skinner and Chapman, 1987; Connell, 1985; Ryan, Connell, and Grolnick, in press; Skinner and Connell, 1986; Harter, 1981; Hightower et al., 1986.
10. Ryan and Grolnick, 1986; Ryan, Connell, and Deci, 1985; Hess and Holloway, 1985; Becker, 1964; Schaefer, 1959; Baldwin, 1949; Baumrind, 1967, 1971; Dornbusch, Ritter, Leiderman, Roberts, and Fraleigh, 1987; deCharms, 1976; Deci, Nezlek, and Sheinman, 1981; Grolnick and Ryan, 1987a, 1987b.
11. Grolnick and Ryan, 1988.

12. Ryan and Grolnick, 1986.

13. See Harter, 1983; Maccoby and Martin, 1983, for review.

14. Grolnick and Ryan, 1987b; Ryan et al., in press; Gordon, Nowicki, and Wichern, 1981; Patterson, 1976; Hatfield, Ferguson, and Alpert, 1967; Loeb, Horst, and Horton, 1980.

15. Baumeister, in press.

16. Baumeister, Tice, and Hutton, in press; Parducci, 1968.

17. One might counter that mania presents just such a condition. However, the grandiose cognitions associated with mania and hypomania are not in themselves regarded as problems that necessitate intervention and treatment. Rather, they may act as an impetus for treatment if they are regarded as predictive of some future more extreme event, such as a full-blown manic episode with its accompanying psychosis or a depressive mood swing. In and of itself, the cognitions of mania and hypomania are not typically a target for clinical intervention.

18. See Nisbett and Ross, 1980; Fiske and Taylor, 1984, for discussions of this issue.

19. One might counter by wondering if the man would not be doomed to repeat the error by failing to recognize the poor quality of his work. If his situation were negative enough, most theories of learning would argue, he would seek a quite different environment in which to pursue his interests, thereby improving his chances for future success.

20. See Fiske and Taylor, 1984.

21. Brown, 1986, p. 375.

22. Janoff-Bulman and Brickman, 1982.

23. See Baumeister, in press.

24. Vaillant paraphrasing Edward Glover.

25. cf., Vaillant, 1977.

26. See, for example, Stipek, 1984.

REFERENCES

Abrams, R. D., & Finesinger, J. E. (1953). Guilt reactions in patients with cancer. *Cancer, 6,* 474–482.

Abramson, L. Y., & Alloy, L. B. (1981). Depression, non-depression, and cognitive illusions: A reply to Schwartz. *Journal of Experimental Psychology, 110,* 436–447.

Abramson, L. Y., Alloy, L. B., & Metalsky, G. I. (in press). The cognitive diathesis-stress theories of depression: Toward an adequate evaluation of the theories' validities. In L. B. Alloy (Ed.), *Cognitive process in depression.* New York: Guilford Press.

Abramson, L. Y., Alloy, L. B., & Rosoff, R. (1981). Depression and the generation of complex hypotheses in the judgement of contingency. *Behaviour Research and Therapy, 19,* 35–45.

Abramson, L. Y., Metalsky, G. I., & Alloy, L. B. (in press). The hopelessness theory of depression: Does the research test the theory? In L. Y. Abramson (Ed.), *Social cognition and clinical psychology: A synthesis.* New York: Guilford Press.

Abramson, L. Y., Seligman, M. E. P., & Teasdale, J. (1978). Learned helplessness in humans: Critique and reformulation. *Journal of Abnormal Psychology, 87,* 49–74.

Adler, A. (1930). Individual psychology. In C. Murchinson (Ed.), *Psychologies of 1930* (pp. 395–405). Worcester, MA: Clark University Press.

Affleck, G., Tennen, H., Pfeiffer, C., & Fifield, J. (1987). Appraisals of control and predictability in adapting to a chronic disease. *Journal of Personality and Social Psychology, 2,* 273–279.

Alicke, M. D. (1985). Global self-evaluation as determined by the desirability and uncontrollability of trait adjectives. *Journal of Personality and Social Psychology, 49,* 1621–1630.

Alloy, L. B., Abramson, L. Y., & Viscusi, D. (1981). Induced mood and the illusion of control. *Journal of Personality and Social Psychology, 41,* 1129–1140.

Alloy, L. B., & Ahrens, A. H. (1987). Depression and pessimism for the future: Biased use of statistically relevant information in predictions for self versus others. *Journal of Personality and Social Psychology, 52,* 366–378.

Allport, F. H. (1955). *Theories of perception and the concept of structure.* New York: Wiley.

Allport, G. W. (1955). *Becoming: Basic considerations for a psychology of personality.* New Haven, CT: Yale University Press.

Alper, T. G. (1952). The interrupted task method in studies of selective recall: A re-evaluation of some recent experiments. *Psychological Review, 59,* 71–88.

American Cancer Society. (1982). *Cancer facts and figures, 1983.* New York: Author.

American Psychiatric Association. (1980). *Diagnostic and statistical manual of mental disorders* (3rd ed.). Washington, DC: Author.

Amkraut, A., & Solomon, G. F. (1977). From the symbolic stimulus to the pathophysiologic response: Immune mechanisms. In Z. P. Lipowski, D. R. Lipsitt, & D. C. Whybrow (Eds.), *Psychosomatic medicine: Current trends and clinical applications* (pp. 228–250). New York: Oxford University Press.

Andersen, S. M., & Lyon, J. E. (1987). Anticipating undesired outcomes: The role of outcome certainty in the onset of depressive affect. *Journal of Experimental Social Psychology, 23,* 428–443.

Anderson, C. A. (1983). Imagination and expectation: The effect of imagining behavioral scripts on personal intentions. *Journal of Personality and Social Psychology, 45,* 293–305.

Anderson, C. A., & Arnoult, L. H. (1985). Attributional style and everyday problems in living: Depression, loneliness, and shyness. *Social Cognition, 3,* 16–35.

Andreason, N. C. (1980). Mania and creativity. In R. H. Belmaker & H. M. Van Praage (Eds.), *Mania: An evolving concept.* New York: Spectrum.

Andreason, N. J. C., & Norris, A. S. (1972). Long-term adjustment and adaptation mechanisms in severely burned adults. *Journal of Nervous and Mental Disease, 154,* 352–362.

Antonovsky, A. (1979). *Health, stress, and coping.* San Francisco: Jossey-Bass.

Arkes, R. M., & Harkness, A. R. (1980). Effect of making a diagnosis on subsequent recognition of symptoms. *Journal of Experimental Psychology: Human Learning and Memory, 6,* 568–575.

Aronson, E., & Linder, D. (1965). Gain and loss of esteem as determinants of interpersonal attractiveness. *Journal of Experimental Social Psychology, 1,* 156–172.

Ashley, F., Jr., & Kannel, W. (1974). Relation of weight change to change in atherogenic traits: The Framingham Study. *Journal of Chronic Diseases, 27,* 103–114.

Atkinson, J. W. (1964). *An introduction to motivation.* Princeton, NJ: Van Nostrand.

Averill, J. R. (1973). Personal control over aversive stimuli and its relationship to stress. *Psychological Bulletin, 80,* 286–303.

Baker, R. (1986, December 14). Don't understand me. *New York Times Magazine,* 26.

Baldwin, A. L. (1949). The effect of home environment on nursery school behavior. *Child Development, 20,* 49–62.

Bandura, A. (1977). *Social learning theory.* Englewood Cliffs, NJ: Prentice-Hall.

Bandura, A. (1981). Self-referent thought: The development of self-efficacy. In J. H. Flavell & L. D. Ross (Eds.), *Social cognitive development* (pp. 200–239). New York: Cambridge University Press.

Bandura, A. (1982). Self-efficacy mechanism in human agency. *American Psychologist, 37,* 122–147.

Bandura, A. (1986). *Social foundations of thought and action: A social cognitive theory.* Englewood Cliffs, NJ: Prentice-Hall.

Bandura, A. (in press). Self-efficacy mechanism in physiological activation and health-promoting behavior. In J. Madden IV, S. Matthysse, & J. Barchas (Eds.), *Adaptation, learning and affect.* New York: Raven Press.

Bandura, A., Taylor, C. B., Williams, L. W., Mefford, I. N., & Barchas, J. D. (1985). Catecholamine secretion as a function of perceived coping self-efficacy. *Journal of Consulting and Clinical Psychology, 53,* 406–414.

Bargh, J. A., & Tota, M. E. (1988). Context-dependent automatic processing in depression: Accessibility of negative constructs with regard to self but not others. *Journal of Personality and Social Psychology, 54,* 925–939.

Bartrop, R. W., Lockhurst, E., Lazarus, L., Kiloh, L. G., & Penny, R. (1977). Depressed lymphocyte function after bereavement. *Lancet, 1,* 834–836.

Batson, C. D., Coke, J. S., Chard, F., Smith, D., & Taliaferro, A. (1979). Generality of the "glow of good will": Effects of mood on helping and information acquisition. *Social Psychology Quarterly, 42,* 176–179.

Baumeister, R. F. (in press). The optimal margin of illusion. *Journal of Social and Clinical Psychology.*

Baumeister, R. F., Hamilton, J. C., & Tice, D. M. (1985). Public versus private expectancy of success: Confidence booster or performance pressure? *Journal of Personality and Social Psychology, 48,* 1447–1457.

Baumeister, R. F., & Scher, S. J. (1988). Self-defeating behavior patterns among normal individuals: Review and analysis of common self-destructive tendencies. *Psychological Bulletin, 104,* 3–22.

Baumeister, R. F., Tice, D. M., & Hutton, D. G. (in press). Self-presentational motivations and personality differences in self-esteem. *Journal of Personality.*

Baumrind, D. (1967). Child care practices anteceding three patterns of preschool behavior. *Genetic Psychology Monographs, 75,* 43–88.

Baumrind, D. (1971). Current patterns of parental authority. *Developmental Psychology Monographs, 4,* 1–102.

Beck, A. T. (1967). *Depression: Clinical, experimental and theoretical aspects.* New York: Harper & Row.

Beck, A. T. (1974). The development of depression: A cognitive model. In R. J. Friedman & M. M. Katz (Eds.), *The psychology of depression* (pp. 3–28). Washington, DC: Winston.

Beck, A. T., Rush, A. J., Shaw, B. F., & Emery, G. (1979). *Cognitive theory of depression.* New York: Guilford Press.

Beck, K. H., & Lund, A. K. (1981). The effects of health threat seriousness and personal efficacy upon intentions and behavior. *Journal of Applied Social Psychology, 11,* 401–415.

Becker, E. (1973). *The denial of death.* New York: Free Press.

Becker, W. C. (1964). Consequences of different kinds of parental discipline. In M. L. Hoffman & L. W. Hoffman (Eds.), *Review of child development research* (Vol. 1, pp. 169–208). New York: Russell Sage Foundation.

Beecher, H. K. (1959). *Measurement of subjective responses.* New York: Oxford University Press.

Benassi, V. A., & Mahler, H. I. M. (1985). Contingency judgments by depressed college students: Sadder but not always wiser. *Journal of Personality and Social Psychology, 49,* 1323–1329.

Berges, M. (1977, January 27). Irving Wallace: A good ear for words. *Los Angeles Times, View,* pp. 1, 6.

Berglas, S. (1985, February). Why did this happen to me? *Psychology Today,* pp. 44–48.

Berglas, S., & Jones, E. E. (1978). Drug choice as a self-handicapping strategy in response to non-contingent success. *Journal of Personality and Social Psychology, 36,* 405–417.

Berkowitz, L. (1972). Social norms, feelings and other factors affecting helping behavior and altruism. In L. Berkowitz (Ed.), *Advances in experimental social psychology* (Vol. 6, pp. 63–108). New York: Academic Press.

Berlyne, D. C. (1960). *Conflict, arousal, and curiosity.* New York: McGraw-Hill.

Blumberg, E. M., West, P. M., & Ellis, F. W. (1954). Possible relationship between psychological factors and human cancer. *Psychosomatic Medicine, 16,* 277–286.

Blumberg, H. H. (1972). Communication of interpersonal evaluations. *Journal of Personality and Social Psychology, 23,* 157–162.

Bohrnstedt, G. W., & Felson, R. B. (1983). Explaining the relations among children's actual and perceived performances and self-esteem: A comparison of several causal models. *Journal of Personality and Social Psychology, 45,* 43–56.

Borysenko, M., & Borysenko, J. (1982). Stress, behavior, and immunity: Animal models and mediating mechanisms. *General Hospital Psychiatry, 4,* 59–67.

Bower, G. H. (1981). Mood and memory. *American Psychologist, 36,* 129–148.

Bower, G. H., Black, J. B., & Turner, T. J. (1979). Scripts in memory for text. *Cognitive Psychology, 11,* 177–220.

Boyce, W. T., Jensen, E. W., Cassel, J. C., Collier, A. M., Smith, A. H., & Ramey, C. T. (1977). Influence of life events and family routines on childhood respiratory tract illness. *Pediatrics, 60,* 609–615.

Bradley, G. W. (1978). Self-serving biases in the attribution process: A reexamination of the fact or fiction question. *Journal of Personality and Social Psychology, 36,* 56–71.

Brehm, J. W. (1966). *Response to loss of freedom: A theory of psychological reactance.* New York: Academic Press.

Brewin, C. (1985). Depression and causal attributions: What is their relation? *Psychological Bulletin, 2,* 297–309.

Briar, S. (1966). Welfare from below: Recipients' views of the public welfare system. *California Law Review, 54,* 370–385.

Brickman, P., Coates, D., & Janoff-Bulman, R. (1978). Lottery winners and accident victims: Is happiness relative? *Journal of Personality and Social Psychology, 35,* 917–927.

Brim, O. G. (1976). Life span development of the theory of oneself: Implications for child development. In H. W. Reese (Ed.), *Advances in child development and behavior* (Vol. 11, pp. 241–251). NY: Academic Press.

Brim, G. (1988, September). Losing and winning. *Psychology Today,* pp. 48–52.

Brockner, J. (1979). The effects of self-esteem, success-failure, and self-consciousness on task performance. *Journal of Personality and Social Psychology, 37,* 1732–1741.

Brodoff, A. S. (1985, October). Resilience. *Vogue,* pp. 235, 238–240.

Broskowski, A. (1981). The health–mental health connection: An introduction. In A. Broskowski, E. Marks, & S. H. Budman (Eds.), *Linking health and mental health services* (pp. 13–15). Beverly Hills, CA: Sage.

Brown, G. W., & Harris, T. (1978). *Social origins of depression: A study of psychiatric disorder in women.* London: Tavistock.

Brown, J. D. (1984). Effects of induced mood on causal attributions for success and failure. *Motivation and Emotion, 8,* 343–353.

Brown, J. D. (1985). *Self-esteem and unrealistic optimism about the future.* Unpublished data, University of California, Los Angeles.

Brown, J. D. (1986). Evaluations of self and others: Self-enhancement biases in social judgments. *Social Cognition, 4,* 353–376.

Brown, J. D., & Siegel, J. M. (in press). Attributions for negative life events and depression: The role of perceived control. *Journal of Personality and Social Psychology.*

Broyard, A. (1985, January 6). Stimuli from inside and out. *Los Angeles Times Book Review,* p. 9.

References

Brunstein, J. C., & Olbrich, E. (1985). Personal helplessness and action control: Analysis of achievement-related cognitions, self-assessments, and performance. *Journal of Personality and Social Psychology, 48,* 1540–1551.

Burger, J. M. (1985). Desire for control and achievement-related behaviors. *Journal of Personality and Social Psychology, 48,* 1520–1533.

Burgess, A. W., & Holmstrom, L. (1979). *Rape: Crisis and recovery.* Bowie, MD: Brady.

Butcher, J. N. (Ed.). (1969). *MMPI: Research developments and clinical applications.* New York: McGraw-Hill.

Calabrese, J. R., Kling, M. A., & Gold, P. W. (1987). Alterations in immunocompetence during stress, bereavement, and depression: Focus on neuroendocrine regulation. *American Journal of Psychiatry, 144,* 1123–1134.

Campbell, J. D. (1986). Similarity and uniqueness: The effects of attribute type, relevance, and individual differences in self-esteem and depression. *Journal of Personality and Social Psychology, 50,* 281–294.

Campbell, J. D., & Fairey, P. J. (1985). Effects of self-esteem, hypothetical explanations, and verbalization of expectancies on future performance. *Journal of Personality and Social Psychology, 48,* 1097–1111.

Cannon, W. B. (1932). *The wisdom of the body.* New York: Norton.

Carnevale, P. J. D., & Isen, A. M. (1986). The influence of positive affect and visual access on the discovery of integrative solutions in bilateral negotiation. *Organizational Behavior and Human Decision Processes, 37,* 1–13.

Carroll, J. S. (1978). The effect of imagining an event on expectations for the event: An interpretation in terms of the availability heuristic. *Journal of Experimental and Social Psychology, 14,* 88–96.

Carsrud, A. L., & Olm, K. W. (1986). The success of male and female entrepreneurs: A comparative analysis of the effects of multidimensional achievement motivation and personality traits. In R. Smilor & R. L. Kuhn (Eds.), *Managing take-off in fast growth companies* (pp. 147–161). New York: Praeger.

Cassileth, B. R., Lusk, E. J., Miller, D. S., Brown, L. L., & Miller, C. (1985). Psychosocial correlates of survival in advanced malignant disease? *New England Journal of Medicine, 312,* 1551–1555.

Chodoff, P., Friedman, P. B., & Hamburg, D. A. (1964). Stress, defenses and coping behavior: Observations in parents of children with malignant disease. *American Journal of Psychiatry, 120,* 743–749.

Cialdini, R. B., Kenrick, D. T., & Baumann, D. J. (1982). Effects of mood on prosocial behavior in children and adults. In N. Eisenberg (Ed.), *The development of prosocial behavior* (pp. 339–359). New York: Academic Press.

Clark, M. S., & Isen, A. M. (1982). Toward understanding the relationship between feeling states and social behavior. In A. H. Hastorf & A. M. Isen (Eds.), *Cognitive social psychology* (pp. 73–108). New York: Elsevier.

Clements, C. D., & Sider, R. C. (1983). Medical ethics' assault upon medical values. *Journal of the American Medical Association, 250,* 2011–2015.

Cobb, S. (1976). Social support as a moderator of life stress. *Psychosomatic Medicine, 38,* 300–314.

Cochran, S. D., & Hammen, C. L. (1985). Perceptions of stressful life events and depression: A test of attributional models. *Journal of Personality and Social Psychology, 48,* 1562–1571.

Cohen, S., & Edwards, J. R. (in press). Personality characteristics as moderators of the relationship between stress and disorder. In R. W. J. Neufeld (Ed.), *Advances in the investigation of psychological stress.* New York: Wiley.

Cohen, S., Glass, D. C., & Singer, J. E. (1973). Apartment noise, auditory discrimination, and reading ability in children. *Journal of Experimental Social Psychology, 9,* 407–422.

Cohen, S., & Hoberman, H. M. (1983). Positive events and social supports as buffers of life change stress. *Journal of Applied Social Psychology, 13,* 99–125.

Collins, R. L., Taylor, S. E., & Skokan, L. A. (1988). *A better world or a shattered vision? Positive and negative assumptions about the world following victimization.* Manuscript submitted for publication.

Connell, J. P. (1985). A new multidimensional measure of children's perception of control. *Child Development, 56,* 1018–1041.

Conway, M., & Ross, M. (1984). Getting what you want by revising what you had. *Journal of Personality and Social Psychology, 47,* 738–748.

Coopersmith, S. (1967). *The antecedents of self-esteem.* San Francisco: Freeman.

Cottington, E. M., Matthews, K. A., Talbott, E., & Kuller, L. H. (1980). Environmental events preceding sudden death in women. *Psychosomatic Medicine, 42,* 567–574.

Cousins, N. (1979). *Anatomy of an illness as perceived by the patient.* New York: Norton.

Coyne, J. C. (1976a). Depression and the response of others. *Journal of Abnormal Psychology, 85,* 186–193.

Coyne, J. C. (1976b). Toward an interactional description of depression. *Psychiatry, 39,* 28–40.

Coyne, J. C. (in press). Interpersonal processes in depression. G. I. Keitner (Ed.), *Depression and families.* Washington, DC: American Psychiatric Press.

Coyne, J. C., & Gotlib, I. H. (1983). The role of cognition in depression: A critical appraisal. *Psychological Bulletin, 94,* 472–505.

Coyne, J. C., Kessler, R. C., Tal, M., Turnbull, J., Wortman, C., & Greden, J. (1987). Living with a depressed person: Burden and psychological distress. *Journal of Consulting and Clinical Psychology, 55,* 347–352.

Crandall, V. J., Solomon, D., & Kelleway, R. (1955). Expectancy statements and decision times as functions of objective probabilities and reinforcement values. *Journal of Personality, 24,* 192–203.

Crile, G. (1972). *What women should know about the breast cancer controversy.* New York: Macmillan.

Crocker, J. (1981). Judgment of covariation by social perceivers. *Psychological Bulletin, 90,* 272–292.

Cutrona, C. E. (1982). Transition to college: Loneliness and the process of social adjustment. In L. A. Peplau & D. Perlman (Eds.), *Loneliness: A sourcebook of current theory, research and therapy* (pp. 291–309). New York: Wiley.

Dahlstrom, W. G., Welsh, G. S., & Dahlstrom, L. E. (1975). *An MMPI handbook: Vol. II. Research applications.* Minneapolis: University of Minnesota Press.

Dance, K. A., & Kuiper, N. A. (1987). Self-schemata, social roles, and a self-worth contingency model of depression. *Motivation and Emotion, 11,* 251–268.

Davis, F. (1961). Deviance disavowal: The management of strained interaction by the visibly handicapped. *Social Problems, 9,* 120–132.

deCharms, R. (1968). *Personal causation: The internal affective determinants of behavior.* New York: Academic Press.

deCharms, R. (1976). *Enhancing motivation: Change in the classroom.* New York: Irvington.

Deci, E. L., Nezlek, J., & Sheinman, L. (1981). Characteristics of the rewarder and intrinsic motivation of the rewardee. *Journal of Personality and Social Psychology, 40,* 1–10.

DeMonbreun, B. G., & Craighead, W. E. (1977). Distortion of perception and recall of positive and neutral feedback in depression. *Cognitive Therapy and Research, 1,* 311–329.

Derogatis, L. R., Abeloff, M., & Melisaratos, N. (1979). Psychological coping mechanisms and survival time in metastatic breast cancer. *Journal of the American Medical Association, 242,* 1504–1508.

Derry, P. A., & Kuiper, N. A. (1981). Schematic processing and self-reference in clinical depression. *Journal of Abnormal Psychology, 90,* 286–297.

DiClemente, R. J., & Temoshok, L. (1985). Psychological adjustment to having cutaneous malignant melanoma as a predictor of follow-up clinical status. *Psychosomatic Medicine, 47,* 81.

Diener, C. I., & Dweck, C. S. (1978). An analysis of learned helplessness: Continuous changes in performance, strategy, and achievement cognitions following failure. *Journal of Personality and Social Psychology, 36,* 451–462.

Diener, C. I., & Dweck, C. S. (1980). An analysis of learned helplessness: 2. The processing of success. *Journal of Personality and Social Psychology, 39,* 940–952.

Diener, E. (1984). Subjective well-being. *Psychological Bulletin, 95,* 542–575.

Donaldson, M. (1978). *Children's minds.* New York: Norton.

Dornbusch, S. M., Ritter, R. L., Leiderman, P. H., Roberts, D. F., & Fraleigh, M. J. (1987). The relation of parenting style to adolescent school performance. *Child Development, 58,* 1244–1257.

Doster, J. A. (1975). Individual differences affecting interviewee expectancies and perceptions of self-disclosure. *Journal of Counseling Psychology, 22,* 192–198.

Douglas, W., & Gibbons, K. (1983). Inadequacy of voice recognition as a demonstration of self-deception. *Journal of Personality and Social Psychology, 44,* 589–592.

Dweck, C. S., & Licht, B. G. (1980). Learned helplessness and intellectual achievement. In M. E. P. Seligman & J. Garber (Eds.), *Human helplessness: Theory and applications* (pp. 197–222). New York: Academic Press.

Dykman, B. M., Abramson, L. Y., Alloy, L. B., & Hartlage, S. (1989). Processing of ambiguous and unambiguous feedback by depressed and nondepressed college students: Schematic biases and their implications for depressive realism. *Journal of Personality and Social Psychology, 56,* 431–445.

Easterlin, R. A. (1974). Does economic growth improve the human lot? Some empirical evidence. In P. A. David & M. W. Reder (Eds.), *Nations and households in economic growth* (pp. 89–125). New York: Academic Press.

Eckland, B. K. (1968). Theories of mate selection. *Eugenics Quarterly, 15,* 71–84.

Ellis, H. C., Thomas, R. L., McFarland, A. D., & Lane, J. W. (1985). Emotional mood states and retrieval in episodic memory. *Journal of Experimental Psychology: Learning, Memory, and Cognition, 11,* 363–370.

Ellis, H. C., Thomas, R. L., & Rodriguez, I. A. (1984). Emotional mood states and memories: Elaborative encoding, semantic processing, and cognitive effort. *Journal of Experimental Psychology: Learning, Memory, and Cognition, 10,* 470–482.

Engel, G. L. (1971). Sudden and rapid death during psychological stress. *Annals of Internal Medicine, 74,* 771–782.

Epstein, S. (1973). The self-concept revisited, or a theory of a theory. *American Psychologist, 28,* 405–416.

Epstein, S. (in press). Constructive thinking: A broad coping variable with specific components. *Journal of Personality and Social Psychology.*

Erikson, E. H. (1950). *Childhood and society* (2nd ed.). New York: Norton.

Erikson, E. H. (1962). *Young man Luther: A study in psychoanalysis and history.* New York: Norton.

Erikson, K. T. (1976). *Everything in its path: Destruction of community in the Buffalo Creek flood.* New York: Simon & Schuster.

Feather, N. T. (1966). Effects of prior success and failure on expectations of success and subsequent performance. *Journal of Personality and Social Psychology, 3,* 287–298.

Feather, N. T. (1968). Change in confidence following success or failure as a predictor of subsequent performance. *Journal of Personality and Social Psychology, 9,* 38–46.

Feather, N. T. (1969). Attribution of responsibility and valence of success and failure in relation to initial confidence and task performance. *Journal of Personality and Social Psychology, 13,* 129–144.

Felson, R. B. (1981). Ambiguity and bias in the self-concept. *Social Psychology Quarterly, 44,* 64–69.

Felson, R. B. (1984). The effect of self-appraisals of ability on academic performance. *Journal of Personality and Social Psychology, 47,* 944–952.

Fenichel, O. (1945). *The psychoanalytic theory of neurosis.* New York: Norton.

Festinger, L. (1954). A theory of social comparison processes. *Human Relations, 7,* 117–140.

Findley, T. (1953). The placebo and the physician. *Medical Clinics of North America, 37,* 1821–1826.

Fingarette, H. (1969). *Self-deception.* London: Routledge & Kegan Paul.

Fischer, C. L., Daniels, J. C., Levin, S. L., Kimzey, S. L., Cobb, E. K., & Ritzman, W. E. (1972). Effects of the spaceflight environment on man's immune system: 2. Lymphocyte counts and reactivity. *Aerospace Medicine, 43,* 1122–1125.

Fischhoff, B. (1976). Attribution theory and judgment under uncertainty. In J. H. Harvey, W. J. Ickes, & R. F. Kidd (Eds.), *New directions in attribution research* (Vol. 1, pp. 421–452). Hillsdale, NJ: Erlbaum.

Fiske, S. T., & Taylor, S. E. (1984). *Social cognition.* Reading, MA: Addison-Wesley.

Forsyth, D. R., & Schlenker, B. R. (1977). Attributing the causes of group performance: Effects of performance quality, task importance, and future testing. *Journal of Personality, 45,* 220–236.

Fowler, H. (1965). *Curiosity and exploratory behavior.* New York: Macmillan.

Fox, B. H. (1983). Current theory of psychogenic effects on cancer incidence and prognosis. *Journal of Psychosocial Oncology, 1,* 17–31.

Frank, J. D. (1953). Some psychological determinants of the level of aspiration. *American Journal of Psychology, 47,* 285–293.

Frankl, V. E. (1963). *Man's search for meaning.* New York: Washington Square Press.

Franks, J. J., & Bransford, J. D. (1971). Abstraction of visual patterns. *Journal of Experimental Social Psychology, 90,* 65–74.

Free, L. A., & Cantril, H. (1968). *The political beliefs of Americans: A study of public opinion.* New York: Clarion.

Freedman, J. (1978). *Happy people: What happiness is, who has it, and why.* New York: Harcourt Brace Jovanovich.

Freud, A. (1966). *The ego and the mechanisms of defense* (rev. ed.). New York: International Universities Press.

Freud, S. (1950). *Collected papers* (Vol. 4) (trans. J. Riviere). London: Hogarth Press.

Freud, S. (1957). Repression. In J. Strachey (Ed.), *The standard edition of the complete psychological works of Sigmund Freud* (Vol. 14, pp. 146–158). London: Hogarth Press. (Original work published 1915).

References

Freud, S. (1961). *Civilization and its discontents* (College ed., J. Strachey, Ed. & Trans.). New York: Norton. (Original work published 1930).

Friedman, H. S., & Booth-Kewley, S. (1988). The "disease-prone" personality. *Health Psychology, 42,* 539–555.

Fromm, E. (1941). *Escape from freedom.* New York: Rinehart.

Fromm, E. (1955). *The sane society.* Rinehart.

Fuentes, C. (1964). *The death of Artemio Cruz.* New York: Farrar Straus Giroux.

Gallup, G. H. (1976–1977). Human needs and satisfactions: A global survey. *Public Opinion Quarterly, 40,* 459–467.

Geer, J. H., Davison, G. C., & Gatchel, R. I. (1970). Reduction of stress in humans through nonveridical perceived control of aversive stimulation. *Journal of Personality and Social Psychology, 16,* 731–738.

Geer, J. H., & Maisel, E. (1972). Evaluating the effects of the prediction-control confound. *Journal of Personality and Social Psychology, 23,* 314–319.

Gibbons, F. X. (1986). Social comparison and depression: Company's effect on misery. *Journal of Personality and Social Psychology, 51,* 140–149.

Gibbs, G. (1981). *Teaching students to learn.* Milton Keynes, England: Open University Press.

Gide, A. (1987). *The journals of André Gide, Vol. 1: 1889–1924.* (J. O'Brien, trans.). Evanston, IL: Northwestern University Press. (Original work published in 1939).

Gilovich, T. (1983). Biased evaluation and persistence in gambling. *Journal of Personality and Social Psychology, 44,* 1110–1126.

Gisler, R. H. (1974). Stress and the hormonal regulation of the immune response in mice. *Psychotherapy & Psychosomatics, 23,* 197.

Glaser, R., Rice, J., Sheridan, J., Fertel, R., Stout, J., Speicher, C., Pinsky, D., Kotur, M., Post, A., Beck, M., & Kiecolt-Glaser, J. (1987). Stress-related immune suppression: Health implications. *Brain, Behavior, and Immunity, 1,* 7–20.

Glass, D. C., & Singer, J. E. (1972). *Urban stress.* New York: Academic Press.

Goffman, E. (1955). On face-work: An analysis of ritual elements in social interaction. *Psychiatry: Journal for the Study of Interpersonal Processes, 18,* 213–231.

Goffman, E. (1963). *Stigma: Notes on the management of spoiled identity.* Englewood Cliffs, NJ: Prentice-Hall.

Goffman, E. (1967). *Interaction ritual.* Newport Beach, CA: Westcliff.

Goldman, R. L. (1947) *Even the night.* New York: Macmillan.

Goleman, D. (1985). *Vital lies, simple truths: The psychology of self-deception.* New York: Simon & Schuster.

Golin, S., Terrell, T., & Johnson, B. (1977). Depression and the illusion of control. *Journal of Abnormal Psychology, 86,* 440–442.

Golin, S., Terrell, T., Weitz, J., & Drost, P. L. (1979). The illusion of control among depressed patients. *Journal of Abnormal Psychology, 88,* 454–457.

Gonzales, A., & Zimbardo, P. G. (1985, March). Time in perspective. *Psychology Today,* pp. 21–26.

Goodwin, F., & Jamison, K. R. (in press). *Manic depressive illness.* New York: Oxford University Press.

Gordon, D., Nowicki, S., & Wichern, F. (1981). Observed maternal and child behavior in a dependency-producing task as a function of children's locus of control orientation. *Merrill Palmer Quarterly, 27,* 43–51.

Gotlib, I. (1983). Perception and recall of interpersonal feedback: Negative bias in depression. *Cognitive Therapy and Research, 7,* 399–412.

Gotlib, I. (1984). Depression and general psychopathology in university students. *Journal of Abnormal Psychology, 93,* 19–30.

Gouaux, C. (1971). Induced affective states and interpersonal attraction. *Journal of Personality and Social Psychology, 20,* 37–43.

Green, S. K., & Gross, A. E. (1979). Self-serving biases in implicit evaluations. *Personality and Social Psychology Bulletin, 5,* 214–217.

Greenberg, M. S., & Alloy, L. B. (in press). Depression versus anxiety: Differences in self and other schemata. In L. B. Alloy (Ed.), *Cognitive processes in depression.* New York: Guilford Press.

Greenfield, S., Kaplan, S., & Ware, J. E. (in press). Expanding patient involvement in care: Effects on patient outcome. *Annals of Internal Medicine.*

Greenwald, A. G. (1980). The totalitarian ego: Fabrication and revision of personal history. *American Psychologist, 35,* 603–618.

Greenwald, A. G. (1984, August). *Totalitarian egos versus totalitarian societies.* Paper presented at the American Psychological Association annual meeting, Toronto, Canada.

Greenwald, A. G., & Breckler, S. J. (1985). To whom is the self presented? In B. Schlenker (Ed.), *The self and social life* (pp. 126–145). New York: McGraw-Hill.

Greer, S., Morris, T., & Pettingale, K. W. (1979). Psychological response to breast cancer: Effect and outcome. *Lancet, 2,* 785–787.

Gregory, L. W., Cialdini, R. B., & Carpenter, K. M. (1982). Self-relevant scenarios as mediators of likelihood estimates and compliance: Does imagining make it so? *Journal of Personality and Social Psychology, 43,* 89–99.

Griffith, W. B. (1970). Environmental effects on interpersonal affective behavior: Ambient temperature and attraction. *Journal of Personality and Social Psychology, 15,* 240–244.

Grolnick, W. S., & Ryan, R. M. (1987a). Autonomy in children's learning: An experimental and individual difference investigation. *Journal of Personality and Social Psychology, 52,* 890–898.

Grolnick, W. S., & Ryan, R. M. (1987b). Autonomy support in education: Creating the facilitating environment. In N. Hastings & J. Schwieso (Eds.), *New directions in educational psychology: Vol. 2. Behavior and motivation.* London: Falmer Press.

Grolnick, W. S., & Ryan, R. M. (1988). *Parent styles associated with children's self-regulation and competence in school.* Manuscript submitted for publication.

Gur, R. C., & Sackeim, H. A. (1979). Self-deception: A concept in search of a phenomenon. *Journal of Personality and Social Psychology, 37,* 147–169.

Gurin, G., Veroff, J., & Feld, S. (1960). *Americans view their mental health.* New York: Basic Books.

Hammen, C., Miklowitz, D. J., & Dyck, D. G. (1986). Stability and severity parameters of depressive self-schemata responding. *Journal of Social and Clinical Psychology, 4,* 23–45.

Hanson, J. D., Larson, M. C., & Snowden, C. T. (1976). The effects of control over high intensity noise on plasma control in rhesus monkeys. *Behavioral Biology, 16,* 333–334.

Harackiewicz, J. M., Manderlink, G., & Sansone, C. (1984). Rewarding pinball wizardry: Effects of evaluation and cue value on intrinsic interest. *Journal of Personality and Social Psychology, 47,* 287–300.

Harackiewicz, J. M., Sansone, C., & Manderlink, G. (1985). Competence, achievement orientation, and intrinsic motivation: A process analysis. *Journal of Personality and Social Psychology, 48,* 493–508.

References

Harari, O., & Covington, M. (1981). Reactions to achievement from a teacher and student perspective: A developmental analysis. *American Educational Research Journal, 18,* 15–28.

Harris, P. R. (1980) *Promoting health—preventing disease: Objectives for the nation.* Washington, DC: U. S. Government Printing Office:

Harris, R. J., Teske, R. R., & Ginns, M. J. (1975). Memory for pragmatic implications from courtroom testimony. *Bulletin of the Psychonomic Society, 6,* 494–496.

Harris, S. (1946). *Banting's miracle: The story of the discovery of insulin.* Toronto: J. M. Dent & Sons.

Harter, S. (1981). A model of intrinsic mastery motivation in children: Intrinsic differences and developmental change. In W. A. Collins (Ed.), *Minnesota Symposium on Child Psychology* (Vol. 14, pp. 215–255). Hillsdale, NJ: Erlbaum.

Harter, S. (1983). Developmental perspectives on the self-system. In E. M. Hetherington (Ed.), *Handbook of child psychology: Vol 4. Socialization, personality and social development* (4th ed., pp. 275–386). New York: Wiley.

Hartmann, H. (1958). *Ego psychology and the problem of adaptation.* New York: International Universities Press.

Hatfield, J. S., Ferguson, L. R., & Alpert, R. (1967). Mother-child interaction and the socialization process. *Child Development, 38,* 365–414.

Hayes-Roth, B., & Hayes-Roth, F. (1979). A cognitive model of planning. *Cognitive Science, 3,* 275–310.

Heider, F. (1958). *The psychology of interpersonal relations.* New York: Wiley.

Henslin, J. M. (1967). Craps and magic. *American Journal of Sociology, 73,* 316–330.

Hess, R. D., & Holloway, S. D. (1985). Family and school as educational institutions. In R. D. Parke (Ed.), *Review of child development research* (Vol. 7, pp. 179–222). Chicago: University of Chicago Press.

Hightower, A. D., Work, W. C., Cowen, E. K., Lotyczewski, B. S., Spinell, A. P., Guare, J. C., & Rohrbeck, C. A. (1986). The teacher-child rating scale: A brief objective measure of elementary children's school problem behaviors and competencies. *School Psychology Review, 16,* 239–255.

Hill, C. T., Rubin, Z., & Peplau. L. A. (1976). Breakups before marriage: The end of 103 affairs. *Journal of Social Issues, 32,* 147–168.

Hinkle, L. E. (1974). The effect of exposure to cultural change, social change, and changes in interpersonal relationships on health. In B. S. Dohrenwend & B. P. Dohrenwend (Eds.), *Stressful life events: Their nature and effects.* New York: Wiley.

Hirata-Hibi, M. (1967). Plasma cell reaction and thymic germinal centers after a chronic form of electric stress. *Journal of the Reticuloendothelial Society, 4,* 370.

Hobfoll, S. E., & London, P. (1986). The relationship of self-concept and social support to emotional distress among women during war. *Journal of Social and Clinical Psychology, 4,* 189–203.

Hobfoll, S. E., & Walfisch, S. (1984). Coping with a threat to life: A longitudinal study of self-concept, social support, and psychological distress. *American Journal of Community Psychology, 12,* 87–100.

Hogarth, R. M. (1980). *Judgement and choice: The psychology of decision.* New York: Wiley.

Hollander, C. (1983). Thanks for the recession. *Newsweek, July 25,* 11.

Horney, K. (1950). *Neurosis and human growth.* New York: Norton.

Horowitz, M. J., & Schulz, R. (1983). The relocation controversy: Criticism and commentary on five recent studies. *The Gerontologist, 23,* 229–234.

Horowitz, M. J., & Schulz, R. (1985). Institutional relocation and its impact on mortality, morbidity, and psychosocial status. In A. Baum & J. Singer

(Eds.), Advances in health psychology (Vol. 3, pp. 319–343). Hillsdale, NJ: Erlbaum.

House, J. A. (1981). *Work stress and social support.* Reading, MA: Addison-Wesley.

Imboden, J. B., Canter, A., & Cluff, E. (1961). Convalescence from influenza: A study of the psychological and clinical determinants. *Archives of Internal Medicine, 108,* 393–399.

Imboden, J. B., Canter, E., Cluff, E., Leighton, E. C., & Trevor, R. W. (1959). Brucellosis: 3. Psychologic consequences of delayed convalescence. *Archives of Internal Medicine, 103,* 406–414.

Irwin, F. W. (1944). The realism of expectations. *Psychological Review, 51,* 120–126.

Irwin, F. W. (1953). Stated expectations as functions of probability and desirability of outcomes. *Journal of Personality, 21,* 329–335.

Isen, A. M. (1970). Success, failure, attention, and reactions to others: The warm glow of success. *Journal of Personality and Social Psychology, 36,* 1–12.

Isen, A. M. (1984). Toward understanding the role of affect in cognition. In R. Wyer & T. Srull (Eds.), *Handbook of social cognition* (pp. 174–236). Hillsdale, NJ: Erlbaum.

Isen, A. M. (in press). The asymmetry of happiness and sadness in effects on memory in normal college students. *Journal of Experimental Psychology: General.*

Isen, A. M., & Daubman, K. A. (1984). The influence of affect on categorization. *Journal of Personality and Social Psychology, 47,* 1206–1217.

Isen, A. M., Daubman, K. A., & Nowicki, G. P. (1987). Positive affect facilitates creative problem solving. *Journal of Personality and Social Psychology, 52,* 1122–1131.

Isen, A. M., Johnson, M. M. S., Mertz, E., & Robinson, G. (1985). The influence of positive affect on the unusualness of word association. *Journal of Personality and Social Psychology, 48,* 1413–1426.

Isen, A. M., & Means, B. (1983). The influence of positive affect on decision-making strategy. *Social Cognition, 2,* 18–31.

Isen, A. M., & Patrick, R. (1983). The effects of positive feelings on risk-taking: When the chips are down. *Organizational Behavior and Human Performance, 31,* 194–202.

Isen, A. M., Shalker, T. E., Clark, M., & Karp, L. (1978). Affect, accessibility of material in memory, and behavior: A cognitive loop? *Journal of Personality and Social Psychology, 36,* 1–12.

Jahoda, M. (1953). The meaning of psychological health. *Social Casework, 34,* 349.

Jahoda, M. (1958). *Current concepts of positive mental health.* New York: Basic Books.

Janis, I. L. (1982). *Groupthink: Psychological studies of policy decisions and fiascoes* (2nd ed.). Boston: Houghton Mifflin.

Janoff-Bulman, R. (1979). Characterological versus behavioral self-blame: Inquiries into depression and rape. *Journal of Personality and Social Psychology, 37,* 1798–1809.

Janoff-Bulman, R. (in press). Criminal vs. non-criminal victimization: Victims' reactions. *Victimology.*

Janoff-Bulman, R., & Brickman, P. (1982). Expectations and what people learn from failure. In N. T. Feather (Ed.), *Expectations and action: Expectancy-value models on psychology* (pp. 207–272). Hillsdale, NJ: Erlbaum.

Janoff-Bulman, R., & Frieze, I. H. (1983). A theoretical perspective for understanding reactions to victimization. *Journal of Social Issues, 39,* 1–17.

Jemmott, J. B. III, & Locke, S. E. (1984). Psychosocial factors, immunologic mediation, and human susceptibility to infectious diseases: How much do we know? *Psychological Bulletin, 95,* 78–108.

References

Jennings, D., Amabile, T. M., & Ross, L. (1982). Informal covariation assessment: Data-based versus theory-based judgments. In A. Tversky, D. Kahneman, & P. Slovic (Eds.), *Judgment under uncertainty: Heuristics and biases* (pp. 211–230). New York: Cambridge University Press.

Jensen, M. R. (1987). Psychobiological factors predicting the course of breast cancer. *Journal of Personality, 55,* 317–342.

Joasoo, A., & McKenzie, J. M. (1976). Stress and the immune response in rats. *International Archives of Allergy and Applied Immunology, 50,* 659.

Johnson, J. E., & Leventhal, H. (1974). Effects of accurate expectations and behavioral instructions on reactions during a noxious medical examination. *Journal of Personality and Social Psychology, 29,* 710–718.

Johnson, J. E., & Tversky, A. (1983). Affect generalization and the perception of risk. *Journal of Personality and Social Psychology, 45,* 20–31.

Jones, E. E., & Berglas, S. C. (1978). Control of attributions about the self through self-handicapping strategies: The appeal of alcohol and the role of underachievement. *Personality and Social Psychology Bulletin, 4,* 200–206.

Jones, E. E., & Davis, K. E. (1965). From acts to dispositions: The attribution process in person perception. In L. Berkowitz (Ed.), *Advances in experimental social psychology* (Vol. 2, pp. 219–266). New York: Academic Press.

Jones, E. E., & Harris, V. A. (1967). The attribution of attitudes. *Journal of Experimental Social Psychology, 3,* 1–24.

Jourard, S. M., & Landsman, T. (1980). *Healthy personality: An approach from the viewpoint of humanistic psychology* (4th ed.). New York: Macmillan.

Kamen, L. P., & Seligman, M. E. P. (1986). *Explanatory style predicts college grade point average.* Unpublished manuscript, University of Pennsylvania.

Kavetskii, R. E. (1958). *The neoplastic process and the nervous system.* Kiev, USSR: State Medical Publishing House. (Trans. from Russian and available from the National Technical Information Service, Springfield, VA 22151, Pub. No. 60-21860).

Keller, S. E., Weiss, J. M., Schleifer, S. J., Miller, N. E., & Stein, M. (1981). Suppression of immunity by stress: Effect of a graded series of stressors on lymphocyte stimulation in the rat. *Science, 213,* 1397–1400.

Kelley, H. H. (1967). Attribution theory in social psychology. In D. Levine (Ed.), *Nebraska Symposium on Motivation* (Vol. 15, pp. 192–240). Lincoln: University of Nebraska Press.

Kelly, G. A. (1955). *The psychology of personal constructs.* New York: Norton.

Keyes, R. (1985, September). The best thing that ever happened to me. *McCall's,* pp. 10, 15, 19.

Kiecolt-Glaser, J. K., & Glaser, R. (in press). Behavioral influences on immune function. Evidence for the interplay between stress and health. In T. Field, P. McCabe, & N. Schneiderman (Eds.), *Stress and coping* (Vol. 2). Hillsdale, NJ: Erlbaum.

Kiesler, S., & Baral., R. (1970). The search for a romantic partner: The effects of self-esteem and physical attractiveness. In K. Gergen & D. Marlowe (Eds.), *Personality and social behavior* (pp. 155–156). Reading, MA: Addison-Wesley.

Kimzey, S. L. (1975). The effects of extended spaceflight on hematologic and immunologic systems. *Journal of the American Medical Women's Association, 30,* 218–232.

Kirscht, J. P., Haefner, D. P., Kegeles, F. S., & Rosenstock, I. M. (1966). A national study of health beliefs. *Journal of Health and Human Behavior, 7,* 248–254.

Klatzky, R. L. (1975). *Human memory: Structures and processes.* San Francisco: Freeman.

Kleck, R. (1968). Self-disclosure patterns of the nonobviously stigmatized. *Psychological Reports, 23,* 1239–1248.

Klerman, G. L. (1979, April). The age of melancholy? *Psychology Today,* pp. 36–38, 42, 88.

Klerman, G. L. (1986, August 15). Depression research advances, treatment lags. *Research News,* pp. 723–725.

Kobasa, S. C. (1979). Stressful life events and health: An inquiry into hardiness. *Journal of Personality and Social Psychology, 37,* 1–11.

Kobasa, S. C., Maddi, S. R., & Covington, S. (1981). Personality and constitution as mediators in the stress-illness relationship. *Journal of Health and Social Behavior, 22,* 368–378.

Kobasa, S. C., Maddi, S. R., & Kahn, S. (1982). Hardiness and health: A prospective study. *Journal of Personality and Social Psychology, 42,* 168–177.

Kobasa, S. C., Maddi, S. R., & Puccetti, M. C. (1982). Personality and exercise as buffers in the stress-illness relationship. *Journal of Behavioral Medicine, 5,* 391–404

Kobasa, S. C., & Puccetti, M. C. (1983). Personality and social resources in stress resistance. *Journal of Personality and Social Psychology, 45,* 839–850.

Kohut, H. (1966). Forms and transformations of narcissism. In P. Ornstein (Ed.), *The search for the self* (Vol. 1, pp. 427–460). New York: International Universities Press.

Kohut, H. (1978). *The search for the self: Selected writings of Heinz Kohut.* P. H. Ornstein, Ed. New York: International Universities Press.

Konner, M. (1988, March 13). Laughter and hope. *New York Times Magazine,* p. 49.

Kraepelin, E. (1921). *Manic-depressive insanity and paranoia.* London: Churchill Livingston.

Kronfol, Z., Silva, J., Greden, J., Dembinski, S., Gardner, R., & Carroll, B. (1983). Impaired lymphocyte function in depressive illness. *Life Sciences, 33,* 241–247.

Kübler-Ross, E. (1969). *On death and dying.* New York: Macmillan.

Kuhn, T. S. (1970). *The structure of scientific revolutions* (2nd ed.) Chicago: University of Chicago Press.

Kuiper, N. A. (1978). Depression and causal attributions for success and failure. *Journal of Personality and Social Psychology, 36,* 236–246.

Kuiper, N. A., & Derry, P. A. (1982). Depressed and nondepressed content self-reference in mild depression. *Journal of Personality, 50,* 67–79.

Kuiper, N. A., & MacDonald, M. R. (1982). Self and other perception in mild depressives. *Social Cognition, 1,* 233–239.

Kuiper, N. A., MacDonald, M. R., & Derry, P. A. (1983). Parameters of a depressive self-schema. In J. Suls & A. G. Greenwald (Eds.), *Psychological perspectives on the self* (Vol. 2, pp. 191–217). Hillsdale, NJ: Erlbaum.

Kuiper, N. A., & Olinger, L. J. (in press). Stress and cognitive vulnerability for depression: A self-worth contingency model. In R. W. J. Neufeld (Ed.), *Advances in the investigation of psychological stress.* New York: Wiley.

Kuiper, N. A., Olinger, L. J., MacDonald, M. R., & Shaw, B. F. (1985). Self-schema processing of depressed and nondepressed content: The effects of vulnerability on depression. *Social Cognition, 3,* 77–93.

Kulik, J. A., & Mahler, I. M. (1987). Health status, perceptions of risk, and prevention interest for health and nonhealth problems. *Health Psychology, 6,* 15–28.

Kunda, Z. (1987). Motivated inference: Self-serving generation and evaluation of causal theories. *Journal of Personality and Social Psychology, 53,* 636–647.

Laird, J. D., Wagener, J. J., Halal, M., & Szegda, M. (1982). Remembering what

References

you feel: Effects of emotion on memory. *Journal of Personality and Social Psychology, 42,* 646–657.

Langer, E. J. (1975). The illusion of control. *Journal of Personality and Social Psychology, 32,* 311–328.

Langer, E. J., & Rodin, J. (1976). The effects of choice and enhanced personal responsibility for the aged: A field experiment in an institutional setting. *Journal of Personality and Social Psychology, 34,* 191–198.

Langer, E. J., & Roth, J. (1975). Heads I win, tails it's chance: The illusion of control as a function of the sequence of outcomes in a purely chance task. *Journal of Personality and Social Psychology, 32,* 951–955.

Larwood, L., & Whittaker, W. (1977). Managerial myopia: Self-serving biases in organizational planning. *Journal of Applied Psychology, 62,* 194–198.

Laudenslager, M. C., Reite, M., & Harbeck, R. J. (1982). Suppressed immune response in infant monkeys associated with maternal separation. *Behavior and Neural Biology, 36,* 40–48.

Laudenslager, M. C., Ryan, S. M., Drugan, R. C., Hyson, R. L., & Maier, S. F. (1983). Coping and immunosuppression: Inescapable but not escapable shock suppresses lymphocyte proliferation. *Science, 231,* 568–570.

Layne, C. (1983). Painful truths about depressives' cognitions. *Journal of Clinical Psychology, 39,* 848–853.

Lazarus, R. S. (1966). *Psychological stress and the coping process.* New York: McGraw-Hill.

Lazarus, R. S. (1983). The costs and benefits of denial. In S. Brenitz (Ed.), *Denial of stress* (pp. 1–30). New York: International Universities Press.

Lazarus, R. S., & Folkman, S. (1984). *Stress, appraisal, and coping.* New York: Springer.

Leach, C. S., & Rambaut, P. C. (1974). Biochemical responses of the Skylab crewmen. *Proceedings of the Skylab Life Sciences Symposium, 2,* 247–454.

Lefcourt, H. M. (1973, May). The function of the illusions of control and freedom. *American Psychologist,* pp. 417–425.

Lehman, D. R., Ellard, J. H., & Wortman, C. B. (1986). Social support for the bereaved: Recipients' and providers' perspectives on what is helpful. *Journal of Consulting and Clinical Psychology, 54,* 438–446.

Lehman, D. R., & Taylor, S. E. (1987). Date with an earthquake: Coping with a probable, unpredictable disaster. *Personality and Social Psychology Bulletin, 13,* 546–555.

Lehman, D., Wortman, C. B., & Williams, A. F. (1987). Long-term effects of losing a spouse or child in a motor vehicle crash. *Journal of Personality and Social Psychology, 52,* 218–231.

Lemoine, J., & Mougne, C. (1983). Why has death stalked the refugees? *Natural History, 92,* 6–19.

Lerner, M. J. (1965). Evaluation of performance as a function of performer's reward and attractiveness. *Journal of Personality and Social Psychology, 1,* 355–360.

Lerner, M. J. (1970). The desire for justice and reactions to victims. In J. R. Macauley & L. Berkowitz (Eds.), *Altruism and helping behavior* (pp. 205–229). New York: Academic Press.

Lerner, M. J., & Lichtman, R. R. (1968). Effects of perceived norms on attitudes and altruistic behavior toward a dependent other. *Journal of Personality and Social Psychology, 9,* 226–232.

Lerner, M. J., & Matthews, G. (1967). Reactions to suffering of others under conditions of indirect responsibility. *Journal of Personality and Social Psychology, 5,* 319–325.

Lerner, M. J., & Simmons, C. (1966). Observer's reaction to the "innocent victim": Compassion or rejection? *Journal of Personality and Social Psychology, 4,* 203–210.

Lettieri, R. J. (1983). Consciousness, self-deception and psychotherapy: An analogue study. *Imagination, Cognition and Personality, 3,* 83–97.

Leventhal, H. (1975). The consequences of depersonalization during illness and treatment. In J. Howard & A. Strauss (Eds.), *Humanizing health care* (pp. 119–161). New York: Wiley.

Levine, J. D., Gordon, N. C., & Fields, H. L. (1978). The mechanism of placebo analgesia. *Lancet, 2,* 654–657.

Levy, S. M. (1983a). Death and dying: Behavioral and social factors that contribute to the process. In T. G. Burish & L. A. Bradley (Eds.), *Coping with chronic disease: Research and applications* (pp. 425–446). New York: Academic Press.

Levy, S. M. (1983b). Host differences in neoplastic risk: Behavioral and social contributors to disease. *Health Psychology, 2,* 21–44.

Levy, S. M., Herberman, R. B., Maluish, A. M., Schlien, B., & Lippman, M. (1985). Prognostic risk assessment in primary breast cancer by behavioral and immunological parameters. *Health Psychology, 4,* 99–113.

Lewicki, P. (1984). Self-schema and social information processing. *Journal of Personality and Social Psychology, 48,* 463–574.

Lewicki, P. (1985). Nonconscious biasing effects of single instances on subsequent judgments. *Journal of Personality and Social Psychology, 48,* 563–574.

Lewinsohn, P. M., Mischel, W., Chaplin, W., & Barton, R. (1980). Social competence and depression: The role of illusory self-perceptions. *Journal of Abnormal Psychology, 89,* 203–212.

Liberman, R. (1962). An analysis of the placebo phenomenon. *Journal of Chronic Diseases, 15,* 761–783.

Lieberman, M. A. (1983). The effects of social supports on responses to stress. In L. Goldberger & S. Breznitz (Eds.), *Handbook of stress: Theoretical and Clinical Aspects.* (764–784). New York: Free Press.

Life Insurance Marketing Research Association (LIMRA). (1983). *The manpower and production survey.* Hartford, CT: Author.

Lindsay, M., & McCarthy, D. (1974). Caring for the brothers and sisters of a dying child. In T. Burton (Ed.), *Care of the child facing death* (pp. 189–206). Boston, MA: Routledge & Kegan Paul.

Linville, P. W. (1982). Affective consequences of complexity regarding the self and others. In M. S. Clark & S. T. Fiske (Eds.), *Affect and cognition: Seventeenth annual Carnegie symposium on cognition.* Hillsdale, NJ: Erlbaum.

Linville, P. W. (1987). Self-complexity as a cognitive buffer against stress-related depression and illness. *Journal of Personality and Social Psychology, 52,* 663–676.

Loeb, R. C., Horst, L., & Horton, P. J. (1980). Family interaction patterns associated with self-esteem in preadolescent girls and boys. *Merrill-Palmer Quarterly, 26,* 203–217.

Lund, F. H. (1975). The psychology of belief: A study of its emotional and volitional determinants. *Journal of Abnormal and Social Psychology, 20,* 63–81.

Lyman, R. D., Wurtele, S. K., & Shannon, D. C. (1980). Parents' perceptions of the psychological and social impact of home monitoring. *Pediatrics, 66,* 37–41.

Lynch, M. D. (1981). Self-concept development in childhood. In M. D. Lynch, A. A. Norem-Hebeisen, & K. Gergen (Eds.), *Self-concept: Advances in theory and research* (pp. 119–132). Cambridge, MA: Ballinger.

Maccoby, E. E., & Martin, J. A. (1983). Socialization in the context of the family:

References

Parent-child interaction. In E. M. Hetherington (Ed.), *Handbook of child psychology: Vol 4. Socialization, personality, and social development* (4th ed., pp. 1–102). New York: Wiley.

MacDonald, M. R., & Kuiper, N. A. (1984). Self-schema decision consistency in clinical depression. *Journal of Social and Clinical Psychology, 2,* 264–272.

MacFarland, C., & Ross, M. (1982). The impact of causal attributions on affective reactions to success and failure. *Journal of Abnormal and Social Psychology, 20,* 63–81.

Marks, G. (1984). Thinking one's abilities are unique and one's opinions are common. *Personality and Social Psychological Bulletin, 10,* 203–208.

Marks, G., Richardson, J. L., Graham, J. W., & Levine, A. (1986). Role of health locus of control beliefs and expectations of treatment efficacy in adjustment to cancer. *Journal of Personality and Social Psychology, 51,* 443–450.

Marks, R. W. (1951). The effect of probability, desirability, and "privilege" on the stated expectations of children. *Journal of Personality, 19,* 332–351.

Markus, H. (1977). Self-schemata and processing information about the self. *Journal of Personality and Social Psychology, 35,* 63–78.

Markus, H., & Nurius, P. (1986). Possible selves. *American Psychologist, 41,* 954–969.

Martin, D. J., Abramson, L. Y., & Alloy, L. B. (1984). Illusion of control for self and others in depressed and nondepressed college students. *Journal of Personality and Social Psychology, 46,* 125–136.

Maslow, A. H. (1950). Self-actualizing people: A study of pyschological health. *Personality, Symposium No. 1,* 11–34.

Maslow, A. H. (1954). *Motivation and personality.* New York: Harper & Row.

Matarazzo, J. D. (1982). Behavioral health's challenge to academic, scientific, and professional psychology. *American Psychologist, 37,* 1–14.

Mayer, J. D., & Salovey, P. (in press). Personality moderates the interaction of mood and cognition. In K. Fiedler & J. Forgas (Eds.), *Affect, cognition, and social behavior.* Toronto: Hogrefe.

McFarlin, D.B., & Blascovich, J. (1981). Effects of self-esteem and performance feedback on future affective preferences and cognitive expectations. *Journal of Personality and Social Psychology, 40,* 521–531.

Mechanic, D. (1977). Illness behavior, social adaptation, and the management of illness. *Journal of Nervous and Mental Disease, 165,* 79–87.

Menninger, K. A. (1930). What is a healthy mind? In N. A. Crawford & K. A. Menninger (Eds.), *The healthy-minded child.* Coward-McCann.

Menninger, K. A. (1963). *The vital balance.* New York: Viking.

Meyer, R. J., & Haggerty, R. J. (1962). Streptococcal infections in families. *Journal of Pediatrics, 29,* 539–549.

Miller, D. T. (1976). Ego involvement and attributions for success and failure. *Journal of Personality and Social Psychology, 34,* 901–906.

Miller, D. T., & Ross, M. (1975). Self-serving biases in attribution of causality: Fact or fiction? *Psychological Bulletin, 82,* 213–225.

Miller, E. (1977, February). A Blaze of Talent. *Seventeen,* pp. 118–119.

Miller, S. M. (1979). Controllability and human stress: Method, evidence and theory. *Behaviour Research and Therapy, 17,* 287–304.

Minkoff, K., Bergman, E., Beck, A. T., & Beck, R. (1973). Hopelessness, depression, and attempted suicide. *American Journal of Psychiatry, 130,* 455–459.

Mirels, H. L. (1980). The avowal of responsibility for good and bad outcomes: The effects of generalized self-serving biases. *Personality and Social Psychology Bulletin, 6,* 299–306.

Mischel, W. (1973). Toward a cognitive-social learning reconceptualization of personality. *Psychological Review, 80,* 252–283.

Mischel, W., Coates, B., & Raskoff, A. (1968). Effects of success and failure on self-gratification. *Journal of Personality and Social Psychology, 10,* 381–390.

Mischel, W., Ebbeson, E. B., & Zeiss, A. M. (1976). Determinants of selective memory about the self. *Journal of Consulting and Clinical Psychology, 44,* 92–103.

Monjan, A. A., & Collector, M. I. (1977). Stress-induced modulation of the immune response. *Science, 196,* 307–308.

Moore, B. S., Underwood, B., & Rosenhan, D. L. (1973). Affect and altruism. *Developmental Psychology, 8,* 99–104.

Morrow, L. (1983, August 1). All the hazards and threats of success. *Time,* pp. 20–25.

Myers, B. A., Friedman, S. B., & Weiner, I. B. (1970). Coping with a chronic disability: Psychosocial observations of girls with scoliosis. *American Journal of Diseases of Children, 120,* 175–181.

Nelson, R. E., & Craighead, W. E. (1977). Selective recall of positive and negative feedback, self-control behaviors, and depression. *Journal of Abnormal Psychology, 86,* 379–388.

Nicholls, J. G. (1975). Causal attributions and other achievement-related cognitions: Effects of task outcome, attainment value, and sex. *Journal of Personality and Social Psychology, 31,* 379–389.

Nielsen, L. E., & Fleck, J. R. (1981). Defensive repressors and empathic impairment. *Psychological Reports, 48,* 615–624.

Nisbett, R. E. & Ross, L. (1980). *Human inference: Strategies and shortcomings of social judgment.* Englewood Cliffs, NJ: Prentice-Hall.

Nolen-Hoeksema, S., Girgus, J. S., & Seligman, M. E. P. (1986). Learned helplessness in children: A longitudinal study of depression, achievement, and explanatory style. *Journal of Personality and Social Psychology, 51,* 435–442.

Novack, W., & Iacocca, L. (1984). *Iacocca.* New York: Bantam.

Oatley, K., & Bolton, W. (1985). A social-cognitive theory of depression in reaction to life events. *Psychological Review, 92,* 372–388.

Oncology Times. (1984). Smoking-related deaths higher for heart disease than cancer. *Oncology Times, 6,* 3, 35.

Ohnstad, K. (1942). *The world at my fingertips.* New York: Bobbs-Merrill.

Ornstein, P. (1980). Self psychology and the concept of health. In A. Goldberg (Ed.), *Advances in self psychology* (pp. 137–159). New York: International Universities Press.

Orwell, G. (1949). *1984.* New York: Harcourt Brace.

Owens, J., Bower, G. H., & Black, J. B. (1979). The "soap-opera" effect in story recall. *Memory and Cognition, 7,* 185–191.

Parducci, A. (1968). The relativism of absolute judgments. *Scientific American, 219,* 518–528.

Patterson, G. R. (1976). The aggressive child: Victim and architect of a coercive system. In L. A. Hamerlynck, L. C. Hardy, & E. J. Marsh (Eds.), *Behavior modification and families: Vol 1. Theory and research* (pp. 267–316). New York: Brunner-Mazel.

Paykel, E. S. (1982). *Handbook of affective disorders.* New York: Guilford Press.

Pearlin, L. I., & Schooler, C. (1978). The structure of coping. *Journal of Health and Social Behavior, 19,* 2–21.

Perloff, L. S. (1983). Perceptions of vulnerability to victimization. *Journal of Social Issues, 39,* 41–61.

References

Perloff, L. S., & Fetzer, B. K. (1986). Self-other judgments and perceived vulnerability to victimization. *Journal of Personality and Social Psychology, 50,* 502–510.

Persson, L. O., & Sjoberg, L. (1987). Mood and somatic symptoms. *Journal of Psychosomatic Research, 31,* 499–511.

Peterson, C., & Seligman, M. E. P. (1984). Causal explanations as a risk factor for depression: Theory and evidence. *Psychological Review, 91,* 347–374.

Peterson, C., Seligman, M. E. P., & Vaillant, G. E. (1988). Pessimistic explanatory style is a risk factor for physical illness: A thirty-five-year longitudinal study. *Journal of Personality and Social Psychology, 55,* 23–27.

Pettingale, K. W., Morris, T., Greer, S., & Haybittle, J. L. (1985). Mental attitudes to cancer: An additional prognostic factor. *Lancet, 1,* 750.

Pettingale, K. W., Philalithis, A., Tee, D. E. H., & Greer, H. S. (1981). The biological correlates of psychological responses to cancer. *Journal of Psychosomatic Research, 25,* 453–458.

Piaget, J. (1954). *The construction of reality in the child.* New York: Basic Books.

Pietromonaco, P. R., & Markus, H. (1985). The nature of negative thoughts in depression. *Journal of Personality and Social Psychology, 48,* 799–807.

Pinneau, S. R., Jr. (1975). *Effects of social support on psychological and physiological stress.* Unpublished doctoral dissertation, University of Michigan, Ann Arbor.

Pruitt, D. G., & Hoge, R. D. (1965). Strength of the relationship between the value of an event and its subjective probability as a function of method of measurement. *Journal of Experimental Psychology, 5,* 483–489.

Pyszczynski, T., & Greenberg, J. (1987). Self-regulatory perseveration and the depressive self-focusing style: A self-awareness theory of reactive depression. *Psychological Bulletin, 102,* 122–138.

Pyszczynski, T., Holt, K., & Greenberg, J. (1987). Depression, self-focused attention, and expectances for positive and negative future life events for self and others. *Journal of Personality and Social Psychology, 52,* 994–1001.

Reite, M., Harbeck, R., & Hoffman, A. (1981). Altered cellular immune response following peer separation. *Life Sciences, 29,* 1133–1136.

Rholes, W., Riskind, J. H., & Neville, B. (1985). The relationship of cognitions and hopelessness to depression and anxiety. *Social Cognition, 3,* 36–50.

Richardson, H. M. (1939). Studies of mental resemblance between husbands and wives and between friends. *Psychological Bulletin, 36,* 104–120.

Ringer, R. J. (1977). *Looking out for number one.* Beverly Hills, CA: Los Angeles Book Corp.

Rizley, R. (1978). Depression and distortion in the attribution of causality. *Journal of Abnormal Psychology, 87,* 32–48.

Robertson, L. S. (1977). Car crashes: Perceived vulnerability and willingness to pay for crash protection. *Journal of Community Health, 3,* 136–141.

Rodin, J., & Langer, E. J. (1977). Long-term effects of a control-relevant intervention with the institutionalized aged. *Journal of Personality and Social Psychology, 35,* 897–902.

Rogentine, G. N., Jr., van Kammen, D. P., Fox, B. H., Docherty, J. P., Rosenblatt, J. E., Boyd, S. C., & Bunney, W. E. (1979). Psychological factors in the prognosis of malignant melanoma: A prospective study. *Psychosomatic Medicine, 41,* 647–655.

Rogers, C. R. (1942). *Counseling and psychotherapy.* Boston: Houghton Mifflin.

Rogers, C. R. (1951). *Client-centered therapy: Its current practice, implications and theory.* Boston: Houghton Mifflin.

Rogers, M. P., Dubey, D., & Reich, P. (1979). The influence of the psyche and the brain on immunity and disease susceptibility: A critical review. *Psychosomatic Medicine, 41,* 147–164.

Rosenberg, M. (1979). *Conceiving the self.* New York: Basic Books.

Rosenhan, D. L., Salovey, P., & Hargis, K. (1981). The joys of helping: Focus of attention mediates the impact of positive affect on altruism. *Journal of Personality and Social Psychology, 40,* 899–905.

Ross, L. (1981). The "intuitive scientist" formulation and its developmental implications. In J. H. Flavell & L. Ross (Eds.), *Social cognitive development: Frontiers and possible futures* (pp. 1–42). Cambridge: Cambridge University Press.

Ross, M., & Fletcher, G. J. O. (1985). Attribution and social perception. In G. Lindzey & A. Aronson (Eds.). *The handbook of social psychology* (3rd ed., pp. 73–122). Reading, MA: Addison-Wesley.

Ross, M., & Sicoly, F. (1979). Egocentric biases in availability and attribution. *Journal of Personality and Social Psychology, 37,* 322–337.

Rubin, Z. (1985). Deceiving ourselves about deception: Comment on Smith and Richardson's "Amelioration of deception and harm in psychological research." *Journal of Personality and Social Psychology, 48,* 252–253.

Ruehlman, L. S., West, S. G., & Pasahow, R. J. (1985). Depression and evaluative schemata. *Journal of Personality, 53,* 46–92.

Ryan, R. M., Connell, J. P., & Deci, E. L. (1985). A motivational analysis of self-determination in education. In C. Ames & R. E. Ames (Eds.), *Research on motivation in education: The classroom milieu* (pp. 13–52). New York: Academic Press.

Ryan, R. M., Connell, J. P., & Grolnick, W. S. (in press). When achievement is not intrinsically motivated: A theory of self-regulation in school. In A. K. Boggiano & T. S. Pittman (Eds.), *Achievement and motivation: A social-developmental perspective.* New York: Cambridge University Press.

Ryan, R. M., & Grolnick, W. S. (1986). Origins and pawns in the classroom: Self-report and projective assessments of individual differences in children's perceptions. *Journal of Personality and Social Psychology, 59,* 226–235.

Ryan, W. (1971). *Blaming the victim.* New York: Vintage Books.

Sachs, P. R. (1982). Avoidance of diagnostic information in self-evaluation of ability. *Personality and Social Psychology Bulletin, 8,* 242–246.

Sackeim, H. A. (1983). Self-deception, self-esteem, and depression: The adaptive value of lying to oneself. In J. Masling (Ed.), *Empirical studies of psychoanalytical theories* (Vol. 1, pp. 101–157). Hillsdale, NJ: Analytic Press.

Sackeim, H. A., & Gur, R. C. (1978). Self-deception, self-confrontation, and consciousness. In G. E. Schwartz & D. Shapiro (Eds.), *Consciousness and self-regulation, advances in research and theory* (Vol. 2, pp. 139–197). New York: Plenum.

Sackeim, H. A., & Gur, R. C. (1979). Self-deception, other-deception, and self-reported psychopathology. *Journal of Consulting and Clinical Psychology, 47,* 213–215.

Salovey, P., & Rosenhan, D. L. (in press). Mood states and prosocial behavior. To appear in H. L. Wagner & A. S. R. Manstead (Eds.), *Handbook of psychophysiology: Emotion and social behavior.* Chichester, England: Wiley.

Sarbin, T. R. (1962). A preface to a psychological analysis of the self. *Psychological Review, 59,* 11–22.

Scarf, M. (1979, April). The more sorrowful sex. *Psychology Today,* pp. 45, 47–48, 51–52, 89.

Schaefer, C., Coyne, J. C., & Lazarus, R. S. (1981). The health-related functions of social support. *Journal of Behavioral Medicine, 4,* 381–406.

References

Schaefer, E. S. (1959). A circumplex model for maternal behavior. *Journal of Abnormal and Social Psychology, 59*, 226–235.

Scheier, M. F., & Carver, C. S. (1985). Optimism, coping, and health: Assessment and implications of generalized outcome expectancies. *Health Psychology, 4*, 219–247.

Scheier, M. F., Matthews, K. A., Owens, J., Magovern, G. J., Sr., Lefebvre, R. C., Abbott, R. A., & Carver, C. S. (1988). *Dispositional optimism and recovery from coronary artery bypass surgery: The beneficial effects on physical and psychological well-being.* Manuscript submitted for publication.

Scheier, M. F., Weintraub, J. K., & Carver, C. S. (1986). Coping with stress: Divergent strategies of optimists and pessimists. *Journal of Personality and Social Psychology, 51*, 1257–1264.

Schleifer, S. J., Keller, S. E., McKegney, F. P., & Stein, M. (1979, March). *The influence of stress and other psychosocial factors on human immunity.* Paper presented at the American Psychosomatic Society annual meeting, Dallas.

Schlenker, B. R. (1980). *Impression management.* Monterey, CA: Brooks/Cole.

Schlenker, B. R., & Miller, R. S. (1977). Egocentrism in groups: Self-serving biases or logical information processing? *Journal of Personality and Social Psychology, 35*, 755–764.

Schmale, A. H., & Iker, H. (1971). Hopelessness as a predictor of cervical cancer. *Social Science and Medicine, 20*, 259–277.

Schmale, A. J., Jr. (1958). The relation of separation and depression to disease. *Psychosomatic Medicine, 20*, 259–277.

Scholzman, K. L., & Verba, S. (1979). Injury to insult: Unemployment, class, and political response. Cambridge, MA: Harvard University Press.

Schulz, D. (1977). *Growth psychology: Models of the healthy personality.* New York: Van Nostrand.

Schulz, R. (1976). Effects of control and predictability on the physical and psychological well-being of the institutionalized aged. *Journal of Personality and Social Psychology, 33*, 563–573.

Schulz, R., & Aderman, D. (1973). Effect of residential change on the temporal distance to death of terminal cancer patients. *Omega, 4*, 157–162.

Schwarz, J. C., & Pollack, P. R. (1977). Affect and delay of gratification. *Journal of Research in Personality, 11*, 147–164.

Secord, P. F., & Backman, C. W. (1965). An interpersonal approach to personality. In B. A. Maher (Ed.), *Progress in experimental personality research* (Vol. 2, pp. 91–125). New York: Academic Press.

Seeman, G., & Schwarz, J. C. (1974). Affective state and preference for immediate versus delayed reward. *Journal of Research in Personality, 7*, 384–394.

Seligman, M. E. P. (1975). *Helplessness: On depression, development and death.* San Francisco: Freeman.

Seligman, M. E. P., & Schulman, P. (1986). Explanatory style as a predictor of productivity and quitting among life insurance sales agents. *Journal of Personality and Social Psychology, 50*, 832–838.

Shaffer, W. J., Duszynski, K. R., & Thomas, C. B. (1982). Family attitudes in youth as a possible precursor of cancer among physicians: A search for explanatory mechanisms. *Journal of Behavioral Medicine, 5*, 143–164.

Shapiro, A. K. (1960). A contribution to a history of the placebo effect. *Behavioral Science, 5*, 109–135.

Shapiro, A. K. (1964). Factors contributing to the placebo effect: Their implications for psychotherapy. *American Journal of Psychotherapy, 18*, 73–88.

Shekelle, R. B., Raynor, W. J., Ostfeld, A. M., Garron, D. C., Bieliauskas, L. A., Liu, S. C., Maliza, C., & Oglesby, P. (1981). Psychological depression and 17-year risk of death from cancer. *Psychosomatic Medicine, 43,* 117–125.

Sherif, M., & Cantril, H. (1947). *The psychology of ego-involvements.* New York: Wiley.

Sherman, R. T., & Anderson, C. A. (1987). Decreasing premature termination from psychotherapy. *Journal of Social and Clinical Psychology, 5,* 298–312.

Showers, C., & Cantor, N. (1985). Social cognition: A look at motivated strategies. *Annual Review of Psychology, 16,* 275–305.

Shrauger, J. S. (1972). Self-esteem and reactions to being observed by others. *Journal of Personality and Social Psychology, 23,* 192–200.

Shrauger, J. S. (1975). Responses to evaluation as a function of initial self-perception. *Psychological Bulletin, 82,* 581–596.

Shrauger, J. S. (1982). Selection and processing of self-evaluative information: Experimental evidence and clinical implications. In G. Weary & H. L. Mirels (Eds.), *Integrations of clinical and social psychology* (pp. 128–153). New York: Oxford University Press.

Shrauger, J. S., & Kelly, R. J. (in press). Global self-evaluation and changes in self description as a function of information. *Journal of Personality.*

Shrauger, J. S., & Terbovic, M. L. (1976). Self-evaluation and assessments of performance by self and others. *Journal of Consulting and Clinical Psychology, 44,* 564–572.

Siegel, B. S. (1986). *Love, medicine, and miracles.* New York: Harper & Row.

Silver, R. L., Boon, C., & Stones, M. (1983) Searching for meaning in misfortune: Making sense of incest. *Journal of Social Issues, 39,* 81–102.

Silver, R. L., & Wortman, C. B. (1980). Coping with undesirable life events. In J. Garber & M. E. P. Seligman (Eds.), *Human helplessness: Theory and applications* (pp. 279–340). New York: Academic Press.

Skinner, B. F. (1971). *Beyond freedom and dignity.* NY: Knopf.

Skinner, E. A. & Chapman, M. (1987). Resolution of a developmental paradox: How can perceived internality increase, decrease and remain the same across middle childhood? *Developmental Psychology, 23,* 44–48.

Skinner, E. A., & Connell, J. P. (1986). Control understanding: Suggestions for a developmental framework. In M. M. Baltes & P. B. Baltes (Eds.), *The psychology of control and aging* (pp. 35–69). Hillsdale, NJ: Erlbaum.

Sklar, L. S., & Anisman, H. (1981). Stress and cancer. *Psychological Bulletin, 89,* 369–406.

Smedslund, J. (1963). The concept of correlation in adults. *Scandinavian Journal of Psychology, 4,* 165–173.

Smith, S. S., & Richardson, D. (1985). On deceiving ourselves about deception: Reply to Rubin. *Journal of Personality and Social Psychology, 48,* 254–255.

Snyder, C. R. (1988, August). *Reality negotiation: From excuses to hope and beyond.* Paper presented at the American Psychological Association annual meeting, Atlanta.

Snyder, M. L., Stephan, W. G., & Rosenfield, C. (1978). Attributional egotism. In J. H. Harvey, W. J. Ickes, & R. F. Kidd (Eds.), *New directions in attribution research* (Vol. 2, pp. 91–117). Hillsdale, NJ: Erlbaum.

Snyder, M. L., & Wicklund, R. A. (1981). Attribute ambiguity. In J. H. Harvey, W. Ickes, & R. F. Kidd (Eds.), *New directions in attribution research* (Vol. 3, pp. 197–221). Hillsdale, NJ: Erlbaum.

Solomon, G. F. (1969). Stress and antibody response in rats. *International Archives of Allergy and Applied Immunology, 35,* 97.

References

Solomon, G. F., Amkraut, A. A., & Kasper, P. (1974). Immunity, emotions, and stress (with special reference to the mechanism of stress effects on the immunity system). *Annals of Clinical Research, 6,* 313–322.

Spuhler, J. N. (1968). Assortative mating with respect to physical characteristics. *Eugenics Quarterly, 15,* 128–140.

Stein, M., Keller, S. E., & Schleifer, S. J. (1985). Stress and immunomodulation: The role of depression and neuroendocrine function. *Journal of Immunology, 135,* 827s–833s.

Stipek, D. J. (1984). Young children's performance expectations: Logical analysis or wishful thinking? In I. Nicholls (Ed.), *Advances in motivation and achievement* (Vol. 3, pp. 33–56). Greenwich, CT: JAI Press.

Stipek, D., & MacIver, D. (in press). Developmental change in children's assessment of intellectual competence. *Child Development.*

Storr, A. (1968). Churchill: The man. In *Churchill: Four faces and the man.* London: Allen Lane.

Strack, S., & Coyne, J. C. (1983). Social confirmation of dysphoria: Shared and private reactions to depression. *Journal of Personality and Social Psychology, 44,* 798–806.

Strecher, V. J., McEvoy De Vellis, B., Becker, M. H., & Rosenstock, I. M. (1986). The role of self-efficacy in achieving health behavior change. *Health Education Quarterly, 13,* 73–91.

Strickland, B. R. (1978). Internal-external expectancies and health-related behaviors. *Journal of Consulting and Clinical Psychology, 46,* 1192–1211.

Sullivan, H. S. (1953). *The interpersonal theory of psychiatry* (H. S. Perry & M. L. Gawel, Eds.) New York: Norton.

Sullivan, H. S. (1956). *Clinical studies in psychiatry.* New York: Norton.

Suls, J. (1982). Social support, interpersonal relations, and health: Benefits and liabilities. In G. S. Sanders & J. Suls (Eds.), *Social psychology of health and illness.* Hillsdale, NJ: Erlbaum.

Suls, J., & Fletcher, B. (1985). The relative efficacy of avoidant and nonavoidant coping strategies: A meta-analysis. *Health Psychology, 4,* 249–288.

Suls, J. M., & Miller, R. L. M. (1977). *Social comparison processes: Theoretical and empirical perspectives.* New York: Wiley.

Svenson, O. (1981). Are we all less risky and more skillful than our fellow drivers? *Acta Psychologica, 47,* 143–148.

Swallow, S. R., & Kuiper, N. A. (1988). Social comparison and negative self-evaluations: An application to depression. *Clinical Psychology Review, 8,* 55–76.

Swann, W. B., Jr. (1983). Self-verification: Bringing social reality into harmony with the self. In J. Suls & A. G. Greenwald (Eds.), *Social psychology perspectives* (Vol. 2, pp. 33–66). Hillsdale, NJ: Lawrence Erlbaum.

Swann, W. B., Jr. (1984). Quest for accuracy in person perception: A matter of pragmatics. *Psychological Review, 91,* 457–477.

Swann, W. B., Jr., & Hill, C. A. (1982). When our identities are mistaken: Reaffirming self-conceptions through social interaction. *Journal of Personality and Social Psychology, 43,* 59–66.

Swann, W. B., Jr., & Read, S. J. (1981a). Acquiring self-knowledge: The search for feedback that fits. *Journal of Personality and Social Psychology, 41,* 1119–1128.

Swann, W. B., Jr., & Read, S. J. (1981b). Self-verification processes: How we sustain our self-conceptions. *Journal of Experimental Social Psychology, 17,* 351–370.

Sweeney, P. D., Anderson, K., & Bailey, S. (1986). Attributional style in depression: A meta-analytic view. *Journal of Personality and Social Psychology, 50,* 697–702.

Sweeney, P. D., Shaeffer, D., & Golin, S. (1982). Attributions about self and others in depression. *Personality and Social Psychology Bulletin, 8,* 37–42.

Tabachnik, N., Crocker, J., & Alloy, L. B. (1983). Depression, social comparison, and the false-consensus effect. *Journal of Personality and Social Psychology, 45,* 688–699.

Tache, J., Selye, H., & Day, S. B. (1979). *Cancer, stress, and death.* New York: Plenum.

Taylor, C. B., Bandura, A., Ewart, C. K., Miller, N. H., & DeBusk, R. F. (1985). Exercise testing to enhance wives' confidence in their husbands' cardiac capabilities soon after clinically uncomplicated acute myocardial infarction. *American Journal of Cardiology, 55,* 635–638.

Taylor, S. E. (1979). Hospital patient behavior: Helplessness, reactance or control? *Journal of Social Issues, 35,* 156–184. Revised version in H. S. Friedman & M. R. DiMatteo (Eds.). (1982). *Interpersonal issues in health care.* New York: Academic Press.

Taylor, S. E. (1983). Adjustment to threatening events: A theory of cognitive adaptation. *American Psychologist, 38,* 1161–1173.

Taylor, S. E. (1986). *Health psychology.* New York: Random House.

Taylor, S. E. (in press). Illusion, mental health and adaptation: Cognitive responses to the stress of life. *American Psychologist.*

Taylor, S. E., & Brown, J. (1988). Illusion and well-being: A social psychological perspective on mental health. *Psychological Bulletin, 103,* 193–210.

Taylor, S. E., & Clark, L. F. (1986). Does information improve adjustment to noxious events? In M. J. Saks & L. Saxe (Eds.), *Advances in applied social psychology* (Vol. 3, pp. 1–28). Hillsdale, NJ: Erlbaum.

Taylor, S. E., Collins, R. L., Skokan, L. A., & Aspinwall, L. G. (in press). Illusions and the processing of negative information. *Journal of Social and Clinical Psychology.*

Taylor, S. E., Lichtman, R. R., & Wood, J. V. (1984a). Attributions, beliefs about control, and adjustment to breast cancer. *Journal of Personality and Social Psychology, 46,* 489–502.

Taylor, S. E., Lichtman, R. R., & Wood, J. V. (1984b). Compliance with chemotherapy among breast cancer patients. *Health Psychology, 3,* 553–562.

Taylor, S. E., & Schneider, S. K. (1989). Coping and the simulation of events. *Social Cognition, 7,* 176–196.

Taylor, S. E., Wood, J. V., & Lichtman, R. R. (1983). It could be worse: Selective evaluation as a response to victimization. *Journal of Social Issues, 39,* 19–40.

Tellegen, A. (1979). *Differential Personality Questionnaire.* Unpublished manuscript, University of Minnesota.

Temoshok, L., Heller, B. W., Sagebeil, R. W., Marsden, S. B., Sweet, D. M., DiClemente, R. J., & Gold, M. C. (1985). Relationships of psychosocial factors to prognostic indicators in cutaneous malignant melanoma. *Journal of Psychosomatic Medicine, 29,* 139–153.

Tesser, A. (1980). Self-esteem maintenance in family dynamics. *Journal of Personality and Social Psychology, 39,* 77–91.

Tesser, A., & Campbell, J. (1980). Self-definition: The impact of the relative performance and similarity of others. *Social Psychology Quarterly, 43,* 341–347.

Tesser, A., & Campbell, J. (1982). Self-evaluation maintenance and the perception of friends and strangers. *Journal of Personality, 50,* 261–279.

Tesser, A., & Campbell, J., & Smith, M. (1984). Friendship, choice and performance: Self-evaluation maintenance in children. *Journal of Personality and Social Psychology, 46,* 561–574.

References

Tesser, A., & Moore, J. (1986). On the convergence of public and private aspects of self. In R. F. Baumeister (Ed.), *Public self and private life* (pp. 99–116). New York: Springer.

Tesser, A., & Paulhus, D. (1983). The definition of self: Private and public self-evaluation management strategies. *Journal of Personality and Social Psychology, 44,* 672–682.

Tesser, A., & Rosen, S. (1975). The reluctance to transmit bad news. In L. Berkowitz (Ed.), *Advances in Experimental Psychology* (Vol. 8, pp. 193–232). New York: Academic Press.

Tetlock, P. E., & Manstead, A. S. R. (1985). Impression management versus intrapsychic explanations in social psychology: A useful dichotomy? *Psychological Review, 92,* 59–77.

Thomas, C. B., & Duszynski, K. R. (1974). Closeness to parents and the family constellation in a prospective study of five disease states: Suicide, mental illness, malignant tumor, hypertension, and coronary heart disease. *Johns Hopkins Medical Journal, 134,* 251–270.

Thomas, C. B., Duszynski, K. R., & Shaffer, J. W. (1979). Family attitudes reported in youth as potential precursors of cancer. *Psychosomatic Medicine, 41,* 287–302.

Thompson, S. C. (1981). Will it hurt less if I can control it? A complex answer to a simple question. *Psychological Bulletin, 90,* 89–101.

Thompson, S. C. (1985). Finding positive meaning in a stressful event and coping. *Basic and Applied Social Psychology, 6,* 279–295.

Thompson, S. C. (1988). *The search for meaning following a stroke.* Manuscript submitted for publication.

Thompson, S. C., & Kelley, J. J. (1981). Judgments of responsibility for activities in close relationships. *Journal of Personality and Social Psychology, 41,* 469–477.

Thompson, W. C., Cowan, C. L., & Rosenhan, D. L. (1980). Focus of attention mediates the impact of negative effect on altruism. *Journal of Personality and Social Psychology, 38,* 291–300.

Thoresen, C. E., & Mahoney, M. J. (1974). *Behavioral self-control.* New York: Holt.

Tiger, L. (1979). *Optimism: The biology of hope.* New York: Simon & Schuster.

Trump, D. (with Schwartz, T.) (1988). *The art of the deal.* New York: Random House.

Turk, D. C. (1979). Factors influencing the adaptive process with chronic illness: Implications for intervention. In I. G. Sarason & C. D. Spielberger (Eds.), *Stress and anxiety* (Vol. 6, pp. 291–311). Washington, DC: Hemisphere.

Tyler, S., & Shopsin, B. (1982). Symptoms and assessment of mania. In E. S. Paykel (Ed.), *Handbook of affective disorders.* New York: Guilford Press.

Vaillant, G. (1977). *Adaptation to life.* Boston: Little, Brown.

Vasta, R., & Brockner, J. (1979). Self-esteem and self-evaluation covert statements. *Journal of Consulting and Clinical Psychology, 47,* 776–777.

Veitch, R., & Griffith, W. (1976). Good news-bad news: Affective and interpersonal effects. *Journal of Applied Social Psychology, 6,* 69–75.

Velten, E. (1968). A laboratory task for induction of mood states. *Behaviour Research and Therapy, 6,* 473–482.

Viney, L. L. (1986). Expression of positive emotion by people who are physically ill: Is it evidence of defending or coping? *Journal of Psychosomatic Research, 30,* 27–34.

Visintainer, M. A., Seligman, M. E. P., & Volpicelli, J. (1983). Helplessness, chronic stress, and tumor development. *Psychosomatic Medicine, 45,* 75 (Abstract).

Visotsky, H. M., Hamburg, D. A., Goss, M. E., & Lebovits, B. Z. (1961). Coping behavior under extreme stress. *Archives of General Psychiatry, 5,* 423–448.

Wagener, J. J., & Taylor, S. E. (1986). What else could I have done? Patients' responses to failed treatment decisions. *Health Psychology, 5,* 481–496.

Wagner, J. (1986). *The search for signs of intelligent life in the universe.* New York: Harper & Row.

Wallston, K. A., & Wallston, B. S. (1980). Health locus of control scales. In H. Lefcourt (Ed.), *Advances and innovations in locus of control research.* New York: Academic Press.

Wallston, K. A., & Wallston, B. S. (1982). Who is responsible for your health? The construct of health locus of control. In G. Saunders & J. Suls (Eds.), *Social psychology of health and illness* (pp. 65–95). Hillsdale, NJ: Erlbaum.

Walster, E., & Berscheid, E. (1968). The effects of time on cognitive consistency. In R. P. Abelson, E. Aronson, W. J. McGuire, T. M. Newcomb, M. J. Rosenberg, & P. H. Tannenbaum (Eds.), *Theories of cognitive consistency: A sourcebook* (pp. 599–608). Chicago: Rand McNally.

Ward, W. D., & Jenkins, H. M. (1965). The display of information and the judgment of contingency. *Canadian Journal of Psychology, 19,* 231–241.

Warfield, F. (1957). *Keep listening.* New York: Viking.

Watson, D., & Clark, L. A. (1984). Negative affectivity: The disposition to experience aversive emotional states. *Psychological Bulletin, 96,* 465–490.

Watson, G. (1930). Happiness among adult students of education. *Journal of Educational Psychology, 21,* 79–109.

Weinberger, D. A. (in press). The construct validity of the repressive coping style. In J. L. Singer (Ed.), *Repression: Defense mechanism and personal style.* Chicago: University of Chicago Press.

Weiner, B. (1979). A theory of motivation for some classroom experiences. *Journal of Educational Psychology, 71,* 3–25.

Weinstein, N. D. (1980). Unrealistic optimism about future life events. *Journal of Personality and Social Psychology, 39,* 806–820.

Weinstein, N. D. (1982). Unrealistic optimism about susceptibility to health problems. *Journal of Behavioral Medicine, 5,* 441–460.

Weinstein, N. D. (1984). Why it won't happen to me: Perceptions of risk factors and susceptibility. *Health Psychology, 3,* 431–457.

Weinstein, N. D. (1987). Unrealistic optimism about susceptibility to health problems: Conclusions from a community-wide sample. *Journal of Behavioral Medicine, 10,* 481–500.

Weinstein, N. D., & Lachendro, E. (1982). Egocentrism as a source of unrealistic optimism. *Personality and Social Psychology Bulletin, 8,* 195–200.

Weisman, A. D., & Worden, J. W. (1975). Psychological analysis of cancer deaths. *Omega, 6,* 61–75.

Weisz, J. R. (1986). Understanding the developing understanding of control. In M. Perlmutter (Ed.), *Minnesota symposia on child psychology: Vol. 18. Cognitive perspectives on children's social and behavioral development* (pp. 219–285). Hillsdale, NJ: Erlbaum.

Weisz, J. R., Rothbaum, F. M., & Blackburn, T. C. (1984). Standing out and standing in: The psychology of control in America and Japan. *American Psychologist, 39,* 955–969.

Welsh, G. S., & Dahlstrom, W. G. (Eds.). (1956). *Basic readings on the MMPI in psychology and medicine.* Minneapolis: University of Minnesota Press.

White, R. W. (1959). Motivation reconsidered: The concept of competence. *Psychological Review, 66,* 297–335.

References

Wilkins, G., Epting, F., & Van De Riet, H. (1972). Relationship between repression-sensitization and interpersonal cognitive complexity. *Journal of Consulting and Clinical Psychology, 39,* 448–450.

Wills, T. A. (1981). Downward comparison principles in social psychology. *Psychological Bulletin, 90,* 245–271.

Wills, T. A. (1983). Social comparison in coping and help-seeking. In B. M. DePaulo, A. Nadler, & J. D. Fisher (Eds.), *New directions in helping: Vol 2. Help-seeking* (pp. 109–141). New York: Academic Press.

Winters, K. C., & Neale, J. M. (1985). Mania and low self-esteem. *Journal of Abnormal Psychology, 94,* 282–290.

Wixon, D. R., & Laird, J. D. (1976). Awareness and attitude change in the forced-compliance paradigm: The importance of when. *Journal of Personality and Social Psychology, 34,* 376–384.

Wood, J. V., Taylor, S. E., & Lichtman, R. R. (1985). Social comparison in adjustment to breast cancer. *Journal of Personality and Social Psychology, 49,* 1169–1183.

Worchel, S. & Goethals, G. R. (1985). *Adjustment: Pathways to personal growth.* Englewood Cliffs, NJ: Prentice-Hall.

Wortman, C. B., & Brehm, J. W. (1975). Responses to uncontrollable outcomes: An integration of reactance theory and the learned helplessness model. In L. Berkowitz (Ed.), *Advances in experimental social psychology* (Vol. 8, pp. 277–336). New York: Academic Press.

Wortman, C. B., & Dunkel-Schetter, C. (1979). Interpersonal relationships and cancer: A theoretical analysis. *Journal of Social Issues, 35,* 120–155.

Wortman, C. B., & Silver, R. (1982, August). *Coping with undesirable life events.* Paper presented at the American Psychological Association annual meeting, Washington, DC.

Wortman, C. B., & Silver, R. (1987). Coping with irrevocable loss. In G. R. VandenBos & B. K. Bryant (Eds.), *Cataclysms, crises, and catastrophes: Psychology in action* (pp. 189–235). Washington, DC: American Psychological Association.

Wright, J., & Mischel, W. (1982). Influence of affect on cognitive social learning person variables. *Journal of Personality and Social Psychology, 43,* 901–914.

Wurf, E., & Markus, H. (1983, August). *Cognitive consequences of the negative self.* Paper presented at the American Psychological Association annual meeting, Anaheim, CA.

Wurf, E., & Markus, H. (in press). Possible selves and the psychology of personal growth. In D. J. Ozer, J. M. Healy, & A. J. Stewart (Eds.), *Perspectives in personality: Self and emotion* (Vol. 3a). Greenwich, CT: JAI Press.

Zigler, E., & Glick, M. (1988). Is paranoid schizophrenia really camouflaged depression? *American Psychologist, 43,* 284–290.

Zimbardo, P. G., Ebbesen, E. B., & Maslach, C. (1977). *Influencing attitudes and changing behavior.* Reading, MA: Addison-Wesley.

Zis, A. P., & Goodwin, F. K. (1982). The amine hypothesis. In E. S. Paykel (Ed.), *Handbook of affective disorders* (pp. 175–190). New York: Guilford Press.

Zuckerman, M. (1979). Attribution of success and failure revisited, or: The motivational bias is alive and well in attribution theory. *Journal of Personality, 47,* 245–287.

Zullow, H. M., Oettingen, G., Peterson, C., & Seligman, M. E. P. (1988). Pessimistic explanatory style in the historical record: CAVing LBJ, presidential candidates, and East versus West Berlin. *American Psychologist, 43,* 673–682.

Zullow, H. M., & Seligman, M. E. P. (1988). *Pessimistic rumination predicts electoral defeat of presidential candidates: 1900–1984.* Manuscript submitted for publication.

INDEX

Index

Index

Soldana, Theresa, 194
Sorrowful Sex, The (Scarf), 212
Stallone, Sylvester, 60
Stevens, Wallace, 121
Stevenson, Adlai, 62
Stipek, Deborah, 9, 35
Storr, Anthony, 207
Stress, 132, 229; control beliefs and experience of, 31–32, 75–80, 82, 83, 91, 95; and depression, 217, 218–19, 220, 224, 262–63n39; and illusions, 74–81; and immune functioning, 105, 106–8, 255n35; mental strategies for control of, 78–80; and personal growth, 81–85; and physical health, 87, 88, 91, 94, 95, 99–105, 106–8, 254n29, 255n35; and social support, 139–43, 257n34; and sudden death syndrome, 99–102
Sudden death, 91, 99–102, 104, 194
Suicide, 201, 208, 212, 233
Superstitious thinking, 70
Survivors of natural disasters, 42, 162, 165, 166–67, 169–70, 175, 197

Tesser, Abraham, 136
Thoreau, Henry David, 48
Tiger, Lionel, 35, 57–58, 207
Tomlin, Lily, 227
Tragedy. *See* Victimization
Truman, Harry, 62
Trump, Donald, 63
Type A behavior pattern, 114

Unipolar depression, 261n18; *see also* Depression
Unrealistic optimism, 6, 49, 245; adaptive functions of, 35–37; de-velopment of, 34–35; effects of outcomes on, 41–43; and illusion of progress, 39–41; incidence and nature of, 32–34, 43–45; maintenance of, 37–43; other illusions bound up with, 37–41; and past experience or new information, 36, 38–39; and placebo effects, 115, 118, 119, 120; seen as defensive reaction, 35–36; *see also* Optimism
Unrealistic pessimism, 215; *see also* Pessimism

Vaillant, George, 198, 244, 256–57n14
Victimization, 83–84; as challenge to illusion, 230; and child's sense of omnipotence, 24; and denial, 123; and efforts to restore lost control, 175–83; forms of, 162–64; and illusions, 161–98; overcoming, 166–98; and search for meaning, 162, 193–98; and social comparison, 170–74; social consequences of, 164–66
Victims for Victims, 194
Voltaire, 35

Wagner, Jane, 227
Wallace, Irving, 60
Weinberger, D. A., 126, 128, 129
Weisz, John, 232–33
West, Adam, 194
West, John, 194, 196
White, Robert, 21, 22
Wills, Thomas, 170
Wixon, D. R., 147
Wolfe, Tom, 107
Woolf, Virginia, 204, 208
Work, 47–48, 58–74, 252n36